CRAG SURVIVAL HANDBOOK

CRAG SURVIVAL HANDBOOK

THE UNSPOKEN RULES OF CLIMBING

MATT SAMET

MOUNTAINEERS
BOOKS

MOUNTAINEERS BOOKS

Mountaineers Books is the publishing division of The Mountaineers, an organization founded in 1906 and dedicated to the exploration, preservation, and enjoyment of outdoor and wilderness areas.

1001 SW Klickitat Way, Suite 201, Seattle, WA 98134
800.553.4453, www.mountaineersbooks.org

Printed in the United States of America
Distributed in the United Kingdom by Cordee, www.cordee.co.uk
First edition, 2013

Copy Editor: Laura Shauger
Cover, Design, and Layout: John Barnett/4 Eyes Design
Cover and text illustrations: Mike Tea
Back cover photograph: *Lauren McCormick cragging in good style on* Porn Star *(5.13d), Little Si, Washington.*
All photographs by Andy Mann unless credited otherwise
Page 6: *Matt Samet getting his crag on, on* East Jesus Nowhere *(5.12d), Wipeyur Buttress, Devil's Head, Colorado.* Photo by Todd Leeson.
Page 272: *Bill Ramsey at Mount Potosi, outside Las Vegas, Nevada*

Library of Congress Cataloging-in-Publication Data
Samet, Matt.
  Crag survival handbook : the unspoken rules of climbing / Matt Samet.
    pages cm
  ISBN 978-1-59485-766-9 (trade paper)—ISBN 978-1-59485-767-6 (ebook)
1. Rock climbing—Handbooks, manuals, etc. I. Title.
  GV200.2.S26 2013
  796.522'3—dc23
                                2013021939

ISBN (paperback): 978-1-59485-766-9
ISBN (ebook): 978-1-59485-767-6

To Kristin and Ivan,
for everything.

To Bob,
my first and most important mentor
on the rocks and in the mountains.

To all the mentors I've had,
past, present, and future, and to any
good soul who takes the time to teach
a fellow climber.

And to my trusted and cherished
climbing partners, without whom this
sport is nothing.

CONTENTS

ACKNOWLEDGMENTS

A BiG THANKS to Mountaineers Books: Kate Rogers, Mary Metz, and all the other great people who helped make this book a reality, and also to Andy Mann for his excellent shots, which comprise the bulk of the photos, and to Mike Tea for his amazing illustrations.

I would also like to thank all the valued contributors and experts who helped me with the writing, research, and art, and without whom I couldn't have pulled this off: the Access Fund, Mike Alkaitis, Susy Alkaitis, Tod Anderson, Brent Apgar, Lisa Aquino, Kristin Bjornsen, Black Diamond Equipment, Tommy Caldwell, Kelly Cordes, Kevin Daniels, Craig DeMartino, Robyn Erbesfield-Raboutou, Herman Feissner, Laurent Filoche, Fixe Hardware, Lynn Hill, Kevin Jorgeson, Joshua Tree National Park, Jim Karn, Jason Keith, Jackie and Jonathan Koehne, Andy Laakman, Ben Lawhon, Leave No Trace, Randy Leavitt, Todd Leeson, Steve Levin, Melissa Lipani, Hugh Loeffler, Maxim Ropes, Metolius Climbing, Mountain Project administrators (www.mountainproject.com), R. D. Pascoe, Eric Pauwels, Petzl America, Rob Pizem, Kolin Powick, Neely Quinn, Bill Ramsey, Bernadette Regan, Corey Rich, Colby Rickard, Brady Robinson, Lucia Hyde Robinson, Rock & Resole, Beth Rodden, Justin Roth, Mikey Schaeffer, Chris Schulte, Jonathan Siegrist, Justen Sjong, Jim Thornburg, Rick Vance, Chris Weidner, Tony Yao, and anyone I may have forgotten.

And thanks also to the amazing mentors I've had over the years—and a big shout out to anyone who takes the time to mentor a fellow climber.

FOREWORD

I BEGAN CLIMBING in 1998 at age 12, on the cusp of a major transition for the sport. Instead of getting my start out on the rock with a friend, I was introduced to climbing when a rock gym opened in my hometown of Santa Rosa, California. In the past 15 years, I've watched climbing change a lot, but most noticeably, it has become more social. Forty years ago, climbing was reserved for rebels, mountain men, and adventurers. Today, sport climbers enter the game in viral numbers, unheard of even five years ago. And they come from all walks of life.

When I transitioned from gym climbing to climbing outdoors, I was too young to drive. So I joined up with others who served as my mentors, instilling a clean aesthetic to *never* alter the rock by hammer, chisel, or other means; to never leave trash and to pack out whatever we found; and to value community, serenity, and respect over crushing your personal tick list.

However, this wave of new participation is outpacing our available mentors, a vital concern since climbing has always been deeply rooted in mentoring. As a result, many longtime climbers, including folks from climbing-gym owners to land managers, the Alpine Club, and the Access Fund, are asking: How do we address this mass exodus from the gym to the outdoors? How can we remain rooted in the process? And what if we lose touch with our traditions?

American climbing has always fostered the cowboy ethic of individual expression. But our sheer numbers mean we no longer can all go Lone Ranger, putting self before

Professional Climbers International cofounder Kevin Jorgeson treading lightly at the Wizard's Gate, Estes Park, Colorado

place. We must account to each other and to *the wilds herself,* or both the sport and the milieu are doomed. So how do we make it all work in the twenty-first century?

There is no silver bullet, but we can each do our part on both macro and micro levels. First, join the Access Fund, our sport's advocacy group for keeping climbing areas open and clean, and join the American Alpine Club, which is doing similar work. Second, seek out a good mentor or instructor. Professional Climbers International (PCI) offers clinics across the nation featuring top climbers sharing their passion and knowledge. And last, make stewardship an integral part of every trip to the rocks, and lead by example. Matt Samet has taken the time to consolidate his vast experience and that of countless others into this book designed to help you thrive and evolve as a climber. As the former editor of *Climbing* and an author of other climbing books, Matt has a unique talent for combining useful knowledge with humor and wit.

The beauty of climbing is that it's open to anyone who's willing to try, with success limited only by our imaginations. This book will help you and our sport thrive. It all begins with you, the reader, and all of us, the climbers.

See you on the rocks.

—Kevin Jorgeson

INTRODUCTION

"DAMNIT, MATT, PAY ATTENTION!" Adair Peterson bellowed. "Stop talking, keep your brake hand on the rope, and keep your eyes on my husband!"

It was high summer in 1988. I was sixteen, out on a New Mexico Mountain Club (NMMC) excursion to the Sandia Mountains, the 10,500-foot granite range above my hometown of Albuquerque, New Mexico. I'd taken the club's introductory rock course a year earlier and had since been going on NMMC trips, small outings mostly to the trad moderates on the crumbly pink cliffs and spires of the upper range. A leader or leaders always took the sharp end and made the routefinding decisions, while the rest of us tagged along, seconded, and soaked up the leaders' wisdom and experience as we served our apprenticeships. It was a great way both to learn and to sample classic routes on the dull end, high above spills of blocky talus and stands of whispering aspen, far from the roaring grid of the hot desert city below. This was simply how you learned back in the day, before rock gyms, summer camps, sport cliffs, and the like began churning out more and more greenhorns.

And now one of my mentors, a woman 40 years my senior, was hollering at me. And she was right to. As her husband, Don, neared the 5.5-mantel crux on a slender spire named the Candle, I jabbered away with a friend, not looking up and focusing as I'd been taught to do, not paying attention to Don's movements or how far he was above his gear, not keeping my eyes peeled for loose rock. Just flapping my piehole and

The author on *Dumpster BBQ* (Rifle, Colorado), at the tender age of 21. *Matt Samet*

feeding rope through my Sticht plate in indifferent flourishes, figuring, "Aww, Don's not going to fall. It's only 5.5."

"I—I'm sorry, Adair," I stammered, turning bright red. And I meant it. I shut my mouth and looked up at Don, who had just passed the crux. I didn't take my eyes off him for the rest of the route. I didn't say another word. A group of us newer climbers stood in the notch between the Candle and its neighboring spire the Cake—one team would climb each to rig a Tyrolean traverse—and Adair had dressed me down before everyone. But she meant it as a lesson for us all: maintain focus while belaying, and never, ever let happenings on the ground distract you, because while you're up there leading, you'd certainly expect the same of *your* belayer.

Adair's lesson was invaluable, one of many such pearls of wisdom I imprinted, often the "hard way," during my formative years. One club leader might teach me the best way to rig a top-rope anchor; another might show me how to place reliable lead pro or how to spot; another might discuss minimum-impact hiking and climbing practices; while yet another might show me how to master overhangs and jam cracks. I was fortunate to have these mentors, and in that hyperenthusiastic honeymoon phase, I soaked up and applied their advice until the right way of doing things became second nature.

I can think of no better way to learn: slowly, carefully, and with thoughtful supervision.

CROWDED CRAGS

Now in the twenty-first century people rarely learn through prolonged apprenticeship, though the crags are more populous than ever. This paradigm shift has contributed to preventable accidents and more frequent cliff closures due to overuse, parking and access issues, and poor climber behavior, including an escalation in confrontations among climbers themselves and between climbers and other user groups. From the glass-is-half-empty perspective, it's getting grim out there. But from the glass-is-half-full perspective, our greater numbers have also meant banner years for the industry: gyms, equipment manufacturers, guides, and so on. They've also meant that we represent an ever-more-powerful land-use lobby, with the power these days to buy crags ourselves.

Two forces seem to be creating all these new climbers: first, the overall growth in world population has increased the sheer number of people heading outdoors. And second, there has been an explosive growth in outdoor sports—and in particular climbing, as fueled by the direct, easy entry facilitated by rock gyms. According to research conducted by the Outdoor Industry Association of America, in the United States in 2011, more than 3.6 million people participated in climbing (sport, indoor, and bouldering are arguably its most popular forms), numbers way beyond what they were when I began in the 1980s. At that time, climbing was a fringe activity with, I'd guess, mere tens of thousands of practitioners.

These days if you don't have a reservation for the bouldering destination Hueco Tanks, Texas, during peak season, for instance, you'll be turned away at the entrance. On a perfect early-spring

Today's crags are always a-hoppin': a very busy Black Corridor at Red Rock, Nevada. *Malcolm Daly*

weekend in March 1987, three friends and I went trad climbing on Hueco's popular Front Side and saw no other climbers. In fact, the legendary Mushroom Boulder barely had chalk on it, and the only other people in the park were bird-watchers and picnickers. Climbing remained largely what it had been—gear-protected trad climbing, a high-commitment activity that took time to learn. Sport climbing was still a fledgling pursuit, you could count the number of US rock gyms on one hand, and bouldering in this pre-crash pad era was relatively obscure. The barriers to entry were much steeper.

Sport climbing is now ubiquitous as are rock gyms; today's modern facilities are all big, steep, bold, and beautiful compared to the dingy, scruffy, chalk-choked facilities of yesteryear. (The first gym in America, Seattle's Vertical Club, now Vertical World, opened in 1987; the gym explosion began in the mid-1990s.) Today there are mega-gyms in most urban centers—even those far from real climbing—not to mention all the artificial walls at health clubs, community recreation centers, on school campuses, etc.

Indoors, climbers might progress to 5.11 or even 5.12 in months, a process that used to take years on rock—a span of time during which you'd learn the skills organically, mastering ever more complex techniques. Now, however, physically fit specimens can charge onto the battlefield in relatively no time. They might also come with more of a *climbing*-centric vs. an *outdoor*-centric perspective: as urbanites schooled in big-city gyms, they might have never been exposed to the outdoors or to low-impact practices and etiquette.

Not surprisingly, two years ago at an informal meeting at the American Alpine Club among a handful of industry veterans, one topic that dominated was the preponderance of new rock climbers, bred and trained in gyms, who'd never been mentored or even taken a basic skills class—and how to address gaps in their skill set. Is the onus on gyms, the new climbers, or experienced climbers who see the newbies doing things "wrong"? Or all of the above? It's a tough question to answer.

TRIBAL LORE

That's where this book, the first of its kind and a book for today's climbing landscape, comes in. The *Crag Survival Handbook* is not your typical instructional manual; it assumes you already have a basic working knowledge of the sport. It covers the things that go *along with* climbing, like the lifestyle and philosophy and care for the rock and nature, including the nuances—like not jabbering away while you're belaying—that were once passed down as tribal lore:

- When should I retire my rope?
- What about oiling my cams?
- How do I warm up my hands on a cold day?
- What's the best way to tape a tweaked finger?

- How do I climb well, not just hard?
- How do I cultivate endurance so that I don't keep pumping out?
- What if I have to go to the bathroom at the cliff?
- Can I bring my dog?

These are the kinds of questions we all had in our early days and should continue to have as we mature with the sport. Such matters are second-tier knowledge, not immediately related to technical proficiency but perhaps no less crucial—essentially pearls of mentorship wisdom. So while this book is not a substitute for a real-life mentor, it serves as the first real-world, all-encompassing climber handbook to compile aspects of the sport that other resources typically gloss over. It focuses on sport cragging, the type of climbing most of us do most of the time—whether we admit it or not.

Think about it: You have a few hours after work, so what do you do? Head to the Himalaya to onsight-solo a 3000-meter mixed line or out to the local cliffs to get in a few pitches? The crags and boulders are close, convenient, and rightfully popular, and it's here in this teeming milieu that most of us ply our skills most of the time—hence the "crag" in *Crag Survival Handbook*.

ROCK MAESTROS

In almost every case I present pointers from various rock maestros or research material, along with a few examples from my own experience. For example, 5.14-climber and technique coach Justen Sjong and professional climber Kevin Jorgeson provided almost all the material for Chapter 3, on movement, while the staff at Access Fund and Leave No Trace, and Joshua Tree climbing ranger Bernadette Regan helped with Chapter 2, on etiquette, access, and impact. In this way, this guide conveys firsthand expertise regarding best practices in easily digested sound bites.

Though this knowledge may seem like common sense, much of it has to date remained uncodified: We know that we know these things, but it takes experts like Sjong and Jorgeson, who think about technique every day, to put them into words. This is exactly how instruction once took place at the cliffs—minute by minute, hour by hour, skill by skill, person to person. Consider this book your pocket mentor. While it won't teach you how to escape the belay, it will teach you why it's important to clean your shoes before starting up a boulder problem and why you should stay hydrated out climbing.

Still not convinced of the need for this guide? I need only think of the new climbers, harnesses still shiny and price tags on their quickdraws, whom I saw recently at the popular Bihedral crag in Boulder Canyon, Colorado. They accidentally dislodged a rock off a ledge toward a lower tier and then stood there clueless and frozen, unaware that they needed to scream "Rock!" as a head-crushing block plummeted down the approach gully. They were not evil kids—no one had ever told them otherwise. There are no loose blocks in the gym. Or there are the countless times I have heard climbers hollering up instructions on how to thread a sport anchor to a terrified beginner, pinned at the top of a route, who should have been ground-schooled before inaugurating this complex maneuver in a do-or-die situation. My hope is that both beginners and veterans alike will benefit from this book. I learned a universe of new things while researching and writing it, and I've been climbing for 27 years.

Since the *Crag Survival Handbook* covers a lot of ground, I've arranged it to be accessible and reader friendly, with sidebars, numbered and bulleted lists, Q&As, photos, illustrations, and other entry points, offering discrete, self-contained blocks of knowledge and information. Although neophyte and moderate-to-intermediate outdoor-going free climbers may find this book more useful, more-experienced climbers will benefit from it as well. *We can all stand to do things better.*

Again, I assume that you already have a working knowledge of the sport; I don't devote space to explaining what a carabiner is or to cataloguing handholds. Other books do exactly that! Instead, I assume that you have enough working knowledge to lead a basic sport or trad pitch but that you might still entertain questions about the slickest way to do things. I've also tried to avoid duplicating material: for example, I haven't included tips such as how to build a stick-clip or clean draws off an overhanging climb since they are already covered brilliantly in other books like Andrew Bisharat's *Sport Climbing*.

These pages offer the collective wisdom of climbing's most avid, expert practitioners, presented as your personal mentorship. Soak it up and put it into play, and we'll see you at the crags being a safe, informed, and considerate vertical citizen!

//// A NOTE ABOUT SAFETY ////

Safety is an important concern in all outdoor activities. No book can alert you to every hazard or anticipate the limitations of every reader. The descriptions of techniques and procedures in this book are intended to provide general information. This is not a complete text on climbing technique. Nothing substitutes for formal instruction, routine practice, and plenty of experience. When you follow any of the procedures described here, you assume responsibility for your own safety. While certain brand-name products appear in this book, these are not recommendations from either the author or Mountaineers Books, but they are instead specific examples uncovered through the author's research and interviews with expert climbers.

Use this book as a general guide to further information. Under normal conditions, excursions into the backcountry require attention to traffic, road and trail conditions, weather, terrain, the capabilities of your party, and other factors. Keeping informed on current conditions and exercising common sense are the keys to a safe, enjoyable outing.

—Mountaineers Books

1 HEADS UP!

Safety, Hazards, and Basic Crag Awareness

FIRST OFF, the crags will *never* be the gym. A rock gym is like a public swimming pool, with the shallow end marked for kids to frolic, lanes divided off in the middle for lap swimming, the deep end sequestered for divers, and lifeguards stationed every 50 feet. Gyms have designated top-roping and bouldering areas, a steep cave with difficult routes, a kids' wall, and staff on the floor to teach, certify, and monitor belay and lead skills. There are bolts every five feet and a soft, padded floor. The ceiling blocks out any sense of exposure, and the temperature is always comfortable. You can climb to your physical limit without having to worry about much more than whether you're spotted, you've tied your knot correctly, and your belayer is set up right.

If the gym is a public pool, then the cliffs are the ocean: vast, indifferent, fluctuating, and elemental. Entire books have been written about the perils of outdoor climbing and how to overcome them. You won't learn basic cliff-side awareness in a gym, but you must cultivate it outside. Failure to apply these fundamentals makes you a liability both to yourself and others—at any phase in your climbing career. *Gravity doesn't sleep, and safety never takes a vacation.* You survive only by constantly being vigilant, avoiding complacency, and being awake, aware, and tuned into your environment.

LOOK UP, LOOK SIDEWAYS, LOOK DOWN

We've all seen it happen or done it ourselves. You ruck up to a busy crag barely sparing a glance upward, throw your stuff down, chat with your friends as you get ready, and then jump on a climb with nary a thought for the unique hazards of your environment: that climber 70 feet up to the side about to bobble a quickdraw; that big drop-off past the belay area that your dog keeps nosing around; that hollow block with the big chalk X, poised directly above your belayer; that loose scree your rope is snaking around; or that thunderhead sneaking up the valley. It's all too easy to think, "Ah, another day out cragging—no big deal. I'll just double-check my knot, and off we go!"

But accidents happen, usually within milliseconds. The day goes from bluebird to nightmare in a snap of the fingers. So be proactive: Start your day by scanning all around you. Each time you climb you should be looking above you, to the sides, and below you, assessing potential threats and taking preventive measures. Outside at the crags in a wild, unpredictable environment, you're never completely safe.

Eyes Up

The number-one hazard at a cliff base is things falling from above: loose rock dislodged spontaneously or by other climbers and dropped gear such as cams, draws, nut tools, water bottles, or carabiners. A helmet will protect you in many cases, but for objects beyond a certain size, it might not. *Wearing a helmet does not make you immune to dropped objects.* A 10-pound rock might bounce off your helmet, but a 100-pound rock won't, and a 1000-pound rock will flatten you. I've seen climbers don their helmets in the parking lot, hike to the crag, and then set up shop in fall zones because they believe their helmet will protect them.

Falling rocks can vary from grains of sand to pebbles to boulders, but the primary rule is to yell "Rock!" the minute anyone spots *any* airborne object—rock, carabiner, helmet, snapping turtle, SCUD missile. When I was 16 and on a National Outdoor Leadership School (NOLS) course, we set out to climb a snow gully on Mount Helen in the Wind River Range. Midway up, the dark granite walls closed in, forming a tight V. It was midmorning, the mountain was thawing out, and from the midst of our six-person pack train, I spotted a rock high in the gully, skittering and bouncing down the snow.

It didn't look very big, so I didn't say anything . . . until it was too late; the "pebble" was caroming off the snow toward us and now as large as a toaster. Our

1

THE CRAGGING 10 ESSENTIALS

Just as anyone who ventures into the mountains should take the 10 Essentials, so too should anyone who "merely" goes out cragging. Here's what I always stash in my crag pack:

- ○ Small first-aid kit
- ○ Extra food
- ○ Extra water
- ○ Raingear and/or a belay parka
- ○ Sunblock
- ○ Cell phone (charged)
- ○ Belay knife for cutting away old slings
- ○ Bail biner(s)
- ○ Assisted-braking belay device and an ATC-type belay or rappel device
- ○ Area guidebook or copies of relevant pages

instructor yelled, "ROCK!" We jumped to either side, and the block shot right down the middle. *"Whew,"* I thought. When I told the instructor I'd noticed the stone earlier and felt bad about not mentioning it, he admonished me, "Matt, if you see a rock, yell 'Rock!' Bottom line: You just don't know how big it is or where it's going, so always yell 'Rock!'"

Got that? *Always yell "Rock!"* If you see something falling, of any size, from any height, yell "Rock!" And if you know a rock is coming, take a half second to look up and gauge its trajectory before fleeing helter-skelter—if you don't, you might run right into it. At a single-pitch crag, it's often best to, counterintuitively, run *toward* the cliff to get under an overhang or avoid a bouncing, ricocheting stone. Finally, always wear a helmet, even when sport climbing or en route to well-trodden crags. Some of the most dangerous spots are, ironically, on approach trails below popular cliffs, such as the Wind Tower in Eldorado Canyon, Colorado, where you might be subject to rockfall, dropped gear, and even airborne climbers.

As much as you don't like having to avoid things others have dropped or dislodged,

1

neither should you intentionally drop anything. *Don't trundle recreationally at the crags, just to see rocks smash things.* It has led to injury and even death when trundlers didn't realize there was anyone below. (See "Trundling Kills" sidebar.)

Eyes to the Side

The best way to avoid falling objects is to not be under them. It all begins with setting up a safe zone or protected staging area at the crag. Mike Alkaitis, a longtime guide in Boulder, Colorado, and former executive director of the American Mountain Guides Association (AMGA), instructs first-time clients in this art before they tie in. The safe zone is a place you can safely drop your pack, get your bearings, take out the guidebook, rack up, and so on. Find a spot that's off to the side of the cliff or that's tucked beneath a low overhang that's not directly beneath your climbs. Alkaitis also conditions clients to beware of exposure; you should ask yourself whether you're above a drop-off and how you can best avoid the edge. Brady Robinson, executive director of the Access Fund and a former Outward Bound instructor, taught his students about a helmet zone, a threshold approaching the cliff that, once you had crossed it, meant you always donned your brain bucket.

If the topography or crowds make it hard to find a safe zone against the cliff, seek staging areas on hardened surfaces (rock, scree, gravel, etc.) without vegetation well out from the rock, and don't set up beneath other parties. In Maple Canyon, Utah, for instance, cobbles often come detached from the sandstone-conglomerate matrix. At Maple's popular Minimum Wall, which has softer, sandier rock, climbers usually stage a good 30 feet from the cobble-littered base.

If you choose to climb under other parties on multipitch routes, realize that they can drop things, that rocks can dislodge, and that you might even be making the other party uneasy. By choosing to climb beneath them, you accept full responsibility for your welfare. If another party is hot on your heels, politely let them know to stay alert as well. Since they chose to climb beneath you, *they* are responsible for whatever might happen. Multiple parties are almost unavoidable on popular multipitch routes these days, so evaluate the risk and decide whether you want to come back another time, perhaps with an earlier start. I avoid climbing under other parties, even on bomber rock like granite. I'd rather find another route than risk having stuff dropped on my head.

1

The pros and cons of a wide range of possible staging areas at the Bowling Alley crag, Boulder Canyon

TRUNDLiNG KiLLS: THE DEATH OF PETE ABSOLON

Pete Absolon was a beloved figure in the Wyoming climbing community, Rocky Mountain Director for the National Outdoor Leadership School (NOLS), a longtime guide, and a skilled, hardcore all-arounder. Absolon lost his life on August 11, 2007, because of a rock heedlessly tossed off a wall in Leg Lake Cirque in the Wind River Range. He and his partner, Steve Herlihy, had climbed to within 200 feet of the top on a 1000-foot first ascent when a man named Luke Rodolph trundled a bowling ball–sized stone. Rodolph, who'd been camping above with family and friends, carelessly dropped the rock off the precipice to see and hear it fall. By the time Rodolph spotted Absolon and Herlihy below, at a semihanging belay with white helmets on, it was too late. The rock hit Absolon on the back of his head, killing him instantly.

It's a given that rocks fall, whether spontaneously or accidentally dislodged. However, there is zero justification for wanton sport trundling. I used to do it myself as a young rowdy, often in places where my friends and I felt sure that we were alone, but such thinking is a trap. Rodolph and friends had knocked rocks off a different part of the cliff earlier in the day and not heard anyone for miles, so he assumed it would be fine to throw that final stone. It wasn't.

A climber was killed, a wife was widowed, and a little girl was left without her father. The lesson is clear: Do not sport-trundle. Not only is it dangerous, but trundled rocks shred the environment by dislodging other rocks, tearing up grasses and soil, and damaging trees.

If you must trundle a loose block for safety reasons, and you can't see the runout, minimize the risk by:

- Staging lookouts below, well to the side of the cliff base or landing zone
- Slinging or tying off the rock and lowering it on a pulley system
- Dropping the rock into your backpack or haul bag

Finally, pay attention to a cliff's natural rockfall—to stones that spontaneously detach. If a cliff has scree and talus at its base, chances are it sheds with regularity; that's how the talus got there! Be extra careful in spring or early summer during the freeze-thaw cycle, especially when it has warmed up after a cold spell or after periods of heavy rain. I've seen giant blocks slide off muddy ledges in Rifle without warning.

Eyes Down

Now to not dropping things and keeping an eye out for folks below you. Fumbled or dropped gear is common, especially at traditional crags where climbers are removing protection as they second. So don't be "that guy," the gear-fumbling bumbler! To avoid bobbling gear, leave it clipped to the rope upon removal. Later, at good stances or once you reach the belay, you can easily unclip the gear and rerack it. This approach also lets you move quickly through a strenuous section. If there's a free, second biner on the piece or sling, clip it into one of your harness's gear loops *before* you unclip the gear from the rope so that the piece is never free-floating.

Dropped nut tools are also common, especially when a second is battling a recalcitrant piece. Here are a few ways to keep your nut tool secure:

- Keep it on a biner that you clip to the rope while you work on the piece.
- Build a keeper leash for it with either a long sling or one of those Slinky-style extendo cords; clip the tool off short to one of your gear loops when you are not using it.
- Place another, more easily removed piece near the stuck one to fifi into, so that both your hands are free to clean.

You also don't want to be that choss monkey who accidentally dislodges rocks onto others. Step on solid rock to travel instead of gravel or scree. Also, avoid staging in steep, loose gullies or on sketchy talus above other parties. I almost inadvertently took out two climbers downhill from me in Smith Rock's steep, gnarly Cocaine Gully when I stepped off a big rock to start a climb and it came loose. They escaped unharmed, but were angry as wolverines and had every right to be. It's better to find another climb rather than endanger others. Remember also that your rope can dislodge loose rocks if it's flaked amid them (see the "Rope Obstacle Course" sidebar); either use a rope bag or flake it on solid ground.

The same rule holds true while you climb: Avoid obviously loose holds. Rap or bang on suspect blocks with your knuckles or palm, listening for telltale bonging or booming or dirt issuing from the bottom. Be especially cautious during a freeze-thaw period, when the rock is most likely to shift. If you can work out a sequence that avoids a loose hold, then use it. If the rock is a big, obvious time bomb, retreating either by downclimbing

1

ROPE OBSTACLE COURSE

Try this drill: Flake your rope on a slab covered in loose stones, or snake your rope through an obstacle course of rocks. Now pull one end sharply like you would when feeding slack to a clipping leader, and see what happens: a choss avalanche, right? It's best to keep the cord in a rope bag, both for safety and for its longevity. Barring that, stack your rope in a flat area without loose rock, or if you are up on a ledge (on a multipitch route), butterfly-coil it over your tie-in tether or foot.

or lowering off an anchor below the block may be the safest option. Finally, if you *must* use a suspect hold, first pull on it lightly to see if it flexes, and then warn everyone below you. Pull down, not out, keeping your rope, legs, and torso to the side of the rock, and move quickly.

STAGING THE BELAY

Now that you've approached the cliff, assessed the hazards, and staged yourself in a safe zone, where should you set up to belay? The primary rule is to face in the direction of pull directly

Rope obstacle course: *1, 2, 3—TUG!*

1

under the first piece for the *entire* pitch. Don't move around for your own comfort and convenience, even when your climber is high on her route. On a steep climb you might be able to turn around and look out at your climber to ameliorate neck strain, but never stray from beneath that first piece. If it's a long pitch with rope-drag issues and the leader unclips her first draw once she has clipped into the second bolt or piece of pro, then orient yourself under the new first draw. If you're tethered to an anchor and can safely move around a bit, leave some play in your tether so you can stay optimally oriented.

I like to set myself up in a "belay box" directly under the first piece. This invisible, four-foot-by-four-foot square serves as my working belay area. It lets me move forward and back to pay out or take in slack, and laterally to avoid my falling climber or loose rock. Set your rope bag beside the box so that you don't trip on it, and ask any climbers who straggle into the box to vacate immediately. Mike Alkaitis says that veterans are less likely than neophytes to respect others' belay boxes. Beginners naturally prefer more space while belaying and will shy away from invaders, perhaps because they're more focused. So keep a beginner's mind.

To see firsthand the importance of good belay orientation and the belay box, practice catching a few falls in the gym or even lowering a heavier climber. The forces can be fierce, sudden, and violent, evidence that will convince you to situate yourself directly under that first piece. Still, we've all seen those knuckleheads who migrate ever farther from the first clip the higher their climber goes, or who most idiotically *begin* lead belaying way back from the wall and remain there with a lazy slack loop dragging on the ground. Catching one fall this way—and perhaps even bobbling your brake hand when you hurtle face-first toward the wall—should change your mind. If you need to step back from time to time to see your climber, do so sparingly and then immediately return to the belay box. Straying also creates rope-drag issues; instead belay actively, judge what's going on from the play in the rope, and perhaps have your leader yell "Clipping!" when he is out of view.

Good, Bad, and Ugly Belayers

Chances are that you *love* having a good belayer. Respect the Golden Rule, and always be that same good belayer for your partners.

The *good* belayer:

- Stays in her belay box, directly under the first piece in the direction of pull, even when lowering; uses good device and rope management and subtle body movements to feed and suck in slack instead of exaggerated movements that exceed the boundaries of the belay box.
- Anchors in at the route base (in the direction of pull) if she has doubts about holding the leader because of a size differential or marginal belay stance.
- Stays hyperfocused on the first three or four bolts on longer routes or at each clip on shorter routes with ground-fall potential.
- Closes the system by tying a stopper knot in the rope or tying in to the bottom end herself before the leader sets off. She makes her stopper knot big and beefy so that it can't possibly squeeze through the belay device. (Knots can compress under pressure.)
- Double-checks herself and her climber before the climber leaves the ground; has her climber sit back on the rope and test the system as a further safeguard.
- Stays out of the fall line of loose rock or dropped gear.
- Wears belay gloves for rope traction and to keep her hands clean for climbing.
- Uses belay glasses (brands include CU, Belaggles, and Belay Specs) for extended belays to reduce neck strain and stay focused.
- Keeps the rope snag-free by neatly stacking it, and then flicks and lasso-whips the rope coming off the stack to avoid hosing her leader on rapid clips. (Snarlier ropes might need a preflight reflaking.)
- Keeps roughly a foot of play, a "lazy smile," in the line (once the climber is up 20 feet or more) to facilitate easy clipping and a soft catch, but not so much slack that it's the proverbial sport loop.
- Jumps up and in a little to give a dynamic belay and bring the leader to a gradual halt instead of sucking in rope ("I don't want you to fall too far, honey!") and locking the device off *hard*, which short-ropes him into the wall like a pendulum.

1

- Is proficient with belay plates and tubes and assisted-braking belay devices, and always keeps her brake hand on the rope.
- Doesn't let distractions take her mind or eyes off her climber, but instead keeps a razor focus on her task; asks anyone who starts talking to her to return once she's done belaying.
- Communicates clearly before the pitch about what the leader plans to do at the anchor: Will the leader remain on belay and be lowered? Will he bring her up as a second? Will he rappel?
- Keeps an eye on how much rope is left and monitors the middle mark and remaining rope.
- Has determined alternative means of communication if vocal signals are ineffective because of ambient noise (traffic, rushing streams, etc.) or a route's geometry or length.

The *bad* belayer:

- Moves around so much that her belay box encroaches on others (e.g., those dim bulbs who lock off the rope and, without looking, run 10 feet backward when their climber says "Take!").
- Moves farther and farther from the first piece as the climber gets higher so that he can "see the leader."
- Doesn't keep enough play in the line, so that the rope locks off on tough clips, nearly pulling the leader off backward when the belay device jams up.
- Short-ropes the leader on falls, giving an ankle-snapping hard catch.
- Chucks out slack indiscriminately when the climber is clipping, without looking up to make sure he's gauging rope correctly; fails to suck in excess slack after the climber clips.
- Stays in the fall line, without noting the hazard.
- Rarely if ever looks up, explaining that his "neck gets sore" or that his climber "will be fine."
- Chats with other climbers.
- Can safely use only one type of belay device and refuses to learn any others.

In addition to all the things that the bad belayer does, the *ugly* belayer also:

- Doesn't double-check herself or her climber before he leaves the ground.
- Neglects to tie a stopper knot.
- Belays from a lawn chair or lying down (yes, I have seen this!).
- Doesn't anchor in when she should, risking being dragged or swung into the rock.
- Pays attention sporadically to her climber, and instead fusses with her crag pack, plays with her dogs, or talks so loudly she can't hear basic commands.
- Takes her brake hand off the rope.
- Gets defensive when anyone points out her bad habits ("I've never dropped anyone! How dare you? This is how I learned at the Mega Crimpfest Indoor Rock Palace.")

NORBERT NOOB'S BiG ADVENTURE

As we move further into the book, let's consider this cautionary tale centered on hypothetical Norbert N00b and his day out cragging. This book is in part intended for climbers like Norbert, an urbanite who is new to the sport and the outdoors in general. Poor Norbert does everything wrong, without even realizing it. He's been climbing six months (four of those at his local gym), thinks he has it all figured out, and doesn't want to hear otherwise. He's never had instruction beyond his gym's basic belay and lead classes, and neither have his friends. They often head out together, in a posse of six or more people, as climbing feels safer that way. But not one among them has taken an outdoor skills or leadership course or been tutored by a mentor. After we and Norbert evolve over the course of this book, we'll check back in with him (see Chapter 7) to see if he's mended his wicked ways.

Norbert N00b stumbles out of bed at 10:00 AM, hungover, with a Burger King crown on his head, left over from that sweet-ass kegger the night before. Leaving the crown on, he wolfs down coffee and a bowl of Froot

Loops and then blows up his buddy's cellie: "Yo, Tommy, where you at, G? I think we're climbing today!" Norbert hollers into Tommy's voice mail before remembering that he was supposed to meet Tommy and their friends in town at 8:00 AM to carpool.

"Ah, well, screw it," thinks Norbert. "I'll just drive out and find those guys."

After jumping into his extended-cab F-250, Norbert rages out to the crag solo with his German shepherd Rommel in the back. The crag is on private property with a modest day-use fee (three dollars) and a waiver sign-in at the trailhead, but Norbert is pretty sure that stuff doesn't apply to him. Anyway, he doesn't have cash and figures that enough other climbers have already kicked down, so why bother? The parking lot is full, so Norbert squeezes his truck in beside a "No Parking" sign. Never mind that there is legal parking back down the road: This looks like the perfect spot. He opens the tailgate and lets Rommel out to roam while he sorts his gear. Rommel heads off to the side, rooting at a groundhog hole right by the "Dogs must be leashed" sign. Norbert has always hated packing, unpacking, and repacking his crag kit, so he stores his gear in his truck bed—rope, draws, harness, and shoes all sitting out in the open.

1

The bed has a liner, but Norbert often hauls construction supplies around in it, and he hasn't cleaned it in awhile. Norbert pulls on his harness in the parking lot; racks draws on it; clips a water bottle, his truck keys, prusiks, a daisy chain, a belay knife, two belay devices, and his chalk bag to the gear loops; and straps on his rope and day pack. He also puts on his rock shoes, comfy planklike rigs he could wear all day with socks. It is time to climb! Norbert whistles for Rommel and heads up the hill with the dog bounding ahead.

It is only a short hike uphill on a switchbacking trail, but since Norbert is in a hurry, he heads directly for the cliff, cutting switchbacks and sidling around a sign that reads "Erosion hazard: Please stay on trail." Then it hits him: He hasn't done his business, and all that beer and fast food are sloshing around in his gut. Norbert has to go, and now!

He leaves Rommel to run up ahead and ducks behind a tree. He briefly considers the pit toilet back at the parking lot but dismisses it as "too far away." Instead he takes off his harness, drops his trousers, and cuts loose; Norbert uses a little toilet paper he has in his backpack, and then plops a rock down atop the mess. He heads back up the hill, repeatedly hollering, "Tommy, YO, TOMMY, where you at, homey?!" and whistling for Rommel. Suddenly, Norbert hears a dogfight up ahead, punctuated by yelping: *"Rommel!"* he thinks.

Norbert charges up to the cliff to find Rommel tussling with a dog leashed to a tree while the dog's owner, who is belaying, tries unsuccessfully to break up the fight. Rommel has also dragged the climber's lunch out of his pack and eaten half a peanut-butter sandwich, including the plastic bag.

"Yo, man, what's up with your dog?" Norbert demands, sticking his hand in to grab Rommel by the collar and yanking him from the fray. "Rommel never gets into fights—Ow, shit, your dog bit me!" he screams as the other dog snaps at him. Norbert drags Rommel away, mumbling epithets, without apologizing for his dog's behavior. The belayer stares after him, dumbstruck.

After hollering for Tommy some more, thrashing through the underbrush off-trail below the cliff so he can get a better view, and discarding an energy-bar wrapper in the woods, Norbert N00b finally locates Tommy and crew at a sector with a handful of classic 5.10s. The gang has set up

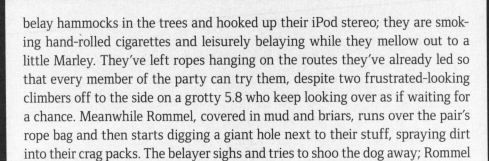

belay hammocks in the trees and hooked up their iPod stereo; they are smoking hand-rolled cigarettes and leisurely belaying while they mellow out to a little Marley. They've left ropes hanging on the routes they've already led so that every member of the party can try them, despite two frustrated-looking climbers off to the side on a grotty 5.8 who keep looking over as if waiting for a chance. Meanwhile Rommel, covered in mud and briars, runs over the pair's rope bag and then starts digging a giant hole next to their stuff, spraying dirt into their crag packs. The belayer sighs and tries to shoo the dog away; Rommel just growls at him and curls up in his nest.

Completely ignoring this tableau, Norbert drops his pack atop a fragile fern away from the main staging area, yells, "What up, homeys!" to his friends, and starts spraying loudly about how he has already ticked this "beginner" sector but is psyched to "warm up for those sick-ass twelves around the corner." He starts pulling random gear out of his pack and tossing it into the dirt while bellowing up to Tommy, who has just reached the anchor on a route, "Which one of you bitches is belaying me?" Tommy is trying to figure out how to thread the chains so that they can top-rope straight through the rings without wearing out his brand-new quickdraws, but he's never threaded an anchor before. Norbert N00b hollers up vague anchor beta while Tommy, sketching, tries to clip in with a daisy chain.

Norbert doesn't stick around to make sure Tommy gets back safely to the ground; he instead jumps on one of the group's pre-slung top ropes to the side. Still wearing his Burger King crown, Norbert hits up his friend Sally for a belay. Without cleaning his muddy shoes or checking his knot or Sally's belay device, Norbert sets off without even a glance upward. "It's only 5.10," he thinks. "I cruise 5.10 in the gym. Whatever . . . " All the shiny metal accessories clank on his harness while Norbert climbs, and he reaches back awkwardly to his dangling chalk bag, futzing with it and barely getting any chalk. Norbert leaves black mud all over the lower holds and ugly dirt-and-rubber streaks down the rock when his feet skate . . . which is often. As the climb steepens and the holds grow smaller, Norbert begins to struggle. Until now, he's had honker jugs and gotten by with awkward, lunging high-steps.

1

About halfway up, feeling pumped, he fumbles a draw while unclipping, and it plummets to the ground. But since Norbert can see that it is going to land out away from his friends, he doesn't yell "Rock!" Nobody notices—they are too busy chatting and hammock-lounging. Then comes the crux: Around two-thirds of the way up, the route requires intricate sequencing on smeary footholds. Sally screams the occasional "You've got it, Norbert," but doesn't look up and maintains a lazy sport loop. Breathing like a freight train and quivering head-to-toe, he sets up for a big jump, walks his feet awkwardly up the wall like Tom Sawyer scaling a fence. He gives off a loud, cursing grunt—"Fawwwwkkk!"—and throws. And misses.

Norbert sags onto the rope and thinks "Uh-oh!" as he drops through space. He looks down and sees Sally with her hands off the rope, the cord zipping through her belay device, horror writ on her face. The last thing he notices before smacking the ground ankles-and-ass-first is that Sally's device is threaded backward. Of course, the other problem could be that his rope came undone from his harness partway down, since he tied-in with a figure 8 follow-through but didn't complete it in his haste to climb.

Norbert N00b rebounds off the deck and comes to rest in a crumpled ball, howling, his ankles broken and tailbone shattered. His friends stare at him dumbfounded and think, "How did this happen? I thought we were just out doing some chill sport climbing. This never happens in the gym." In shock, crying, and panting with agony in the cold, hard dirt, Norbert looks off to the side and right before the world goes dark notices a shiny gold object: It is his Burger King crown, resting against the flanks of his sleeping dog, Rommel.

STAYING ALIVE

To the nonclimbing public, we're a bunch of Mountain Dew–slamming, adrenaline-junkie thrill-seekers. Aunt Martha from Omaha will never understand the difference between top-roping a 5.8 sport route and soloing the Kangshung Face, so there's no point in explaining to her our sport's infinite gradations of risk and the infinite variables that

1

inform them. *Despite the best skill set and preparation, accidents can and do happen.* Still, we must control the known variables so that we're better equipped to face the known-unknowns and the unknown-unknowns when they go down. Much stems from how you approach each technical skill. Being humble and proactive about safety every step of the way minimizes your chances of disaster.

The Top Five Ways to Stay Alive

Staying alive to climb another day is the ultimate goal. There is no great nobility in dying while climbing, only the end of life and the pain of those left behind. *Dying doing "what you love" is small consolation for dying a preventable death.* The following five tips are culled from my own experience and conversations with other veteran climbers. They are as much guiding philosophies as they are methodologies, the sort of foundational notions that infused every lesson back in the day.

1. Be Humble

I try to live by this tenet just as much now as when I started. If I don't understand a technique or piece of gear, I ask questions of those in the know, study product litera-ture, or have someone show me until I'm certain I have it right. Knowing and admitting what you don't know are both important! If an exposed section of scrambling seems to merit a rope or I want a belay where others don't, I ask. If a lead feels off or too risky that day, I back off. If I'm pumping out on a strenuous clip and fear falling with the rope out, I grab the quickdraw.

And I never ask my partners to do something they're uncomfortable doing, nor should they ask such things of me. Climb with people who are also humble, and avoid those out to show you up; competition is good only when it's friendly and focused on bringing both partners to higher levels. We are all fragile, all mortal, and climbing 5.whatever-plus does not confer immunity from accidents. Despite all the bravado on internet climbing forums, there is no such thing as a stupid question or wimping out; there is only the omnipresent specter of gravity.

2. Ground-School Everything

At moderate sport areas around Boulder, I've noticed an alarming trend of beginners being instructed *on the rock* by "leaders" barely more qualified than themselves. Before

1

gym and sport climbing became the dominant gateways to our sport, you apprenticed for months and years because there was so much to learn about trad climbing. We spent hours on the ground placing protection and inspecting those placements, building anchors, and drilling and redrilling every last skill. The idea was, you needed to master the basics in a milieu without fatal consequences before exercising them in the real world.

There is no reason to change this formula, even in the gym era. If you are teaching someone to use a new belay device, simulate a lead or two on the ground with the belayer feeding out slack, taking it in, and then lowering—and then have a third party supervise him or slap a back-up device on the rope behind him when he really belays. If you are teaching someone to thread top anchors, again, do it on the ground (see the "Anchors Away" section). If you are teaching someone to lead, belay her on top rope at the gym while she uses a second cord to simulate clipping and rope management.

3. Double-Check and Double Down

As the survivor stories presented later illustrate, failure to double-check even one system component can lead to catastrophe. *Double- and triple-check everything:* your harness, your knot, your gear, your belayer, your rope, your rappel device.

And when you can, *double down.* Build redundancy into every part of the system: double up on slings and lockers at anchors, stack two pieces on a trad lead at a crux or runout or to back up fixed pro like bolts and pitons, use a locking and/or two reversed (opposed) quickdraws at critical bolts, preclip your rope to both the first and second bolts on a climb with a difficult opening sequence, and so on. *As the saying goes, one is good but two is always better.*

4. Research Everything, Including the Rating

With modern full-color guidebooks, online route databases like Mountain Project (www.mountainproject.com), and guidebook apps, there is more route information available today than ever. You have zero excuse not to do your due diligence; spend a few minutes learning about an area and its routes before you go. Scrutinize the number of clips or rack requirements (bring extra quickdraws or gear), the rope length necessary for lowering, the rock quality, the condition and age of fixed hardware, the descent, and the danger or protection rating (e.g., G, PG, PG-13, R, or X). At the

1

THE "DADDY DRAW"

Before I became a parent, I made fun of locking quickdraws ("daddy draws"), deriding them as gumby overkill. But daddy draws are superb for hard climbs with cruxes down low or for when you are passing a mission-critical bolt from which the rope must not accidentally come unclipped. To build a daddy draw:

- Remove the carabiners from a quickdraw dogbone.
- Attach lockers on the draw's bolt and rope sides, with their gates facing the same direction; don't swap the biners around, as the bolt-side biner accrues nicks and scratches that are hard on the rope. Also, use screw-gate lockers, which are easier to lock and unlock one-handed than twist-locks (aka auto-lockers).
- Use daddy draws on low or crux bolts and also at top-rope anchors; ignore the derision of your jerk-butt partners.
- If you don't have a daddy draw, tape the gate shut on your rope-side biner (say, when stick-clipping) or double up on quickdraws, opposing the rope-side gates on both.

same time, think for yourself because guidebooks contain errors and beta can be subjective. Also, ask people who have climbed the route recently for the latest beta—conditions change.

Never put too much stock in a route's rating, because grades may vary wildly even within a single area. They should be taken only as useful guidelines. Also, anything with a "plus" or "d" rating, particularly from the 1960s-through-1980s era of grade compression, is probably a sandbag. Don't fall prey to the notion that just because you've climbed 5.10d, for instance, in one place that you should necessarily try 5.10ds everywhere. *Ratings are not the same at all cliffs.* A 5.9-plus offwidth at Vedauwoo (Wyoming) will be lightyears harder than a four-bolt 5.9-plus at the Red River Gorge, so don't let the rating dictate your choices. Look instead for appealing climbs within a certain grade range. You'll be much happier for it. Trust me: I spent years at Rifle chasing numbers, and it turned me into a miserable, perpetually frustrated shell of a man. Grades are empty calories.

1

Also, beware the sandbag! I recall in 1989 cockily jumping on a radically over-hanging "5.11c" at Hueco Tanks called *Secret Sharer,* a grade I'd climbed back in New Mexico. *Secret Sharer,* however, turned out to be a slippery, dynamic scarefest put up by the Hueco pioneer Mike Head, with only four bolts in 60 feet. After barely sketching through greasy, sloper huecos to a high second clip over a death-block pit, I left a carabiner and lowered, whining like a kicked puppy. Then I asked around and learned the truth—*Secret Sharer* was a sandbagged 5.12! When I returned a year later to redeem myself, I knew better than to think of it as a 5.11c.

5. Build Lasting Partnerships and Follow the Golden Rule

One of the most intimate bonds you'll share in life is with a trusted climbing partner, yet so much of that seems lost in the modern era of school clubs, rock-gym meet-and-climbs, group outings, and online partner finders. These are all useful tools, but any old salt will tell you to compile a short roster of A-list partners who are also friends you trust implicitly. At the heart of any solid partnership is an unspoken pledge to do right by your partner, double-checking each other's systems and providing unimpeachable belays. "We use the word *partner* nonchalantly, but we really are in it together," as climbing guide Mike Alkaitis puts it. "Gravity works 365 days a year, and it doesn't care how experienced you are. Accidents can happen to anyone, so use that partnership to your advantage."

That random dude at the gym who wants to trade belays: what do you know about his skill level, and should you trust him to hold your lifeline? My sister-in-law did this once in London and ended up taking a 40-foot ground fall thanks to belayer inatten-tion. A true partner is much more than a belayer, but you should ask the same of every belayer that you would of a trusted partner: competence and his undivided attention.

By the same token, what responsibility do we have to climbers beyond our party? If you see a stranger doing something unsafe, should you speak up or go hide? I warrant that it's the former. If you take five minutes to *talk* to someone, you may even save his life. And by not saying something you may become involved anyway, in the rescue.

Some years ago during an unfortunate, arrogant period in my climbing career, I set off to lead a pillar during only my second day on ice, well before I had become profi-cient with crampons and tools. A friend and mountain guide at the cliff gently warned that I "might not want to do that, as tools can pop way more easily than you think." I backed off below the slender crux icicle and was glad for it when later I found the climb spooky even on top rope.

1

ANCHOR THREADING

1 First clip off to upper points on both anchors with the quickdraws equalized, keeping the bottom lowering rings free.

2 Next, pull up a big bight of rope and clove-hitch it off, to retain the rope while you untie and thread.

3 After you thread the lowest points on the anchors, tie back in, and undo your clove hitch, call down "Take!" Then have your belayer reel in slack to get you tight to the anchors and confirm that you're ready to be lowered. Don't forget to unclip your draws.

40

1

That is the way to speak up: point out in a friendly manner that what someone is doing is dangerous, what the consequences could be, and that there are safer alternatives. You might also cite precedents where this practice has led to an accident. If you see an entire group engaging in an unsafe practice, identify the leader and then take him aside for a quiet chat to avoid disrespecting him before his charges. Nine times out of ten people respond well, and if they don't, then you can walk away knowing you tried.

Anchors Away

Since anchor threading is such a key skill—it's one of the only times you come fully out of the belay system, plus we do it quite frequently—let's review the best way to do this, as well as possible practices to avoid. Mike Alkaitis says that he spends a full *two hours* in his courses teaching students how to clean quickdraws off a bolted sport anchor. Even though more experienced climbers might have other methods for cleaning sport anchors, this one remains the simplest, fastest, and best (to understand why, see the "Daisy Chains" section below):

1. When you reach the anchor, clip one quickdraw from your belay loop directly into one of the anchor points, and another draw into the other anchor point, equalizing the two draws. Clip into the hangers so that the rings or chains remain free for lowering.
2. Pull up eight feet of rope, and clip it off to your harness with a clove hitch or figure 8 on a bight. Call down "Slack" to your belayer as you do so—but never "Off belay."
3. Untie and thread the rope through the *lowest* anchor points, usually rings or quick links (mallions) at the end of the chains, such that your rope doesn't cross itself coming up from below (i.e., thread from left to right if the anchor is up and right of the bolt line and vice versa).
4. Tie back in, undo the clove hitch, and drop the slack.
5. Verify verbally that you're still on belay, ask your belayer to "Take" to get you snug on the rope, confirm that you're ready to lower,

1

double-check everything a final time, and then unclip your draws from the anchors and descend.

To ground-school someone in this method, demonstrate the process using simulated bolts like two slung trees or two protection points. Put locking carabiners (lockers) on the two points to simulate lowering rings. Now, as your pupil works each step, quiz him about the consequences of a mistake; ask him what would happen if he did a particular step incorrectly.

You also can prethread the anchor so that your rope is already through the rings for your second in a slingshot top rope. As a community service to preserve the rings, rig your anchor such that the rope weights the two carabiners and not the rings themselves. Because it wears out the metal, *it is poor form to top-rope directly through fixed anchors*. With a classic ring-and-chain set-up, this means clipping two lockers or short quickdraws directly to the bolt hangers after threading the rings. When your second reaches the anchors, he need only remove the carabiners and lower.

Daisy Chains and Rappeling Off Lowering Rings

Newer climbers unfortunately have been girth-hitching daisy chains through their harness tie-in points to clip into sport anchors when threading. While climbing, these climbers then string up their daisy chains through their nether regions and clip them off to a gear loop—oh, the humanity! More and more climbers are also rappeling off perfectly good ring-style lowering anchors. The justification for the former seems to be that a daisy chain's multiple pockets let you more easily equalize between the two anchor bolts and is somehow more reliable than your belay loop. While for the latter, these rings are deemed "for rappeling only" or it's thought that repeated lowering will wear grooves in the metal. Let's examine these hypotheses.

Daisy Chains

Daisy chains are three- to four-foot slings with looped ends and myriad bar-tacked clipping pockets. They were designed so that aid and wall climbers could fifi into protection and also into ascenders, letting them adjust their jumar stroke length on the fly. Unlike newer purpose-designed anchor tethers like the Metolius Personal Anchor System (PAS), which can hold 22 kilonewtons (4950 foot-pounds), daisy

1

Anchor prerigged for safe top-roping but also for lowering, in case the second feels uncomfortable with threading

1

chains are not intended for loads grossly exceeding average body weight, such as you'd generate if one anchor bolt failed or you slipped from above the anchor while cleaning. Daisy chains are meant for *static* loads, and their sewn pockets typically pop around 500 to 1000 foot-pounds says Kolin Powick, director of global quality at Black Diamond Equipment.

Moreover, the daisy chain can become *disconnected* if you've clipped in across a pocket's bar tack—that is, used the top biner on the end loop to clip into a lower pocket also. In this scenario, you've clipped into two loops separated only by stitching. If the stitching blows in a chain reaction, you're suddenly clipped to *nothing*, and you'll fall right to the ground. If you insist on using a daisy, go in short only by clipping a separate locking biner to the lower pocket and then to the top locker. Better yet, use a sling, or anchor tether specifically designed for anchor work. Always girth-hitch slings, daisies, or the anchor tether through your tie-in points, never through your belay loop.

Powick, with a decade of experience at Black Diamond Equipment and a bachelor's degree in mechanical engineering, says that he uses the quickdraw method to clean anchors, and trusts his belay loop. This little loop is far and away the strongest part of your harness, and if it is in good condition, it should not spontaneously fail. For a harness to get its European Community (CE) certification, its belay loop must withstand three minutes of 15 kilonewtons (3372 foot-pounds) of force, and most exceed that. You can also girth-hitch a short sewn runner through the tie-in points alongside the loop as a backup.

Ring Anchors

As someone who installs many new anchors, I know that there are no absolutes with steel anchor rings: they are neither only for lowering nor only for rappeling. (Only those flimsy aluminum rappel rings are rappel only.) True, a weighted rope running through rings will erode the steel until eventually they need to be replaced, but a route popular enough to see that volume of traffic will eventually need new rings anyway, even if everyone climbing it rappels. A well-placed modern sport anchor is designed to have its components updated, and often community initiatives provide the funding for hardware. Don't be shy about lowering if the situation calls for it.

With fixed anchors, be situationally aware:

- Keep your rope clean and flaked in a rope bag so that it doesn't pick up dirt and rock particles, which erode anchor metal.

- If you want to rappel to preserve an anchor, then do so—it's a thoughtful gesture! If, however, draws are still hanging from bolts or the route is overhanging or traverses, it's often safer to lower so that you have both hands free to retrieve draws. You might need to tram into the rope's belayer side (that is, clip into it with a quickdraw attached directly to your belay loop) to stay in anyway, making rappeling impracticable.
- If an anchor is over a ledge or lip and lowering will maul your rope, consider rappeling or bringing up your second.
- Rappel also if the two lowering points are widely spaced horizontally—a foot or more—or the anchor has an uneven number of chain links (and no rings or mallions). Both scenarios will turn your rope into spaghetti, the former by introducing double 90-degree bends and the latter by kinking and pinning the rope. If you must lower, pull the rope through the long way (via the end you're tied into) once down to work kinks out through the anchor.

The Many, Many Ways to Die

Unfortunately, there are as many ways to die climbing as there are routes. The interested should pick up the American Alpine Club's annual *Accidents in North American Mountaineering,* a grim but informative resource. Let's examine some hard facts and figures from my backyard, Boulder County, Colorado, to segue into three case studies of competent, veteran climbers who made common mistakes that nearly claimed their lives. My hope is that by examining the errors climbers make most, we can strive to avoid them.

In 2012, the Rocky Mountain Rescue Group (RMRG) released two studies: one on rock-climbing rescue causes, injuries, and trends in Boulder County and the other on Boulder's mainstay trad area, Eldorado Canyon. Boulder is notable both for its thousands of climbers (including many from the greater Denver metropolitan area) and thousands of single- and multipitch sport and trad routes. None of our cliffs stand much taller than 1000 feet, so you could say that Boulder County represents a microcosm, distilled to pure concentrate, of the overall American cragging scene. The studies focused on 14 years (1998 through 2011) during which RMRG responded to

1

345 climbing incidents involving 428 victims; 85 percent of these incidents occurred in Boulder's most popular areas: Eldorado and Boulder Canyons and the Flatirons.

The findings were enlightening. First off, rock-climbing rescues in Boulder only came to 19.5 percent of total mountain and wilderness search-and-rescue (SAR) victims. Thus more than 80 percent of rescues were for nonclimbers, even in an area this vertiginous—so much for the public's perception of "reckless" climbers overtaxing SAR resources! Meanwhile, technical roped climbers accounted for 11 percent of all SAR victims and 58 percent of total climbing victims, while unroped climbers (free soloers and scramblers) clocked in at about half of that: 6.5 percent of SAR and 34 percent of total climbing victims. Looked at another way, some 190 roped-climbing incidents involved 247 victims, while some 120 unroped incidents involved 145 victims. In third place came bouldering, with 24 incidents involving 26 victims, and in fourth place was bystanders hit by rockfall (5 incidents involving 4 victims). Unroped climbing by far caused the most fatalities—9 incidents or 39 percent of the 23 total climbing fatalities—followed by lead falls (5 deaths), lowering accidents (3 deaths), and anchor failure, rockfall, and mountaineering mishaps (2 deaths each).

Although accidents while roped were more numerous, clearly your chances of survival are better with a rope—a reflection both of how few people free solo vs. climb roped and of the almost universally fatal consequences of a large, unroped fall. Per the study, "For all rescues of persons involved in technical roped climbing, lead falls are the dominant cause, followed by belay incidents . . . and then by climbers who became lost during the descent—thus necessitating SAR assistance, predominantly after sunset." To break it down even further, here are the top five roped-climbing incidents by cause:

1. Lead fall: 39 percent
2. Belay incident (lost control, lowered off the rope, rappeled off the rope, rope became stuck while rappelling, or tied knot incorrectly): 21.5 percent
3. Lost: 10 percent
4. Stranded: 10 percent
5. Unknown: 6.5 percent

Lead climbing thus emerges as the most dangerous pursuit behind free soloing. The consequences of a huge, upside-down, ledge-smacking, or gear-ripping whipper are abundantly clear: you get injured or worse. But note that belaying and rappeling incidents are also a major subset of roped-climbing incidents, probably because climbers rely so completely on a system easily affected by user error. As the study states, "Belay and rappeling incidents in which the rope was not long enough for the climber to reach the ground accounted for 21 victims, 16 of whom had severe or fatal injuries and 3 of whom received severe rope burns while belaying." Meanwhile, "Belay-related climbing incidents (51 individuals) included 8 belayers losing control of the rope while lowering and 20 climbers stuck on rappel." Thus whether your slacker belayer drops the ball or you botch the rappel, inattention and poor technical skills—both preventable scenarios—are likely culprits.

The study also offers some great takeaways, synthesized at RMRG's website (www .rockymountainrescue.org):

- Anchors rarely fail (anchor failure accounts for only 2.5 percent of total climbing incidents), but when they do it is most likely because the person setting them up is inexperienced.
- Of all accidents, 20 percent could have been prevented by better belay practices, such as tying a knot in the end of the rope or wearing belay gloves.
- Rockfall causes a small number of accidents (4.5 percent of total) and may be related to the freeze-thaw cycles of spring and climb-er-use patterns. Checking the rock you're about to climb on is a prudent preventive measure (even on well-frequented trade routes).
- Being knowledgeable about a climb's rappel anchors and walk-off and taking a headlamp would prevent a lot of rescues (up to 45 percent of total).
- The most common injuries sustained are to the legs and ankles (30 percent) and to the head and spine (30 percent). Knowing how to improvise a splint and how to assess spinal injuries is a great addition to a climber's toolkit.

What else can you do to stay alive? Well, lots of things! Before we go to our survivor stories, here are a few, simple, proactive life-saving steps:

- Carry a headlamp and extra batteries.
- Bring suitable raingear (impermeable or semi-impermeable) and warm clothing (hat, gloves, thermal shirt and tights, fleece, parka, etc.).

1

- Get trained in first aid and basic life-support skills, and consider becoming certified as a Wilderness First Responder.
- Bring a small first-aid kit.
- Bring a cell phone.
- Always tell a responsible person where you are going, who you are climbing with (your contact person should have the phone number of your partner's contact person), what your climbing plans and alternate plans are, when you will return, and the time at which, if you haven't yet returned, your contact person should alert the authorities.

Three Survivor Stories: Even Veteran Climbers Make Mistakes

Lecturing about safety only goes so far—*nag, nag, nag, nag, nag*—until you have the misfortune to either witness or experience an accident yourself. No one among us, from the birthday-party kid tying in for her first time at the gym, to the 40-year veteran leading his ten-thousandth pitch, is exempt. Gravity pulls us all toward earth at 32.2 feet per second squared, and pilot error, chance, and a moment's inattention will let gravity have its way. The three examples below are all veterans who through simple haste or inattention fell victim to common mistakes, many also made by climbers in the RMRG study. Let their stories serve as a reminder that we must treat every time we tie-in as attentively as the first.

Craig DeMartino: Miscommunication about Lowering

Colorado climber Craig DeMartino had 18 years in the game the day he fell 100 feet . . . to the ground. On July 21, 2002, DeMartino, a solid all-arounder who cruises 5.12 sport and 5.11 trad, had just completed the first pitch of a 5.11 called *Whiteman* on Sundance Buttress at Colorado's Lumpy Ridge. His trusted partner of seven years, Steve Gorm, had suggested the route after they'd been stormed off another climb.

As they'd hiked up to *Whiteman*, Gorm had said, "Let's top-rope it," but the men didn't discuss the details. DeMartino believed that he would lead *Whiteman*, set up a slingshot top rope, have Steve lower him, and then belay Gorm from the ground. But in Gorm's mind, *top rope* meant DeMartino would belay him from above—that

Craig DeMartino, a hard man to slow down, crushing at the boulders not long after his 100-foot ground fall. *DeMartino Collection*

Gorm would second the pitch. The men had been up in Rocky Mountain National Park almost every weekend that season, ticking routes left and right, and had become "pretty lax on our belay commands and all that," as DeMartino said in an interview at The Enormocast (www.enormocast.com). In other words, they were so comfortable with each other that they didn't confirm a game plan before DeMartino left the ground.

DeMartino ably led the pitch and reached the belay ledge, clipped into the anchor bolts, and hollered "Off belay." Out of sight below, Gorm promptly removed the device from the rope, hollered up "OK!" and went to fetch his rock shoes. DeMartino took a minute to sort himself out, checking that the anchors were equalized for top-roping; everything looked good. He hollered "OK" to let Gorm know he was ready to be

1

lowered just as Gorm was rooting through his backpack and facing away from the climb. Gorm reflexively hollered up "OK" again—as in, "OK, about ready to second"—which DeMartino took to mean that he was back on belay.

DeMartino unclipped from the anchor and leaned back, expecting to be lowered. Unbelayed, slowed only by the nominal friction of the rope through the 15-odd pieces below him, DeMartino plummeted backward. Years of bouldering conditioned him to push off from the wall and get his feet under him, but he had a long way to go. The fall flipped him backward, and he fell horizontally; 20 feet from the ground he hit a tree with his head, which flicked him back upright. DeMartino landed standing in almost his exact starting point, traveling 55 miles per hour. The impact compound-fractured both his ankles and both his heels, exploding the rubber on his climbing shoes. "I hit so hard that my back actually didn't snap; it crushed itself," DeMartino said, pulverizing his L2 vertebrae and breaking his neck at C6. He also sustained broken ribs, a punctured lung, a torn rotator cuff, a hurt elbow, and a ruptured artery in his right leg.

DeMartino's epic fight for life merits a separate book (in fact it's called *After the Fall*), but the good news is that he survived. Eighteen months later he chose to amputate his lower right leg, which had refused to heal. DeMartino still deals with chronic pain and neurological issues, but he's climbing as hard as ever with a prosthetic limb, and he has put the emotional trauma of the accident behind him.

Lessons. Confusion over lowering vs. seconding vs. rappeling at anchors is an all-too-common and potentially lethal scenario. Phil Powers, executive director of the American Alpine Club and a man who has summited K2 without supplemental oxygen, was hurt badly in a 50-foot ground fall in Clear Creek Canyon in 2011 because of a similar misunderstanding. Nobody is exempt, *ever*. Take these few quick, easy steps:

- Agree upon a game plan for anchor logistics with your partner before every pitch. Do not deviate unless you can visually and verbally confirm your new strategy.
- Ambient noise, such as cars, flowing water, wind, and crag chatter, contributes to miscommunication, as can the climber being out of view. If you know that you'll be unable to see or hear each other at the anchors, reconfirm your game plan before starting.

1

- Use communication signals with unequivocal meanings. "OK" can mean a million different things. Be precise: "You got me?" "I got you." Or: "Ready to lower" and "Lowering." Never say "Off belay" unless you truly are going off belay, either to bring up your second or rappel. Don't say "Off belay" to haul up slack to thread the anchors; technically, if you're threading and lowering, your belayer keeps you *on belay* and merely pays out slack. So request "Slack." "Off belay" means one thing only: "Remove your device from the rope because you no longer need to belay me." Don't say it unless you mean it.
- *Never* unclip from the anchor until you've sat on the rope and confirmed that it's taut—that your belayer indeed has you.

Lynn Hill: Failure to Double-Check

Even Lynn Hill, the first woman to climb 5.14 and the rock artist who made the first free ascent of the *Nose* (VI 5.14a) of El Capitan in 1993, makes mistakes. Her legendary ground fall from atop a 5.10d sport route at Buoux, France, is a tale that bears repeating because of the central lesson: Always double-check yourself and your partner.

It was 1989, and Hill was already an established force in rock climbing, one of the few women redpointing 5.13. She earned her living with her fingertips, winning prizes, fame, and sponsors through her dominance of the ascendant World Cup competition circuit. Hill was sport-climbing world champion that year and would, between 1987 and 1992, win Italy's prestigious Arco Rock Master competition an incredible five times. She split her time between the United States and Europe and had become a household name. Standing only 5 feet 1.5 inches but with preternatural power, finger strength, focus, and flexibility from her years as a gymnast, Hill never fails at her goals.

That day, May 9, she was at the Styx Wall at Buoux, a venerable pocket-climbing area in the bucolic south of France. Hill climbed with her husband at the time, Russ Raffa, and the two started on a warm-up called *Buffet Froid*. At 5.10d it was well within Hill's ability; Raffa would lead the pitch, then Hill would top-rope it after him and clean the draws.

1

WHAT DO YOU DO WHEN YOU'RE OUT OF EARSHOT?

Multipitch climbing is a more common scenario for this dilemma, though it can happen on single-pitch crags too: Your partner has reached an anchor out of voice and sight range, and you're both hollering vague and increasingly desperate things trying to divine what's going on. "Erfff belarrgh!" "What?" "Ern rawrary?" "HUH?!" "Swarkkkkkk!"

Some solutions:

- Use CB headsets if you're true safety nuts.
- Use each other's names in crowded areas: "On belay, *Kendall!*"
- Drop the word "belay," and just yell "on" or "off." On a windy day "on belay" can sound a lot like "off belay."
- Whoop: On a multipitch climb, after the leader has built and clipped into an anchor, she whoops at the expected point near the end of the rope to communicate "Off belay." The leader then pulls up rope until it's taut, puts the second on, and whoops again for "On belay." The second gets ready, undoes the anchor, and whoops once to signal that he is ready to climb.
- Use tugs: Two sharp tug-and-releases from the leader means "I'm off belay"; then when she's anchored in, has pulled up rope, and put her second on belay, she uses three sharp tugs for "On belay."
- Use hand signals if you can see each other: one signal for "on" and another for "off."

As Hill writes in her autobiography, *Climbing Free,* while Raffa led up and threaded the anchor, "My thoughts had drifted to my next competition, which would be held in Leeds, England." Hill was in a mellow, contented mood and let her mind wander as she prepared to climb. She threaded her rope through her harness intending to tie in with a bowline, and then walked over to retrieve her climbing shoes 20 feet away. There she chatted with a Japanese woman, came back to *Buffet Froid* where Raffa had put her on belay, had the fleeting thought that there was "something I needed to do before climbing," and wondered if it was to remove her jacket. But then she dismissed the notion and set off climbing.

Lynn Hill deciphers the *Doric Dihedral,* Skunk Canyon, Boulder, Colorado.

1

In those few distracted moments, Hill had failed to tie her bowline; the rope hung only by friction through her tie-in loops, obscured by her jacket and unsecured "like a ticking time bomb" as Hill writes. As she moved fluidly up the pitch, the rope stayed looped through her harness. Hill reached the anchors 72 feet off the ground, saw that Raffa was talking to someone, grabbed the belayer's side of the rope to reel in slack, and leaned back. She plummeted immediately toward earth.

As the air rushed past and the ground hurtled up, she let out a bloodcurdling scream so loud it was heard a half mile away. Falling backward, Hill windmilled her arms to stay upright. She aimed for a tiny oak tree below—something, anything to break her fall—curled up, plunged through the tree limbs, and then hit the ground so hard she rebounded three feet into the air "like a rubber ball" before face-planting in the dirt and losing consciousness.

But Hill had survived, thanks in no small measure to her falling instincts (i.e., windmilling her arms), which kept her from rotating backward and landing on her head. Fortunately, Hill only sustained trauma to one buttock, a puncture wound in her chest from a tree root, and a dislocated arm. In the following years, Hill became not only the first person to free climb the *Nose*, but in 1994, the first to free climb it in a day, initiating a new era of big-wall free climbing.

Lessons. Distractions at the cliffs are many: other climbers chatting with you, enticing sports action, road or river noise, dogs, kids. The gym is even worse—loud, blaring music and a high density of climbers, not to mention people falling beside or practically onto you. Thus whether you're the only two people at an alpine crag or two of forty climbers at a roadside area, always follow the same protocol, which is to *double-check your systems and double-check each other.*

Don't let distraction invade your space, especially while tying-in and prepping to belay. The only world that should exist when you're starting up is the six-foot-bubble surrounding you and your partner; politely evict anyone or anything that enters your physical or mental space until you've completed your preflight checklist.

As the climber, I follow a three-point inspection. I check that:

1. My harness is on correctly and the buckles are doubled back.
2. The rope is threaded through *both* tie-in points.
3. I tied my knot correctly, and it's dressed for action.

1

As the belayer, I follow a three-point inspection. I check that:

1. My harness is on correctly and the buckles are doubled back.
2. My belay device is threaded correctly, and my brake hand is ready to go.
3. The locking carabiner on the belay device is secured to my belay loop and *locked.*

The climber should always check the belayer after checking herself, and vice versa: "Four eyes are better than two." Both climbers are doing a six-point inspection. Make a game of it until it becomes habit. Try pointing six times, once at each inspection item, and listing them.

Test your system by weighting it: If the first piece or an anchor is preclipped, sit back on the rope to make sure your belayer has you. Or if you are not yet clipped in, simply walk to the end of the rope, and have your belayer keep you taut to see what happens.

As the climber, inspect your knot periodically as you climb. A knot shouldn't spontaneously come undone, but you never know—you might have inspected it poorly on the ground.

Don't tie-in with a bowline; instead use a figure 8 follow-through. Some climbers favor the bowline because it comes untied more easily after being weighted (figure 8s can freeze after a big fall), but the inconvenience of undoing a stubborn knot pales beside the risk of using one that can come undone more easily. Some years ago at Rifle a correctly tied bowline spontaneously came undone on a slick, stiff new rope—not good! Moreover, the figure 8 is much easier to inspect and tie correctly; it's very simple and clean.

Kelly Cordes: Rope Behind the Leg

Coloradan Kelly Cordes seems to be made of Teflon. A veteran alpinist with a blitzkrieg ascent of Cerro Torre and the world's longest rock climb (the 7400-foot *Azeem Ridge*, VII 5.11 R/X M6 A2) to his credit, Cordes had already survived a heavy dose of accidents and injury by summer 2010. He had major back reconstructive surgery in 2005, fusing his L4 and L5 vertebrae to correct chronic degeneration in his spine. And in February 2010 Cordes sustained a heinous pilon (lower shinbone) fracture to his right leg in Hyalite Canyon, Montana, when a sudden burst of slack while lowering deposited him rudely on an ice ledge.

HOW TO LOOSEN A FIGURE 8 AND A FROZEN BELAY LOCKER

If you've welded your figure 8 in a fall, there are a couple ways to break the knot:
- Grab the doubled strands on both sides of the knot and repeatedly push and pull them back and forth (like stretching taffy).
- Find a flat surface, such as a rock or hard floor, and roll the knot back and forth beneath the side of your fist to soften it; you may have to take your harness off.

Big falls can also freeze the locking mechanism on a screw-gate locker. To loosen it, have your climber tie back in and weight the rope. Now try unscrewing the gate.

A bucket of heavy metal (rods, pins, plates, screws, external fixators) and multiple surgeries later, Cordes was walking again and then, inevitably, climbing. By that summer he'd switched his focus to sport climbing to rehabilitate his body. Being less perilous than alpinism and ice, it seemed like a logical reentry.

Then, Cordes took an upside-down fall. If there's one thing that can get you sport climbing, it's the rope sneaking behind your leg and upending you. It can even happen to a world-class alpinist.

It was late July 2010, and Cordes was with two friends at a bolted cliff called the Wizard's Gate, on the Crags formation high above his home of Estes Park. Cordes set out to onsight a radically overhanging 5.13a called *Magic Dagger*. The route moves across a flat face onto a suspended prow that juts wildly over the hillside, necessitating half-controlled slap moves to sloping jugs. Cordes climbed easily to the crux, started slapping, and then fell off almost backward, bombing out of the roof.

He dropped into space for what should have been a clean volley, but suddenly found himself launched into a backflip. Cordes's left heel, hooked on a small protrusion, had stayed on longer than the rest of his body. Combined with a hard catch, he'd somehow caught the rope behind his leg as he fell—Cordes pile-drove headfirst into the slabbier stone below. Both his head and face hit *hard,* and blood drizzled off his forehead into the void as his belayer lowered him. Though he did not have a helmet on, Cordes never lost consciousness.

Despite his spectacular fall, Cordes essentially felt OK. A friend wrapped his dome in a sweatshirt, and he and his friends stumbled out, "freaking people out on the trail," as Cordes blogged. At the ER, he received 13 staples in his scalp and 14 stitches to his face. "Just what I need," Cordes wrote. "I got uglier."

Lessons. Don't allow the rope to sneak behind your leg (ankle, calf, shin, knee, or thigh), because if it does you risk taking a topsy-turvy fall, as Cordes did. When the cord becomes taut, it will catch on your gam, upend you, and swat you against the rock like a gnat. In the heat of battle, however, it's not always easy to monitor your rope's position. The goal is to never set yourself up for this worst-case-scenario whipper, which can cause severe head and neck trauma:

Kelly Cordes on *The Guillotine* (5.11) at the Wizard's Gate, Estes Park, Colorado, the crag where he took his upside-down header

- When you are climbing straight above a piece, as on a face route with a clean, straight line, or in a splitter crack or dihedral, let the rope

hang between your legs. Keep it away from your heels and ankles, flicking it away with your foot as needed.

○ The instant you move laterally, up and to the side of protection, situate the rope so that it lies across the top of the hip or thigh opposite your direction of travel. If you're moving right, the rope should come off your left hip and vice versa, in effect keeping you below the rope instead of above it. If you can't situate the rope above your hip or thigh, try to at least keep it above and away from your feet.

○ Beware of wild moves like heel hooks or kneebars that put the rope in nontraditional positions. Before you throw in that heel hook,

1

A Virgin No More. (5.13a), Penitente Canyon, Colorado. Nathon Welton gets the rope behind his leg and takes the rude ride.

ensure that the rope is still running cleanly *over* your hooking leg (if applicable) or is otherwise well situated.

If you do flip, grab for the rope above your knot as you career into the wall, and do a sit-up so that your buttocks and back take the impact instead of your head and neck.

If your climber has fallen with the rope behind her leg, give her a soft catch that gradually slows her and reduces the chance that she'll smack the wall. It's better that she fall farther rather than be turned into a human pendulum.

Wear a helmet, even when you are sport climbing.

1

BACKCLiPPiNG AND BiNER ORiENTATiON— WHY THEY MATTER

"Matt, your rope is backward," my friend Adam admonished me. Two years into sport climbing, I was dithering on the first bolt of a route at Shelf Road, Colorado.

"You've backclipped it! It could unclip itself!"

I looked but couldn't spot my error. I'd never heard of this *backclipping* before.

"What do you mean, Adam?" The biner looked fine. I mean, my rope was *in it* after all.

"Your rope needs to come up from the belayer side against the rock, and exit the carabiner coming toward you—away from the rock," he explained. "Otherwise the rope can unclip itself."

Aha: I finally got it!

Don't backclip: If you climb past a backclipped draw and fall, the rope doubles back on itself and can unclip. A few additional tips for proper clipping:

- Orient your quickdraw's bolt- and rope-side biners in the same direction: Being opposed places undue torque on the top biner and can shorten its life span.
- Face the biner gates away from your direction of travel. This keeps the rope where it needs to be—on the bottom biner's spine not the gate—and prevents your introducing a half-twist into the draw, which again leads to a backclipping scenario. Also, if you fail to do so, as you climb past the draw, the rope tugs the top biner up toward you, in your direction of travel, which distributes the load toward the biner's nose (much weaker than the basket) or even places it on the gate notch where the biner could fail under a very low load.
- Keep your bolt-side and rope-side biners separate. Because of metal-on-metal wear, bolt-side biners get nicks, chips, dings, and other flaws that can damage or cut your rope's sheath. With most modern quickdraws, which have bent-gate rope biners fixed in place by rubber toggles or a tight dogbone loop, it's pretty obvious which biner is which. But on extendo or trad draws you might be using them interchangeably. Mark each biner separately, perhaps with one dash of nail polish for your bolt-side biner and two dashes for the rope-side clipper.

1

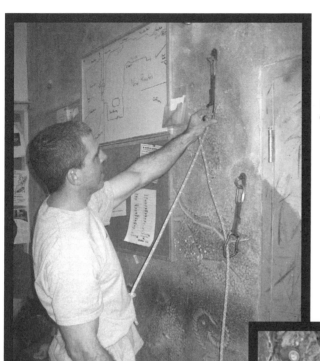

Both draws in this photo are backclipped: can you spot the error? *Matt Samet*

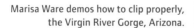

Marisa Ware demos how to clip properly, the Virgin River Gorge, Arizona.

1

2 ETIQUETTE, ACCESS, AND IMPACT

You're Not the Only Fish in the Aquarium

CLIMBERS DON'T LIKE BEING TOLD WHAT TO DO. I know I don't. I'd warrant that many of us got into the sport precisely because we're at liberty to roam the hills and do as we please. The act of climbing itself has no official structure. It's just you and the rock, and you vs. your fears and physical limitations.

However, the rock is also a shared medium. Our venues lie in the public domain, and the cliffs are always managed by somebody, be they on private property or on public lands paid for by us all. It's almost never *your* climb or *your* cliff—you're merely a tourist passing through. It's up to all of us to respect the cliffs.

When I began climbing in the 1980s, it was a fringe activity. The United States had all of three rock gyms; sport climbing was brand-new and neither largely accepted nor popular, with few entirely bolted cliffs; crash pads were not yet being sold; bouldering was seen as training; and most climbers either top-roped or trad climbed for a day's outing. Rock climbing was riskier, and as a result attracted rougher, scruffier characters. There were fewer cliffs but also fewer of us bouncing off each other at those cliffs. Land managers barely noticed our presence, and you could camp out on Bureau of Land Management or US Forest Service land for months at a time.

Things have changed. Every urban center has at least one big gym; sport climbing is everywhere, with mega-destinations like Rifle, Colorado; Maple Canyon, Utah: Red River Gorge, Kentucky; New River Gorge, West Virginia; Rumney, New Hampshire; and Boulder Canyon, Colorado, offering thousands of well-bolted climbs; bouldering has exploded, and chalk and crash pads have infiltrated even high-alpine boulder fields; formerly deserted campgrounds at cragging venues now require reservations; parking lots fill up, and climbers have to seek alternate cliffs on busy days; there are university climbing clubs, gym teams, youth teams, and regional and national competition circuits; climbing has developed a substantial media presence both endemically (through print, videos, and the internet) and in the nonclimbing world (movies, TV shows, and advertisements); and land managers definitely know about us. Our tiny sport has matured and even gone a little mainstream. This change can be a tough reality for old crusty climbers like me to accept, but it's where we find ourselves today.

So what does this growth mean in terms of etiquette, access, and impact? Our every action en route to, at the base of, up on, and leaving the cliffs affects other people. We should expect someone, at some point, to notice our presence. Greater user numbers are creating greater cumulative impacts, and the more we shrink our footprint now, the better the cliffs will look down the road. *You can view climbing as a right or a privilege.* If you take the latter approach, you'll be a better crag citizen. It all starts with how you treat the rock, the environment, and others.

CRAGGING ETIQUETTE

Let's cut to the chase: You don't leave your manners at home when you go climbing, even out in the boondocks. It doesn't matter how 5.14c/d rad you are, whether you discovered and developed an area, or if you're just in a surly mood; as in every other avenue of life, you're going to get as good as you give. Send out positive or at least neutral vibes.

Crag-side etiquette begins with acknowledging that you're neither special nor unique, that your fellow climbers are worthy of respect, and that cliffs are public spaces. These Ten Commandments of Cragging Etiquette have been developed after many discussions with other longtime climbers. Read and agree, or read 'em and weep—it's up to you.

2

1. Thou Shalt Not Covet

Have you ever shown up to try that one, specific climb only to find somebody's rope hanging through the first quickdraw without a climber in sight? It's frustrating to be "rock-blocked," yet such route squatting happens all the time. Ergo: *Learn to share.* Even if I've left my draws on a route, I don't assume that it's somehow mine for the duration. I'll tell other climbers to feel free to jump on it, or to pull my rope if it's pre-clipped; then, as a courtesy, they can rehang the rope on their way down.

By the same token, "quickdraw tourists" should be considerate of the original climber: They should first ask to use the draws, always brush the holds, and, if they see you arrive and know you're ready to go, let you into the queue. Those are *your* carabiners seeing wear and tear, and chances are you'll climb through quickly anyway.

I've also seen climbers hog popular routes all day, often with one member of the party leading the climb and then leaving a top rope for his group—this isn't cool. If other climbers show up and you're on a four-star classic, courtesy dictates that you endeavor to let other parties have their turn. Ask if they're waiting, and strive for a mutually agreeable solution—you'd certainly hope they'd do the same for you. Similarly on multipitch routes, if a faster party is coming up and can safely squeak by, let them. Holding them up because your fragile ego can't handle being passed only creates a pointless, potentially perilous logjam.

And when you are overtaking a slower party, don't crowd them—stop a respectful distance below and discuss with them the logistics of passing. If two parties arrive below a route at once and it's unclear who should go first, they should politely discuss expectations, experience, and speed, and the faster party should prevail. At popular multipitch venues with an obvious, dedicated parking area, you could also leave a note on your windshield informing other parties which route you're trying, so they can make alternate plans.

2. Thou Shalt Not Crowd

Gym routes are set close together—as in, three or four feet apart—to exploit finite wall space. Climbing indoors, then, we get used to belaying, staging, and even making moves in close proximity. Don't bring this mentality outdoors: It's annoying, intrusive, and hazardous. Be conscious of your own and others' space both on the rock and below it. Don't drop your pack where someone is already staged, don't drop your rope bag where someone's already belaying, and if an area is already swarming with climbers, don't add to the chaos. Instead, head elsewhere to climb. Chaotic, noisy, crowded crags are much less safe and satisfying for everyone. Finally, respect the orderly staging area by repacking your crag pack once you've racked up. A gear explosion is inevitable when you first arrive, but after that it takes only seconds to repack and free up staging space for other parties.

If you're dead-set on queuing up for a popular route, place your rope bag near the belay and staging area, quickly mention that you'd like to try the route next or discuss it with the party already on the rock, and then move out of their way to wait. If someone else shows up, politely explain that you've been waiting and are up next. As the party ahead of you lowers, be ready to roll with your rope tied in and shoes and harness on, to speed up the queue.

3. Thou Shalt Not Steal

It's pretty simple: Quickdraws hanging on a route are not "booty"; someone trying the climb left them, so don't take them. The same holds true for chains, rings, and lowering carabiners at anchors—they've been placed for *everyone* to use, so don't purloin them. Similarly, bail gear left on trad climbs or for emergency rappel anchors also belongs to *someone*.

If you harvest it, describe when and where you found the gear on Mountain Project (www.mountainproject.com) or a similar forum, and ask the owner to get in touch and describe it so you can return it. It used to be much harder to return gear, and I know climbers who would (and still do) solo popular moderate routes after rainstorms to harvest bail pieces. This is bad karma. We all have to bail sometimes, so help your fellow climbers out by returning their equipment.

4. Thou Shalt Not Spray

If you don't know someone at the cliff and maybe even if you do, don't hang out spraying unsolicited beta while they climb. It's loud and distracting. Most of the beta-sprayers I've met don't do so out of altruism, but instead to telegraph to everyone within earshot that they've ticked said climb. What could be needier?

Also, if you're having a personal or potentially offensive conversation with your partner, keep your voices down or take it elsewhere (I'm looking at you, bickering

2

crag couples!). Once, at a quiet, empty cliff in the South Platte (Colorado), my climbing partners and I had two bozos descend on us babbling at top volume about how much they hated Boulder climbers—where we live. Never mind that we had been climbing quietly, minding our own business at a backwater crag; they still saw fit to burst onto the scene like spraylord imbeciles.

5. Thou Shalt Not Cluster

Gym teams, university and school clubs, guided courses, and mountain clubs are many a modern climber's introduction, and they condition him or her to climbing in a posse, with multiple partners throughout the day, ropes hanging everywhere, a group staging area, and so on. But at its best, climbing is about solitude, the inner journey, and sharing an adventure with a trusted partner. There's not necessarily greater safety in numbers—big groups tend to knock down more rocks, create more noise, have laxer oversight over each individual, and drop more gear. They also hyperfocus impact and potentially hog the crag. (A smaller group will by default create less human waste and less cliff-base impact with backpacks and crash pads, etc.)

If you arrive at a crag with, say, four or more people, break into two-person teams and spread out to be considerate to others. Also, if you're an instructor who strings multiple top ropes on a wall first thing in the morning to claim them, courtesy dictates that you let other climbers work in or use them when your pupils are idle. Considerate group leaders post info on climbing sites about when and where they're leading an outing, and some even invite others to come use their ropes. If you have an issue with a group's behavior or simply want to work in on their ropes, it's best to pull the leader aside for a quiet chat instead of bringing up a thorny issue in front of his pupils.

Finally, if you are climbing in a big group on public land, know the rules about group size and permits. Joshua Tree National Park, for example, asks that groups not use more than half the available parking, attend all ropes, and not monopolize crags. Also certain crags are closed to climbing on weekends and holidays.

6. Thou Shalt Not Vibe

Even worse than crowded crags is CCWA (crowded crags with attitude)—the kind where you walk up and elitist climbers give you the alpha-dog stink eye to assert their territorial dominance. It's toxic. If you're already at the cliff, smile and say hello to anyone who comes up to let them know that they're just as welcome as the next guy. Being friendly or at least cordial goes a long way. Even a quick smile, a snippet of joking conversation, or a little wave keeps the vibe upbeat and pleasant.

7. Thou Shalt Not Whine on the Internet

The forum posts, missives of outrage from the American cragscape venting about some execrable fellow-climber behavior encountered over the weekend, crop up every Monday morning. Soon the flame wars start. Land managers read our forums, and I often wonder how pathetic we must look to them. "Jeez, these guys can't even have a rational discussion about some minor bone of contention," they surely think as they scroll down page 17 of the "To those jack wagons I saw at Mega Mondo Headwall last weekend!!!" discussion.

Consider this: If another climber's actions offend you or jeopardize access, your best bet is to offer constructive criticism in the moment or through direct correspondence instead of airing your grievances online. Too many climbers have been tried, convicted, and sentenced in impromptu kangaroo courts in online forums, without both sides of the story being told. And I'd say very few people are likely to change their behavior based on outrage expressed on the internet.

8. Thou Shalt Not Dag

I'm not sure when it became a la mode to complete a route *at any cost,* including hours of flapping, scrapping, quickdraw grabbing, and hanging, but perhaps it's a gym thing—"Hey, look, I got to the top of the wall!" In any case, hopping on a route *way* over your head will not help you learn to climb better. Moreover, it punishes your belayer and gums up a line others might be waiting to try.

Although we all need to hang sometimes, if entire sections or sequences continue to elude you, you're barely making moves without your belayer assisting you and you're mostly using quickdraws and other gear to pull yourself up, then you're dagging. And dagging sucks. The best way to improve is one letter grade at a time, not by trying to jump entire numbers, like from 5.10a to 5.12a.

AUTHORITY OF THE RESOURCE

It's often hard to know how to proceed when you see someone exhibiting poor etiquette or creating unnecessary impact. Getting up in their face, and shouting, "You moron, you're messing this up for all of us!" won't get you anywhere, so what can you do to graciously help others rethink their behavior?

Rangers use a concept called authority of the resource technique (ART), first codified by Dr. George N. Wallace, who holds a PhD in natural resources and is a professor at Colorado State University, in his paper "Law Enforcement and the 'Authority of the Resource,'" available at Wilderness.net (www.wilderness. net). Instead of invoking the official authority of the ranger or land-management agency, ART calls upon the authority imposed by nature itself—to "those things in nature (resources) that have their own requirements," as Wallace writes. This reasoning compels the visitor to correct such undesirable behavior as leaving food out in bear country to meet nature's exigencies instead of to follow a rule or the law. ART is best done standing shoulder to shoulder, not face to face in the classic confrontation pose; together with the other party, you look at the sticky situation and then outline a solution *together*.

Say you've come out on a Saturday and found a school group hogging your local cliff with top ropes, their stuff yard-saled across fragile grasses away from the usual staging area. First, identify the group leader, because this is the only person you should talk to about the situation. You and she stand shoulder to shoulder, looking at the dangling ropes and the backpacks and pupils on the grass:

1. You give an objective description of the situation, avoiding, as Wallace writes, "value-laden terms . . . [or] phrases like 'You really shouldn't' . . . or 'It's against regulations to . . .'" In this case, you might say, "I noticed you guys got to the crag first and strung up most of the climbs, which is great. And also that you guys are set up on that grassy area."

2. You explain the implications of their actions, including both social impacts and impacts on others' ability to commune with nature. You might say, "I realize it's a small cliff and that these routes are perfect for instructing, but since there's not much else to climb, it's going to be hard for any other climbers who come here. Also, just as a

heads-up, that grass doesn't see much rain, so leaving backpacks and things on top of it will likely kill it."

3. Tell them how you feel about it and what can (should) be done to improve the situation. You could say, "I'd hate for us not to get to climb today, so we'd love to work in on your ropes. We'll even set up our own top rope over there, and you guys can feel free to jump on that. Also, if you don't mind restaging off the grass, say on that rock, that's usually where we set up, and it will keep the cliff looking nice."

The goal is to keep the message focused, positive, and in the vein of constructive criticism so that you and the other climbers still have a great day out—everyone benefits, *especially* the resource. Finally, even with ART on your side, let your desired experience dictate your choice of venue. If you want solitude, don't go to a roadside top-roping area on a perfect Saturday and then go ballistic when you find it's crowded and invoke ART to bully into the fray. If it's quiet you seek, hike an hour into the backcountry to that obscure crag. Match your destination to your expectations.

9. Thou Shalt Not Alter Existing Climbs

Don't chip or aggressively brush holds (no wire brushes!) on existing climbs, and don't add protection to existing climbs except with the express permission of the first-ascent party or through community consensus. Also, do not add permadraws to existing climbs without consensus. Any time you add or replace hardware, make sure you're in compliance with the management agency's or landowner's official rules or regulations pertaining to installation.

10. Thou Shalt Communicate Logistics with Thy Fellow Climbers

When you're pulling your rope, always yell "Rope!" even if you haven't seen anyone else. At a crowded cliff, give everyone a polite preliminary heads-up before that final pull so that they can clear out. You should also remind people on the ground to stay alert for loose rock, especially if you know about the hazard. Other hazards you should warn others about include any dropped gear or the rope itself if they have to walk

2

near it while you're belaying. I also like to remind others that I'll be returning to a route if I leave my draws on it to go belay elsewhere. That way we can time our efforts accordingly. The main thing is *to communicate.* If you think others may find something relevant, especially related to matters of safety, then tell them.

KICKING ACCESS

In the United States, climbing is a peculiar pastime. It lacks the deep, rich history reaching back to the golden age of mountaineering that climbing has in Europe, and aside from a few rare climbing centers, you don't find high concentrations of climbers. The general public has little understanding of what we do. Throw in the litigious nature of American society and the perception of rock climbing as an extreme sport, and it's a wonder we're able to get on rock at all. Looked at this way, climbing in America is more sideshow than main attraction, more privilege than right.

In fact, "There is no right to climb," says Brady Robinson, executive director of the Access Fund (AF), the national organization dedicated to keeping crags open and conserving the climbing environment. "People always talk about 'my right to climb,' but the truth of it is you *don't* have a right to climb." This observation might sound pessimistic from someone whose job it is to keep crags open, but Robinson knows what he's talking about. He's seen what can go wrong and how quickly access (the "right to climb") can be revoked.

Climbing creates a unique set of impacts. As climbers, we take these things for granted as quotidian, as part of the landscape, and barely register them. But nonclimbers might see things otherwise. We are not the only ones who have a relationship with the rock—there are also hikers, bird-watchers, the birds themselves and other wildlife, wildlife biologists, ecologists, land managers, and so on. Like everyone else, we're just passing through. The fact that a given rock can be climbed does not automatically confer on us an unalienable right to climb it.

Meanwhile, our impacts include:

- **Chalk.** Over time and especially on overhanging rock, holds can become so chalky that even if the cliff were closed tomorrow, it might take years for the chalk to disappear.
- **Shoe rubber.** Our black-soled shoes leave rubber polish, especially on softer or more porous stones.

- **Visitor-created trails (aka social trails).** Climbing areas often lie off main trails or up hillsides. Undesignated climber-created access trails develop over time, in general without preliminary work to mitigate erosion (because trail-building on public land is illegal!).
- **Fixed hardware.** Such hardware includes brightly colored slings at anchors and around trees, fixed pitons, and of course fixed bolts and anchor hardware as well as permadraws. To date, climbers have enjoyed a fortunate freedom to bolt new climbs on national lands, to do so through a permit system in other areas, and to self-manage and update our hardware.
- **Cliff-base impact.** All those people below a cliff change the environment. Rope bags, crash pads, climbers, dogs, and so on impact the soil and vegetation, though many cliff bases are often dry, dusty places to start with. We might also leave litter in the form of food wrappers, shredded tape, cigarette butts, and so on. And we likely will need to do our "potty business" near the cliff too (see the "Minimum Impact" section later in this chapter).
- **Noise.** Because climbers aggregate at a cliff and stay there, we produce a certain amount of chatter, as well as the grunting and, unfortunately, screaming that can attend falling off.
- **Parking issues.** These issues crop up at trailheads, along roads, in campgrounds, on private land, and so on.
- **Perception of risk and rescue.** Most nonclimbers don't understand the sport well enough to grasp the real risk. Seeing only sensationalized news reports about those rare instances in which a climber is hurt or killed (requiring a SAR operation) or hearing tales of an injured or killed scrambler who is labeled a "climber" leads to concern over liability (lawsuits) and the misplaced notion that climbers consume disproportionate amounts of taxpayer money through SAR operations.

This list is not meant to be an indictment; it simply states the side effects of and perceptions around climbing. *Not one of us who visits the cliffs is without a footprint, and we should never pretend otherwise.* Everyone who ventures outdoors has impact,

Hardpacked soil and erosion from hiking along the crag base from route to route. Stone steps could help this.

Random debris, perhaps to keep rock shoes clean

Heavily impacted, devegetated soil from climbers' feet, rope bags, backpacks, etc.

Erosion at edge of belay platform caused by repeated usage and stepping on the edge of the slope.

2

The well-used base of a popular Colorado crag shows various climber impacts.

from the ATV enthusiast to the vegan, barefoot hippie who walks contemplatively off into a meadow to play didgeridoo. But when climbing's effects don't sit well with other users or land managers, or we don't keep them in check, access gets sticky.

What Closes Crags

Jason Keith, senior policy advisor at the Access Fund (AF), has been fighting on the access front for a dozen years, liaising between climbers, land managers, and regulatory agencies both on the local level and in Washington, D.C. He's seen cliffs closed or threatened with closure for every reason under the sun. Keith has learned that most access issues don't occur at established crags with high or growing visitor numbers; they instead crop up either when a new crag is being developed or shortly thereafter, as it becomes known in the larger community. In nonclimber and land-manager eyes, what was once a lonely, silent lump of rock has morphed into a three-ring circus with the need for oversight or regulation.

Keith says some of the more contentious situations arise when a cliff is developed secretly by a clique of friends. Then, when a land manager or other climbers shine a light on what they're doing, all hell breaks loose. First ascentionists tend to want all the gems for themselves, but the peer-review process ensures that the climbs and ancillary logistics (trails, staging areas, etc.) are developed as thoughtfully as possible.

Keith cites cases in which climbers have, illegally on public lands: chipped Moki steps (footholds) in a slab to access a new cliff, cut down trees wholesale in a burn area to create a climber trail and staging areas, bolted rocks into and used come-alongs (ratcheting pulleys) to flatten landing zones for bouldering, and left blatant landscaping and climbing tool caches in places where a ranger or nonclimber eventually found them. These are all hallmarks of industrial-level activity that we're best off not having associated with our sport, even if we need certain tools to groom a new cliff. Some of these scenarios have even led to criminal actions against climbers.

To combat the nefarious "secret-crag mind-set," Keith urges climbers to expand their circles of buddies or be more willing to include other climbers as they develop a cliff, so that decisions are made by consensus and with an eye toward the ultimate outcome. "Know that your crag is going to be found some day," Keith says, "and that your name is going to be associated with it." Above all, when putting up new climbs, be smart and low-key.

2

FiVE TiPS FOR LOW-KEY ROUTiNG

1. **Research land ownership** and determine if the established routes have followed a set hardware precedent. If the cliff is on private land, approach the owner before you drill.

2. **Ask yourself whether the route is worth it.** Trailside, roadside, and bouldering-height sport climbs provoke controversy within the climbing community, and they stick out to nonclimbers. So perhaps your new two-bolt testpiece above the main trail in a national park was just fine as a top rope.

3. **Be aware of cultural and biological resources.** The discovery of Native American pictographs, burial sites, pottery shards, and so on has led to closures and even removal of bolts. If you suspect that your new find contains an archaeologically or culturally important site, find another cliff or establish routes well away from any artifacts. Similarly, don't aggressively clean or devegetate the rock.

4. **Camouflage all hardware** *before* you install it. Paint your hangers, bolt heads, and anchor to blend in with the rock, or buy prepainted hardware like that sold by Fixe Hardware or Metolius Climbing.

5. **Use permadraws sparingly.** Steel gym-style screw-on quickdraws have come into vogue at high-traffic areas, particularly on overhanging routes, but are they necessary? Nonclimbers are hard-pressed to spot even shiny new hangers, but they won't miss a two-foot-long cable or chain quickdraw. Consider the context, community consensus, and visual impact.

2

With modern tools like the internet, Google Earth, and public records, there's little excuse for taking a bolt-first, research-ownership-later perspective. "Understand who owns the property and what that means," says Keith, be it a private landowner who might not want fixed hardware and liability issues or a land-management agency with its own hardware regulations and special designations (wilderness, designated natural area, etc.). He also urges developers to remember that land managers have to manage for the lowest common denominator; don't make their jobs harder by using visible tactics in high-profile, sensitive, or wilderness areas. "A third party, say someone hiking around looking for butterflies, looks at these things—grid bolting, permadraws, shiny chain anchors—and becomes outraged, which puts the land manager in a tough spot even if he wants to be permissive to climbers," says Keith.

At this point you're probably thinking, "Wait a minute, this doesn't pertain to me. I don't even put up routes." Well, OK, sure, you probably don't. Very few climbers (maybe 1 percent) put up routes, so it's not like there are hundreds of thousands of new climbs every year overwhelming land managers. For most climbers, establishing routes is too gnarly. But once a climb is established, we *all* climb on it, so how and where it goes in is an access question in perpetuity. We're certainly within our rights to provide constructive feedback through community discussion, local climbing organizations, or personal interface. *A poorly thought-out route can affect access for us all!*

Keith sees a shift coming, one in which it's no longer easy to show up on public land and bolt at will. Land managers are too cued in to climbing for the status quo to continue. "There are more and more smaller crags popping up around the country," says Keith, "and more and more agency people going, 'Wait a minute, we didn't authorize this crag.'" When other user groups want a new access route (e.g., a hiking, biking, or ATV trail), they have to approach an agency and undergo an environmental analysis and legal process. So why, land managers are wondering, should climbers be any different? Perhaps the sheer number of new crags has tipped the balance, or perhaps the growing numbers of climbers have, or perhaps land managers across geographic regions are sharing notes. In any case, this developing situation demands our attention.

"It's not about right and wrong and being the crag police," concludes Keith. "It's about considering the predictable consequences of your actions."

What Keeps Crags Open

There are many ways to reduce or reverse the climber impacts cited earlier. Let's look at ways to keep existing crags open and healthy.

Tick Marks

The latest rage, especially among boulderers, is to make tick marks: giant, thick, obvious chalk lines pointing to holds. Well, not all climbers love them, to nonclimbers they look like graffiti, *and* they take forever to wear off. Instead of bringing the gym

2

outside, substituting your chalk line for colored tape, learn to read the rock using other visual cues (seams, crystals, or patches of different-colored stone). Barring that use small, easily brushed-off ticks or simple chalk dots, and clean them up as well as marks made by others when you leave. Carry a toothbrush or even a hand towel and extra water for this purpose.

Shoe Rubber

Besides improving your footwork, there's not much you can do about residual shoe rubber, though starting up a climb with clean soles certainly helps. Dirty, muddy, or gravel-covered kicks muck up the rock, and then said muck grinds into the holds, polishing, eroding, and staining them; picture the filthy, black, glassy overused starting footholds at your local boulders. Begin by thoroughly cleaning your soles front to back while standing atop a towel, jacket, crash pad, flat rock, etc. below the stone. More meticulous climbers even use water or rubbing alcohol and a rag. I wipe my shoes with my palm, wipe them against each leg, and then step onto the rock from my clean surface. You can also clean your shoes up on a wet or muddy route by doing this same "cricket rub."

Visitor-Created Trails

Stay on the main or most hardened trail, even if it means taking a longer, more circuitous route. Also, research the approach in the guidebook or with a guidebook app. With visitor-created trails (aka social trails) among routes or boulders, likewise select the most well-used and durable path to avoid creating new ones. Durable walking surfaces include rock slabs or outcrops, gravel, sand, dry grasses, washes, stable talus fields, and snow. Avoid stepping on live vegetation or beelining straight up sliding gullies or the fall line of a hillside—work *with* the topography to find the least erosion-prone approach. If the trail is wet, walk directly through the mud to avoid site creep (in this case widening the path). Finally, avoid wearing heavy-tread shoes like hiking boots.

In pristine areas without trails (or without biological soil crust, see below), spread your group out, and have each member take a slightly different course. If six climbers take the same path to and from an unvisited cliff, they might beat down a visible track with only one visit. Also, be proactive by not falling into the herd mentality, blindly following the leader, on the approach. If you see your friends taking shortcuts or a less-than-ideal approach, speak up and lead by example. Finally, if you're concerned about visitor-created-trail multiplication at your local crag, write letters to the land-management agency in support of designated climbing access, or organize an official trail day with the agency.

For off-trail travel on cryptogamic or cryptobiotic soil (aka biological soil crust) such as that found in the US desert, avoid crust whenever possible. If an approach involves travel through crusted terrain, walk in each other's footprints; spreading out in this environment could wipe out hundreds of years of soil development in seconds. These crusts, according to Bernadette Regan, a climbing ranger at Joshua Tree National Park, contain a complex community of microorganisms that helps to keep sand in place and provides plants nutrients and moisture. "Thick crusts can be seen as lumpy black areas, much like fungus," she says. "When you walk on these living soils, the micro-organisms die."

If you're bored between burns at a cliff gridded out with social trails, do some good-karma work by dragging brush, sticks, or dead wood across redundant paths to block off or obscure them, leaving only the most durable tracks open. You can also put rock rings around trees or plants in the access trail to protect against foot traffic. And while it's not technically legal, climbers have used cairns to mark approach trails. For example, at Queen Mountain in Joshua Tree, says Regan, the park ended up giving a silent nod to a cairned climber approach trail after realizing it had greatly reduced impact.

Fixed Hardware

Carry a belay knife and use it to cut away ancient, unsightly tat at rappel anchors. When you install new slings, use earth-toned ones that match the rock. Meanwhile, don't leave your draws hanging so long on a high-profile project that they become de facto permadraws.

Cliff-Base Impact

Over time at frequented cliffs, the staging area or visibly human-impacted areas expand out from the rock as repeated visits tamp down the soil, compromise vegetation, and so on. Considering climbing's explosive growth, it's easy to see why cliff-side site creep has, well, crept onto land managers' radar. Some solutions:

2

1. **Stage yourself and your things on durable surfaces,** including rock, sand, or stable talus, but never live vegetation. Or choose

sites that have already been co-opted as staging areas; this concentrates impact within a contained area.

2. **Be a conscientious parent or dog guardian.** Don't let your child or dog pillage the crag environment out of boredom. If your kid won't be climbing, bring a game or book to keep her occupied. And tie Fido up or leave him at home. Dogs can stress critters out by chasing them. (See the "Kids and Dogs" section later in this chapter.)

3. **Go potty the right way.** (See the "Doing the Dirty Deed" section later in this chapter.)

4. **Don't litter, ever, and pick up and pack out trash even if it isn't your own.** Even small items like pistachio shells, bar-wrapper ends, and tape scraps add up and can, along with food particles, attract wildlife. Critters can get sick or die if they ingest inedible items like energy-bar wrappers. Also, to keep curious fauna from chewing holes in your backpack, hang all food and scented items (sunscreen, bug repellent, etc.) in a stuff sack from a sturdy tree limb, especially while away from your pack.

5. **Don't crush or trample vegetation,** for example, by dragging your rope bag or crash pad instead of carrying it, and don't cut down trees or trim vegetation. Some climbs are better left alone if climbing them means harming or killing flora.

6. **Respect cultural and wildlife closures.** These aren't arbitrary rules put in place to keep climbers out; they're monitored closures that allow the birds and animals—many of them endangered—to thrive and reproduce in peace. A nesting bird that has had its habitat violated will expend precious energy to drive off intruders or might even abandon its nest. We are visitors. Raptors depend on the cliffs for survival.

7. **Don't stash gear, especially crash pads.** Critters get into pads and ropes and can shred or even eat the foam or nylon (to their detriment). Land managers hate seeing this; it smacks of laziness.

2

Noise

Leave your portable stereo at home if you are visiting a crag frequented by other climbers. Your music sucks; I know because I've heard it. And save the fits for your garage wall where you can scream all you want like a psycho in a padded room. Some grunting and effort or emotional yelps are inevitable, but hollering epithets is immature and pathetic, and it jeopardizes access.

Parking Issues

Pay your day-use and parking fees; don't park anywhere you're not supposed to. If a lot is full, go elsewhere, and don't block other cars in. When feasible, carpool to the crag to conserve gas and leave space for others.

Perception of Risk and Rescue

Unforeseen accidents are inevitable, but being prepared and not getting in over your head reduce your chance of needing to be rescued. If you're not sure what being ready for a given route means, then you should choose a different climb.

Closing Thoughts on Access

At its core, access mostly comes down to how nonclimbers (the overwhelming majority of the American public) and land managers perceive us. *Do they find us likable and sympathetic, and will they rally to our cause? Or have they written off climbers as a bunch of elitist jerks?* It is up to us to bridge the gap: to educate the public; to show them that what we do is a respectful, worthwhile use of the resource; and to demonstrate that we're ecoconscious, considerate, and friendly.

A few final tips:

- **Be nice to hikers and tourists:** Sure, they ask dumb questions, but that's because they're curious about climbing. Be a friendly, patient ambassador for our sport, and answer their queries, even the ever-popular "How did you get the rope up there?"
- **Be nice to land managers.** Leave your antiauthoritarian attitude at home. Many land managers are also climbers and are in our court. Land managers tend to roll with the punches more in any access discussion if they already have a strong rapport with climbers. In Joshua

2

79

Tree National Park, for example, the park holds a regular Climber's Coffee event during which rangers and climbers talk climbing, get to know each other better, and establish enduring friendships.

- **Volunteer.** Help out with trash and chalk cleanup events, and volunteer for trail days. Brady Robinson says that climbers have amazing turnout for volunteer days and that it's one of the best things for access, because then land managers see climbers as a *solution* to problems like litter and erosion.
- **Get involved.** Join your local climbing organization, and lend them financial support. The Access Fund (AF) can't be in all places at all times, and regional situations are often resolved through the AF's support of local groups.
- **Join the AF and the American Alpine Club (AAC).** For only $35 and $75 a year, respectively, you can belong to the two organizations doing the most to promote and protect climbing in the United States. Visit www.accessfund.org and www.americanalpineclub.org to learn more.
- **Donate to the American Safe Climbing Association (ASCA).** The ASCA, through a hardware fund, enables volunteers to update sketchy bolts and anchors, reducing the chances of hardware failure and accidents. Visit www.safeclimbing.org to learn more.

MINIMUM IMPACT

As a teenager, I was lucky enough to take two National Outdoor Leadership School courses. Out in the mountains for weeks, we were schooled on minimum-impact practices, the goal being to leave behind zero trace of our group's passage. With a pack of 20 people, this approach was a necessity, or we'd have left behind a telltale wake of trash, human waste, and trampled meadows. The mountain club I learned from urged similar conscientiousness. The goal then, as ever, was to preserve the cliff and environs in their natural state—or as natural a state as possible. Think of the difference between a pristine, remote cliff and that urban bouldering area with spray paint, broken glass, and fast-food wrappers. Where would you rather climb? Which one comes closer to the reason you love the sport?

ROADSIDE CRAG, RED RIVER GORGE: A CASE STUDY IN CLIMBER STUPIDITY

Lest you think I'm being alarmist about access, consider the sad case of Roadside Crag at Red River Gorge, Kentucky. This well-established mainstay cliff with 50 climbs ranging from 5.6 to 5.12 was closed to climbers—*by its climber owners*—in May 2011 and has not reopened since. One of the Red's original sport areas, Roadside boasts a five-minute approach and crowd-pleasing jug hauls. When development threatened access in the mid-2000s, two climbers, Grant Stephens and John Haight, bought the property and formed the 80-acre Graining Fork Nature Preserve, keeping the cliff open to hiking and climbing. They are the ones who also eventually closed it.

Why would climbers close a cliff they'd bought expressly to keep open for climbing? Basically, it was out-of-control visitor numbers coupled with users' failure to follow the preserve's few simple rules. The catalysts were a clandestinely bolted new climb as well as the installation on several climbs of sketchy homemade permadraws. Both advents broke rule No. 5 at the preserve: that you cannot "establish any new rock climbing routes (sport)" without the express consent of the owners. Moreover, Stephens and Haight feared that the convenient permadraws would lure even more climbers to an area already seeing unsustainable traffic—often in violation of rule No. 4: "Groups of more than 4 people are discouraged. More than 8 are prohibited."

In an open letter posted on Red River Climbing (www.redriverclimbing.com), Haight and Stephens lamented, "There were over 35 cars in the parking lot on Saturday and Sunday [before the closure]. Every route had multiple parties on or waiting for them. There were dogs digging deep holes, hammocks in trees, people pissing wherever they wanted, and the already severely eroded areas continue to be decimated. The Preserve aka Roadside cannot sustain that much traffic."

The same scenario had played out earlier at Torrent Falls, a privately owned cliff on resort property just up the road. There, bad-seed climbers had been ignoring parking regulations and a suggested day-use donation and were relieving themselves in the woods right above the resort cabins, letting their dogs roam free, and using profane language. This behavior predictably soured the formerly pro-climber owners who, after nine years of permitting climbing, shut the cliff

2

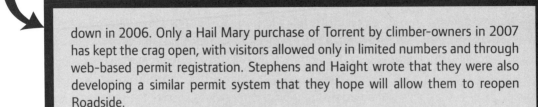

down in 2006. Only a Hail Mary purchase of Torrent by climber-owners in 2007 has kept the crag open, with visitors allowed only in limited numbers and through web-based permit registration. Stephens and Haight wrote that they were also developing a similar permit system that they hope will allow them to reopen Roadside.

While it's clear that both Roadside and Torrent suffered from their own popularity, it's also clear that too many climbers were breaking the rules, a handful of basic common-sense regulations. Though we'll never know for sure why these climbers acted this way, it might have as much to do with coming straight from the gym and never being mentored as it does with being selfish human beings. The message, again, is that we should never assume that we have a right to climb. Had climbers behaved conscientiously, like access was a privilege, Roadside might still be open. For now, I'll leave you with this parting thought: "Remember, every one of you are guests at the preserve," wrote Stephens and Haight. "It is not a climbing gym."

We've already covered a few minimum-impact practices in the sections on etiquette and access, with ideas about some small yet very meaningful steps. But three other issues are cropping up at crowded areas, all creating either new levels of impact or tension among climbers. While not necessarily removed from questions of access and etiquette, they are complex enough to merit separate discussions. The issues are using the bathroom and managing children and dogs.

Doing the Dirty Deed

Do climbers sometimes provoke land-manager ire because we—unlike mountain bikers or trail runners—stay in one place all day, and therefore create a focused potty impact? Namely, clumps of toilet paper, poorly buried feces, and a strong odor of urine in certain "piss caves" or on boulders that have become de facto latrines? Don't let this happen to your crag! You'll have to urinate multiple times during the day, and you might even have to go number two, so do it right and consider the compounded impact.

Urinating on the same spot over time will create lingering odor issues thanks to a buildup of uric acid. If that spot happens to be the cliff base, then the cliff will stink to an ungodly degree, especially on hot days. Pretend that the cliff is a water source and walk at least 200 feet (70 paces) away, staying the same distance from lakes or streams. Seek out rocks or nonvegetated areas, off the beaten path and far from trails. Don't go in the same place repeatedly, even in the woods, and avoid peeing in shady nooks and crannies where the sun can't evaporate your urine. Finally, never relieve yourself on vegetation, as your urine attracts foragers like mountain goats and marmots that will defoliate the plants in search of salts.

Just as babies struggle with object permanence—the knowledge that an object still exists even if they can't sense it, like when you hide a baby's toy behind your back—so too do climbers struggle with "doo-doo permanence," the idea that once they take a dump and walk away, their offering has somehow vanished no matter how poorly they disposed of it. Unfortunately, it doesn't work this way. Taking a dump atop the soil, wiping your heinie, leaving the TP, and plopping a rock down atop the mess is lazy and unhygienic. Never mind how they do it in Europe—the Continent has never been known for its civility. Fecal matter contaminates water, wildlife, and other users; it carries disease; and when it shows up in and around a cliff, land managers will certainly know who's responsible. (The same goes for feminine-hygiene products, which take ages to decompose; always pack them out.)

We should all aim to do better. If you have to go at the cliff, you have a couple of viable options according to an article by Buck Tilton of the Wilderness Medicine Institute and suggestions from Access Fund and Leave No Trace.

From best to worst, you can:

- Find a bathroom or an outhouse at the trailhead. Walk back from the cliff if you have to. Don't be a lazy sod.
- Use a disposable wag-type bag (name brands include Restop, GO Anywhere, and Biffy Bag). You can do your business directly into the bag, seal it, pack it out, and dispose of it as instructed. You can also build a screw-top poop tube out of PVC piping like big-wall climbers use (go in a bag and then place the bag in the tube), or fill a brown paper sack with kitty litter and then double-bag it for transport back to a portapotty, where you dump the contents.

2

TP OR NOT TP?

Toilet-paper blossoms are heinous, but what can you do to prevent them? Here are three solutions, in ascending order of impact, with the final one being your last (not-recommended) resort:

1. **Don't use it:** Smooth sticks and rocks, leaves, pinecones, and even snow work well in a pinch. Dispose of these in the cathole. Beware of stinging or rash-inducing plants like poison ivy or poison oak.
2. **Use TP, but pack it out:** Carry a designated plastic bag for used TP.
3. **Bury TP with your waste:** This option is the least desirable because TP decomposes slowly and animals can dig it up. Use unscented, dye-free organic paper, and pee on it or wet it in the hole to pack it down. Never burn used TP—you don't want to be the guy who starts a forest fire by burning his used paper.

○ Sneak off into the woods, and dig a cathole. The goal is to let nature (microorganisms in the soil) break down feces and the bacteria such that they're no longer a contaminant. Always make sure that you're 200 feet (70 paces) from water.

To dig a cathole:

1. Find a level, secluded, inconspicuous area with a layer of organic soil, and dig a hole six to eight inches deep by four to six inches across with a small trowel, a rock, or the heel of your shoe.
2. Do your business.
3. Stir it into the soil with a stick (make "poop soup"), which helps the waste to break down quicker.
4. Fill the hole back in, and cover it up with duff, sticks, native rocks, etc., to disguise it. If you've done the job correctly, you should be comfortable laying down a sleeping bag and camping there. You also want to bury the waste and disguise the hole well enough so that animals won't dig it up.

If you don't have time to dig a hole beforehand, go on the ground and then dig a hole next to your business. Now use a stick to move the waste into the hole, following the steps above to finish.

Desert Places

Being dry, sandy, and largely inorganic, desert soil can't break down feces like moister dirt can. In arid areas, pack it out, or dig a shallow cathole in the sun so that the heat will be able to bake the bacteria. Avoid washes, drainages, slickrock, and anywhere water might run, as fecal matter filters down through the ground.

Kids and Dogs

You see it all the time on climbing forums: "Kids and dogs don't belong at the crags. They're loud, disruptive, and a hazard to themselves and other users!" This tired argument is often presented as if it contained the absolute God-given rules of crag comportment. However, people without children or dogs seem to be doing most of the grousing. In reality, the complainers are merely expressing how they want things to be or how they once were. You can legally bring your child to every public cliff in the United States, and your dog to almost all of them with the exception of national parks (more than 100 feet from the road). I advise those internet mavens arguing against their presence to take a good, long look in the mirror and ask themselves why they're unable to share the resource.

As a parent and dog owner, I love sharing these places with my son and hound, and I believe I should be able to on our taxpayer-funded lands. The real question is whether a particular venue is appropriate for a particular child or dog. So when you do head out together, how can you make the experience safe, fun, and low impact, as well as ensure the quality of other users' experience?

Kids and Cragging

Being at the cliffs can be amazing for children in today's sad, sedentary epoch of TV, video games, and rampant childhood obesity. It teaches fitness, self-awareness, self-sufficiency, courage, a sense of adventure, and a connection to nature. For parents, climbing can be an incredible gift they share with their children, especially if the kids become lifers themselves. At the same time, climbing is scary: It's not for everyone, kids included. Not every child will push through that initial fear. Meanwhile, the

2

LEAVE NO TRACE

A great clearinghouse for information on minimum-impact practices and their interface with outdoor sports is the Leave No Trace Center for Outdoor Ethics (www.lnt.org), a nonprofit that comprises the most widely employed outdoor-ethics program on lands used for recreation. Besides just being generally good juju, minimum impact is also important because of our cumulative impact. Think about it: If you take a leak behind that tree one time, not much will come of it. But if this happens a thousand times, there starts to be a problem.

As with all the issues presented thus far, the Leave No Trace teachings are about making a series of choices every time you go out. They're about participation, not perfection. As Susy Alkaitis of Leave No Trace says, "Leave No Trace is not rigid or about rules; it's a spectrum and a framework for making good decisions about how to enjoy the outdoors responsibly."

For further reference, Leave No Trace's seven core principles are:

- Plan ahead and prepare.
- Travel and camp on durable surfaces.
- Dispose of waste properly.
- Leave what you find.
- Minimize campfire impacts.
- Respect wildlife.
- Be considerate of other visitors.

For only $2.95, Leave No Trace offers a great booklet on rock climbing from their "Skills and Ethics" library.

risks to children at the crags are real, omnipresent, and specific to them, compounded beyond the standard perils we all face. Significant factors include children's fragility, lack of mobility and spatial awareness in early-development stages, and small size relative to dangers like rockfall, dropped gear, falling climbers, and dogs.

New parents ourselves, my wife and I have so far brought our toddler son to the cliffs only once, when we had the grandparents along to help. We have, however, taken him to the gym plenty and noted how he likes to watch us climb, and we plan to get out more with him soon. While researching this section, I spoke to climbing-and-parenting veterans Lucia Hyde Robinson, a dedicated boulderer who's been taking her first daughter out since birth, and Jonathan and Jackie Koehne, who have always brought along their two daughters, who are now happily into climbing themselves. (Note: You can also find many great kids-specific climbing programs, including, in my hometown of Boulder, Colorado, the venerable ABC Kids climbing school and rock gym, a motivating, play-based program pioneered by former World Cup champion Robyn Erbesfield-Raboutou that has produced a long list of champions and phenomenal climbers, including her own children, Shawn and Brooke.)

Brooke Raboutou romps up a limestone sport route on one of her earliest leads. *Robyn Erbesfield-Raboutou*

In any case, all the parents I spoke to emphasized that things tend to go best at empty crags—where the kids are freer to roam and there is less risk of hazards like rockfall or of being overwhelmed by crowds, dogs, noise, etc. They also recommended venues with quiet, pleasant natural settings and water nearby (lakes or streams to play in) over loud, dirty, or roadside venues. And they emphasized approaching the experience as a family trip on which you *might* happen to climb a little instead of as a goal-focused sendathon, which can be a recipe for dashed expectations as well as child meltdowns.

It's useful to look at climbing with children in terms of three stages of childhood development: infant, toddler, and child.

2

Climbing with an Infant

This is the easiest phase because your child is not yet mobile and often sleeps for hours. Knowing that you'll have to carry her in her car seat or backpack, hit up crags with short approaches or go bouldering, where you can make a quick escape. Bring warm clothing, portable shade (an umbrella or sun shade), a crash pad, and your car seat or a portable crib. Climb in mild, comfortable conditions—not too hot, not too cold. Stage your child on flat, durable, protected ground well away from rockfall or occupied routes, and don't overstay your visit. Nothing is worse than trying to pack up with a baby in "Feed me now!" crisis mode.

Climbers who don't have children can also help by having more empathy toward parent-climbers, just as parents need to be aware that not everyone will get it. The Koehnes cited a trip they took to Shelf Road, Colorado, right after their first daughter was born. They were at an empty crag and had found a zone with a perfect nap spot for their daughter when another couple showed up wanting to do a route directly above the baby—at a cliff with unlimited options! While the Koehnes accommodated the couple and relocated their daughter, it certainly would have been better not to. "Ultimately, it's our responsibility as parents to educate nonparents," says Jackie Koehne, "though these types of things still happen because some people don't care."

A final thought for maintaining domestic harmony: When new parents begin to climb together, they should lay out the groundwork first thing in the day for childcare logistics and divvying up climbing time. Communicating about your plan can do a lot to prevent bickering later.

Climbing with a Toddler

From about one to three years of age, your child is mobile (crawling or walking) and full of energy, but not old enough to notice all the cliff's perils. Now is a good time to hook up with other climbers with kids or who enjoy children's company. Climbing in threes works well—two people climb while the third, resting, looks after the toddler. "A third set of hands is so critical," says Jonathan Koehne. "You can't belay two people at once, so you shouldn't be watching two people at once either."

Hyde Robinson, meanwhile, says she had good luck with bouldering at this stage. "It's a little more casual and social," she says. "You're not up on a route, you're not engaged for long periods of time, and other people in your group can help watch the kid." My wife and I have also had success going to a local rock gym with auto-belay machines and taking turns climbing and watching our son.

Visiting crowded cliffs with a toddler can be dangerous, especially if there are dogs. Dogs love the food crumbs on toddlers' faces and fingers and might inadvertently knock a child over trying to lick them off. Big dogs or the dog packs that congregate off leash can also be intimidating for toddlers. "If we know there will be a big group of people or a big group of dogs, we just don't go to that cliff," says Jackie Koehne. Also, seek out kinder venues with short approaches (since you're probably still using a child carrier), and without punishing elements (too much sun or wind), rockfall issues, or drop-offs.

To keep your toddler from becoming fussy, bring abundant snack food and toys, like you would when going anywhere. As he gets older, you can also come up with fun diversions that

Wunderkind Shawn Raboutou on *Bad Attitude* (5.13c), Saint-Antonin, France, a route first established by his father, Didier.
Laurent Filoche

incorporate the cliff environment, like hunting for pinecones or flowers (not picking them, of course), stacking rock cairns, counting bolts, building log cabins from twigs, and so on. If you can get him to play in and appreciate nature, he'll be more likely to want to return.

Climbing with a Child

Beginning around age three or three and a half, your kid can try climbing herself. She's mature enough to understand and take more responsibility for her safety. She'll also be old enough to approach more-distant crags (up to a quarter mile or more away), which expands your options.

When you visit a crag, begin by setting up in a safe zone, where your kids can hang out and where you can all drop your packs. Accustom your kids to seeking out protected staging and hangout areas, such as off in the trees or under overhangs.

As a family unit, revisit basic safety rules each time you get to a crag:

- Don't walk under occupied routes, rockfall zones, or other climbers.
- Don't step on ropes.
- Keep your helmets on when climbing or at the cliff base; be aware of rockfall or dropped gear.
- Don't wander out of sight (children make easy pickings for predators like mountain lions), and always know where mom and dad are climbing.
- Don't go near drop-offs.
- Keep an eye out for crag dogs, and ask their owners if they're friendly before approaching them.
- Be respectful of other climbers.
- Don't run around, throw rocks, scream, fight with siblings, etc.

Explain the reasons for these rules, and discuss how they pertain to each cliff. Be patient and help kids see that these aren't just more rules from mom and dad. Your goal is to introduce a crag education that they assimilate over the long haul.

Now to getting your kids started climbing. Your goal is to make the outing fun and low-pressure, because if you push them too hard, they'll hate climbing, hate you, or never climb again. They are their own people and should decide whether to climb for themselves. Some suggestions:

- **Start bouldering low** to accustom children to the shoes, chalk, and holds. Being close to the ground also lets your child experience climbing in an unintimidating way, with you spotting. Try the kid's bouldering wall at the gym, which often has bright, playful holds or fun shapes like animals.
- **Accustom your child to wearing a harness.** A full-body harness designed for children is a sure bet for the smallest kids (for about

2

ages four to nine and up to about 60 pounds). Encourage your child to wear it around the house, and then sample a few rope swings off a tree limb, gym rope, or overhanging climb.

- **Use fun gear examples.** "This rope could hold up our car," or "Helmets are cool," or "These rock shoes are magic shoes."
- **As your child graduates to top-roping, keep things playful.** If she wants to swing instead of climb, let her. If she wants to come down after four feet, let her. Perhaps the next time she'll go five feet, then six, then seven all of her own volition.
- **The first few times your child top-ropes, climb alongside her or station someone up at the anchor so that she's not alone when she gets there.** Encourage her while she climbs and prepares to lower.
- **Make something other than the climb the goal.** Instead of saying, "Daddy wants you to get to the anchors, honey, because then you'll be a good little climber," try this approach: "Hey, let's do this route, and find the fossil halfway up." Or you could say, "Let's climb up to that ledge together and look at a really neat crystal." You can also try bribery by promising a treat, such as ice cream, later.
- **Keep things quiet.** It's natural for parents and onlookers to cheer a kid on, but the clamor can be overwhelming. Keep your beta and encouragement mellow, low-key, and more focused on being in the moment (e.g., "Try putting your hand here, sweetie, by this cool patch of yellow lichen").
- **Avoid the anchor meltdown.** Station yourself or someone else up top to welcome your child, and then try this trick: Attach a second rope to the back (haul loop) of her harness, and then have someone on the ground tug it gently to pull her away from the wall so that she naturally walks her feet down. This approach especially helps you lower very small or light children.
- **Be flexible.** If your kid wants to climb that day, great; if not, that's OK too. Let him be the guide, and be ready to leave early or move on to other activities if he's not interested in climbing.

2

- **Bring friends or siblings.** Older kids love to play with and entertain each other, so be social and climb with other families.
- **Avoid frustration.** As your child gets more into climbing, she may become more goal oriented. To take the edge off when she fails, encourage her with positive feedback. Also, emphasize that you're there to have fun and that she can come down to try another climb or save this one for another day. You can also jump on the route yourself, hang, and say something like, "Wow, it *is* really hard right here!" Remember that your kids will model your behavior; if you pitch giant wobblers, they will too.

Dogs and Cragging

Look on any climbing forum and odds are you'll see some heated thread about whether dogs belong at the crags, with opinions tilting to each pole: "I bring Poochie every time I climb, and it's my God-given right," vs. "Leave your dog at home. He digs holes, fights with other dogs, steals food, bites people, craps everywhere, and is ruining my nature experience." Both answers are essentially correct. Unless dogs are expressly forbidden, you can legally bring your dog no matter how other users might feel. Dogs love being out in the woods.

Yet not all climbers are dog people (some are even dog phobic), not all crags are good dog venues, not all dogs make good crag dogs, and dogs can create impact and user conflict. It's poor etiquette to let your dog raise hell at the cliffs, which will stress out you, your dog, and other climbers. I should know. My diabolical Plott hound, Clyde, is a brindled 80-pound wildebeest with a super-sniffer nose that causes him to wander, invariably to steal food. And as I've learned over the years, it's not always a good idea to bring him.

It all begins with awareness. If you set your dog up for success, things can go swimmingly. If, however, you don't pay attention to cues from your dog and other climbers, things can get ugly.

Venue

Before you even leave the house, consider the venue. Are you going to a cliff at which both you and your dog will be safe and happy, or would it be better to leave him at home?

A chillaxed crag dog always wears his Doggles. *Matt Samet*

Cliffs that make *good* venues:

- Have flat, wide bases and a good mix of sun and shade.
- Have nontechnical approaches and unexposed staging areas.
- Have single-pitch climbs so that you're always in range of your dog.
- Do not have too many other people, dogs, or children so that your pooch doesn't get overstimulated.
- Do not have extreme temperatures (too hot or too cold).
- Do not have dangerous fauna (such as rattlesnakes, ticks, or poisonous spiders) or flora (such as poison oak or ivy or stinging nettles) or special environmental considerations (such as cryptobiotic soil).

Cliffs that make *poor* venues:

- Have rocky, overly sunny, or semiexposed bases.
- Have somewhat technical, scrambling approaches.
- Are busy with lots of climbers and dogs (Even if your dog is well

2

trained, you can't account for other dogs and their owners.).
- Are known for having chossy rock.
- Have small or tight staging areas, such as cramped belay zones where there's barely room for your crag kit, much less a dog.
- Are known for objective nuisances like dangerous flora or fauna.

Cliffs that make *awful* venues:
- Have multipitch routes, which will prevent you from reaching your dog in an emergency or keeping track of him.
- Have technical approaches (rope ladders, rappels, Tyroleans, etc.) and exposed staging areas such as ledges with drop-offs. (If you feel the exposure, your dog will too.)
- Have hiking trails (not just climber trails) along their bases. Dogs obstructing hiker traffic have caused access issues.
- Experience extreme temperatures. Consider especially how much sun or exposure the base has.

Don't ever feel guilty for leaving your hound at home. Rover might see the climbing pack come out, get fired up, and then look at you with "sad panda" eyes when you don't load him into the car, but dogs have short memories. When I don't bring Clyde climbing, I'll walk him first thing in the morning or when I get home so that my conscience doesn't gnaw at me. Sometimes I'll walk him before bringing him climbing so that he's more docile at the cliffs.

Dog Management 101

Since the venue looks good, you've opted to bring Fido. Now how do you make it work? Melissa Lipani, who works for a large national animal welfare and rescue organization, has been climbing for 13 years and has at various times owned one to four crag dogs. "We are responsible for ourselves and the environment that we're climbing in," she says. "It's the same thing with dogs at the cliffs. My role as a dog owner is to set my dog up so that he succeeds. If he screws up, it's on me—not him."

First, consider temperature, particularly on an approach on a hot day. Like humans, dogs are most comfortable between about 50 and 75 degrees Fahrenheit, so let your own comfort level be a guideline.

CANINE FRIEND TOOLKIT

Bring the following to keep your crag pooch happy.

- Doggie pack. Dogs should carry no more than 25 to 30 percent of their body weight; my mega-beast, Clyde, carries my water too, which is awesome
- Collapsible water bowl
- Long leash like an old piece of rope (for tying your dog to a tree or other anchor) and carabiners for rigging
- Dog jacket for cold days
- Cooling vest for hot days
- An old blanket or towel for your dog to lie on and for interrupting fights
- A spray bottle filled with water to deter bad behavior or cool off your dog, and as extra drinking water
- Pet first-aid kit, which will contain many of the same essentials as your own first-aid kit
- Consider a rattlesnake vaccine for your dog if you live in snake country; dogs are much more likely to be bit than humans, and the vaccine can delay the onset and mitigate the severity of a reaction.
- Animal deterrent spray: Melissa Lipani recommends Spray Shield (formerly Direct Stop), a citronella spray used to break up dogfights, stop a charging dog, or deter other undesirable behavior
- Poop bags or a small spade for burying waste. If you're at a crowded cliff or on a trail, pick up the poop or bury it, and endeavor to do so even in remote or light-use areas. Dog feces have a high nitrogen content that can negatively affect the environment, and they carry pathogens such as toxocaria and parvovirus, so it's best to remove them when you can.

Before taking Poochie into the outdoors, check off these common-sense boxes:

- ☐ Your dog has a microchip (which can often be done cheaply, frequently at your local humane society) and collar with current ID tags. How often have we read about that missing crag dog that ran off with old tags or no collar?
- ☐ Your dog is current on his vaccinations and is spayed or neutered.
- ☐ You know where the nearest vet is, especially on a road trip.
- ☐ You've completed an obedience class with your dog and understand basic training principles.

2

The majority of a dog's sweat glands are in his paws, with some also concentrated around his nose. Unlike people, dogs cool off mainly through panting. On a hot day, your dog will naturally pant, but he can quickly overheat with too much sun exposure or strenuous activity. Warning signs of hyperthermia (aka heatstroke) include excessive drooling, dehydration (dry, sticky gums are an indicator), gums and mucous membranes turning brick red, excessive panting or trouble breathing, refusing to move, and vomiting. Hyperthermia is a serious condition requiring veterinary intervention; don't let your dog reach this state.

Lipani recommends preventive cooling first:

- **Squirt your dog with the spray bottle.** Spray his entire coat so the water will cool him as it evaporates, and wet the tops and bottoms of his paws and the backs and inside flaps of his ears. Lipani sprays the water onto her hand first and then rubs it all over her dog's ears.
- **Use a cooling vest**, and spray it down from time to time.
- **Give your dog access to drinking water.** A common error occurs when an owner ties up a dog next to a water bowl and goes climbing, and then the dog upsets the bowl. Place the bowl in a secure spot where your dog won't lie down on it, or try a no-spill bowl.
- **Ensure that your dog is in the shade.**

Signs of a frozen dog are obvious: shivering, curling up into a ball, or snuggling close to you for body heat. Bring a dog jacket (easily supplemented by building a warm nest with a towel, blanket, or your own extra jacket) and snow booties for winter travel. Sustained travel over snow or ice can also freeze and crack a dog's paws, so watch for bleeding.

Staging

Once you reach the cliff, set your dog up in a comfortable staging area, just like you do for yourself: flat, shady or sunny as need be, away from rockfall, and away from any center-stage action. From what I've seen, most conflict among dogs or between dogs and climbers occurs over territory. It usually goes something like this: You plunk your stuff down below a route and leave or tie your dog up there. Then other climbers show up, and suddenly your dog barks or growls at them or tussles with their dogs. Things

2

quickly escalate to an all-out war! Or worse, you leave your dog to wander, and thinking the whole cliff is his dominion, he starts Project Mayhem: picking fights, biting people, stealing food, chasing critters, and digging holes.

Put a stop to such behaviors by training your dog to go to his personal staging area. Lipani brings a towel or blanket; what you want is a portable dog nest that you condition your dog to view as his hangout. Treat-and-clicker training can accustom your dog to his place, and you can bring treats to reward his good behavior. A towel also makes a great place to give a misbehaving dog a timeout, keeps your dog out of the crag dust, prevents him from digging holes, and can be used to clean his paws at day's end. Plus, having his own spot keeps your dog from chasing wildlife. Dogs are predators whose mere presence, even leashed, can stress prey animals, such as deer, rabbits, and squirrels, disrupting their daily routine and provoking energy-sucking escape measures.

When you tie your dog up, be aware of leash reactivity. Think about how your leashed dog will react if other dogs, climbers, or children approach. If someone shows up with an unleashed dog and your own is tied up, ask the other climbers to leash their dog until you sort the situation out. Do the same with parents and children: warn them that your dog is on a leash and might be better off left alone. Meanwhile, monitor your dog's stress signals (see the "Canine Stress Signals" sidebar) to make sure an eruption isn't building.

A tired climber and his tired crag dog (Captain Cowpants) chilling in the Utah desert. *Melissa Lipani*

Dogs and Bouldering

Staging your dog in a safe zone is even more important while bouldering because boulderers fall onto their crash pads frequently, often in a helter-skelter, unpredictable fashion, and to dogs

2

CANINE STRESS SIGNALS

Dog owner and climber Melissa Lipani emphasizes the importance of knowing your dog's stress signals, the cues he gives off when he is anxious, angry, sad, or scared. By recognizing his most common stressors and his unique body language, you can train your dog or reassure him.

Common stressors include:
- Weather (thunderstorms or high winds, for instance)
- Being tied up
- Separation anxiety
- Drop-offs and exposure
- Having other dogs or kids in his space

Common stress signals include:
- Yawning
- Licking his nose
- Barking or whining
- Flattening his ears or tucking his tail
- Excessive scratching

crash pads look like giant dog beds! You see the problem, right? A dog running underfoot or lounging on your pads might get hurt, and so might you in the bargain. The worst dog-related accident I've seen out climbing was a boulderer landing on a puppy that had sprinted underneath him as he fell. The dog lived—that day—but eventually had to be put to sleep. Climbers have torn knee ligaments and broken ankles when they landed on large breeds. Either tie your dog up far from the action, or make sure he'll stay put.

Breaking Up a Fight

Even with good training some dog conflict is inevitable. The trick is to keep things from escalating. The first sign of an imminent conflict is usually preemptive low growling; you might also see raised hackles, bared teeth, or the dogs circling each other. Curtail this behavior by squirting your dog in the face with a spray bottle, especially if he's guarding his territory. In the event that a battle breaks out, try these measures:

- Throw a backpack between the dogs or a blanket over their heads. Never stick your hands into the fray to grab a dog by the collar; this is a recipe for getting bit.
- Grab a dog—preferably the aggressor—by the rear legs, lift him, and then pull him toward you, turning your face away from gnashing teeth.
- Spritz animal deterrent spray on both dogs, and then quickly separate them.
- Throw water on them.

RESPECTING THE ROCK

This ancient medium was here long before us and will be here long after; we must respect it. Without further ado, here are the Five Ultimate Rules for Respecting the Rock:

1. **Clean your rock shoes.** Don't start up any route, ever, with dirty feet. Take off your muddy socks or filthy approach shoes, and put on proper rock shoes. Now wipe the major chunks of dirt or gravel off your soles with your hands or on a crash pad or your pants leg, and then lick your palm and rub it on the front of your sole until it squeaks. You can also use a little towel with water or rubbing alcohol. There are also some great tools out there specifically for cleaning climbing shoes, such as the Boreal Shoe Tool.

2. **Brush the holds.** Caked-on chalk is not only an eyesore, it reduces friction by interposing a spongy layer between skin and rock. Brushing, even a quick once-over on the crux holds, is a courtesy for yourself and the next guy. (See the "Hold Cleaning 101" sidebar for brushing tips.)

3. **Don't chip.** Don't add holds that never existed, and don't alter or enhance existing holds unless loose rock needs to be removed for safety reasons. This rule includes not using metal-bristled brushes, such as steel or brass, which some people have used to create grips on established lines. Wire brushes also polish the rock, removing

2

critical texture. Neither should you overzealously brush soft stone with a stiff-bristled nylon brush, for similar reasons.

4. **Don't climb on soft rock after rainy periods.** Especially on porous sandstone, fragile crimpers and horns are more prone to snapping when they are damp. Let at least one windy or sunny day pass after a big rainstorm. At Red Rock Canyon, Nevada, the locals will have some choice words for you if you violate this ethic. And don't slather chalk on or use a chalk ball to dry out wet climbs: As the water evaporates, the chalk melds with the rock to create a pasty mess.

5. **Don't draw chalk graffiti.** You might think it's cute to draw a smiley face around that hueco, but it isn't. Even if chalk eventually fades, nonclimbers might mistake your "rock art" for paint.

HOLD CLEANiNG 101

A brush is an essential part of any climber's kit because clean holds are happy holds. On a well-traveled route, not only do the grips gunk up with chalk, but also with a patina of hand oil, dead skin, sweat (salt), shoe rubber, and dust. Brushing both removes this layer and also reduces the chalk's visibility. *Failure to brush, especially if someone is coming up right after you, is bad etiquette.*

Boulderers are notoriously fussy about cleaning holds. Ace Colorado boulderers Chris Schulte and Herman Feissner both recommend starting with a kit that has multiple brushes and different tools for different scenarios. Buy a commercial kit, or assemble the tools yourself with a trip online or to the grocery, hardware, or climbing store.

Look for:

○ A large brush for large or sloping holds, for softer stone, or for volumes (indoors). One good supermarket option is a long-handled, nylon-bristled dishwashing brush without a soap reservoir; some even come with dual-sided heads (one with bigger, softer bristles and the other a toothbrush head with stiffer bristles). Schulte also recommends a midsized horsehair shoe-shining brush.

2

- An oversized boar's-hair or horsehair toothbrush for mid-range holds, harder rock, and general-purpose scrubbing. (The Lapis Boar's Hair Brush has a cult following.)
- A stiff-bristled toothbrush, nylon denture brush, or climbing-specific brush for detail work
- A hand, tea, or dish towel
- A spray bottle or bottle of water

When your brushes are ready, it's time to demank those holds:

- Use bigger brushes for bigger holds and smaller brushes for smaller holds, so that you don't wear out your small brushes on big jobs.
- Employing soft-bristled brushes on harder rock like fused limestone, granite, or quartzite will wear them out quickly: use a stiff-bristled brush instead.
- With softer rock such as sandstone, use a softer rig like your big nylon brush or boar's-hair brush, and make small, circular motions across the hold. Grinding aggressively can damage the rock. "You don't need that much force to clean a fine-grained stone," says Schulte. "So be delicate." As Feissner puts it, more generally: "Brushing a hold well requires a gentle touch. There's no reason to smash the bristles down with too much pressure or to use an aggressive back-and-forth motion. I believe brushes are more effective with light pressure."
- Use a stiff-bristled toothbrush on harder rock like granite, such as the patina crimps of the Buttermilks, California. The chalk sits atop compact stone more than it absorbs into it, so you can brush with greater vigor.

Finally, do a touch-up:

- Blow on the hold to remove loose chalk.
- Whap the hold with your tea towel to remove excess dust or humidity and even cool the hold.

2

Holds on trade routes can become so caked that they're in need of hydrotherapy. To give a hold a bath:

- Pour water from your water bottle, or spit it directly onto the hold. (Rinse out your mouth first so that you

A light touch helps when brushing holds.

  don't spew food particles.) A spray bottle works well too, though they are more delicate and are perhaps best for dedicated situations, such as when you are close to sending.
- Use a nylon-bristled brush (not boar's hair or horsehair) to clean the hold, making circular scrubbing motions.
- As you scrub, greasy white bubbles of chalk and skin will froth up on the hold. Add water and keep scrubbing until the froth disappears.
- Dry the hold with your towel, or let it air dry. Let the grips on soft rock like sandstone dry for a couple hours or even overnight to keep from ripping off any fragile holds.

IT'S ABOUT CHOICES

2

We all make choices every time we climb, from where we'll go, to which routes we'll try, to who we'll try them with, to which piece we'll place at the crux. The same can be said of the choices we make off, below, or around the stone. My hope is that the information in this chapter will help you to make informed decisions that respect the rock, the natural environment, and other users, with the goal of keeping our cliffs healthy, friendly, clean, and open.

Climbers have always been great at self-policing, as well as largely cognizant of our impacts. There is a long tradition of environmentalism woven into the fabric of our sport. Take John Muir's writings about and involvement to protect the Sierra Nevada, David Brower's leadership of the Sierra Club, and the clean-climbing movement of the 1960s and '70s when climbers eschewed pitons for low-impact passive protection like nuts and chocks. It behooves us to recognize our cumulative impacts, step in to fix them where we can, and work with land managers as allies for the access cause. A world in which the crags have been closed forever and the only climbing left is the gym is not a world I'd want to live in. Climbing is about freedom, and we must all work to keep it that way.

2

3 MOVEMENT PhD

Crouch Like a Tiger, Hide Like a Dragon

DESPITE WHAT YOU MIGHT have read elsewhere, climbing is not a strength sport. It is rather a technical sport in which strength is a *factor* but is by no means the foundation. The foundation is a good head and smooth, deliberate, controlled motion. Free climbing has always had this Zen aspect to it: Give a gorilla a nine iron, and he'll hit the unholy hell out of the ball, but probably not toward the hole. But give him a nine iron and teach him how to aim, and he'll nail a hole in one. The infinitely diverse medium of the rock is like every possible golf shot in the world rolled into one. Power is nothing without proficiency, and sequencing is nothing without creativity.

Still don't believe me? How many top climbers are what the general public would label "strong looking"? Consider Adam Ondra, the world's leading sport climber, who onsights 5.14c: Tall, skinny, and wearing nerdy Harry Potter glasses, he's the last person you'd label a "crusher" yet he dispatches routes like Schwarzenegger curling a one-pound dumbbell. Consider also the top women climbers: Lithe, small, and slender, very few have über-bulging She-Ra builds, yet all flow over the stone. Sure, these people are all physically fit and have crazy-strong fingers, but first and foremost they are students of technique. They have mastered the ability to control and apply their strength at their outermost physical limits.

To use another analogy, I could go out and spend thousands of dollars souping up my 1997 Honda Civic. But if I don't take a car-racing class first, and instead apply my usual commuter skill set, I'll peel out at stoplights and burn through my fancy new tires, leaving skid marks like an amateur. This is how most of us climb: like amateurs. We focus on numbers and goals and impressive feats of vertical strength, but rarely on technical improvement. Even though we know we're being lazy, we fall back into our bad habits. When we hit a plateau, we train to get stronger and break through. But we're still climbing in the same sloppy way, albeit with a few more horses under the hood. And so the cycle continues . . .

The key to advancing is improving your technical game. Whether your ceiling is 5.9 or 5.14-plus, you must bring the same level of technical excellence to each and every move. Anything else is just souping up a car you don't know how to drive.

The bulk of this chapter relies on the theory and teachings of Justen Sjong, a routesetter and coach at Movement Climbing + Fitness in Boulder, Colorado. Sjong is a phenomenal climber with redpoints up to 5.14c as well as, with Tommy Caldwell in 2008, the first free ascent of one of El Capitan's hardest big walls, the VI 5.13d/5.14a *Magic Mushroom*. When Sjong coached my wife, Kristin, she went from 5.11a to 5.12a in a month. When you

consider that nothing changed about her physique or fitness, her rapid improvement seems miraculous. Sjong helped Kristin refine her technique so that she could better tap her innate strength, a process we'll examine now in terms of the three big concepts of footwork, composure, and flow.

(Sjong recommends that you do the drills that accompany the teachings only during your warm-ups. This way, a little bit of each teaching resonates throughout the day without your becoming a neurotic, overly self-conscious wreck.)

Justen Sjong, aka the "Sensei," in his element in Yosemite National Park.
Corey Rich / Aurora Photos

FOOTWORK

As the saying goes, "The key to climbing better is good footwork." But what makes footwork "good," and how does it improve your climbing? Kevin Jorgeson is a powerhouse boulderer and highball specialist who in 2009 made the first ascent of a 45-foot V11 boulder problem called *Ambrosia* outside Bishop, California. He is also a cofounder of Professional Climbers International (PCI), a body of pro climbers that offers the public a series of killer technique clinics (http://clinics.proclimbers.com). A polished and strong climber, Jorgeson has put a lot of thought into the nuances of footwork.

You've probably heard another truism: that your leg muscles, since they are larger, are slower to tire than your arms and hence should be your main weight-bearing points. But as Jorgeson frames it, footwork is simply one facet of being an *active* instead of a *reactive* climber. By using your feet and legs to propel you in the desired direction as part of a deliberate sequence, you become the architect of your climbing motion. Unfortunately, this tactic is not always our first instinct. Before we rock climb,

Kevin Jorgeson stays on his toes on the very tall *Footprints*, Grandpa Peabody, Buttermilks, California.

we might scale ladders, fences, and trees, where an opposing hand-foot monkey shuffle (focused on pulling with our hands) works best. In his clinics, Jorgeson urges people to hit the reset button and focus on their feet. Grabbing the next hold should be the product of placing your feet and moving your body correctly, not moving your feet *in reaction* to where the hold is (overextending and then bringing your feet up out of necessity). This backward paradigm leads to sloppy technique and traps climbers at moderate grades. You can fake it up through 5.10, but from 5.11 upward, the holds are simply too small.

Precise footwork begins in your big toe, the *point of power* or *pivot point* for your entire foot. Our big toes stick out the farthest, are our strongest toes, and cue our other piggies kinesthetically. They are *action points* for move initiation, transferring tension across our feet, up through our ankles and heels, and along our legs to the rest of our body. We rotate around them to complete a move, like the tip of a spinning dreidel. So much hinges on such a small body part!

Your big toe, however, cannot do its job unless it is partnered with a properly sized climbing shoe. If your shoes are too tight, you'll barely weight your feet for the pain, while if they are too loose, you'll roll off small footholds and edges. To find your match, attend a shoe demo or visit an equipment shop with a demo wall. *Don't just buy the latest, hottest shoe or any old pair sight unseen and assume it will meet your needs—the wrong shoe can even be lethal, by making you slip where you wouldn't otherwise.*

Here are some buying tips gleaned from Jorgeson and Lisa Aquino, who works at La Sportiva USA and sold shoes in a Denver shop for years:

- **Ask the salesperson what type of climbing he's into** to get a sense of which shoes he'll recommend and why. Make sure you discuss what type of climbing you are into and what you are looking for in a shoe.
- **Be aware of your personal foot shape.** Some brands fit wide, high-volume feet better, while others cater to people with narrow, low-volume feet. Have the salesperson assess your bare feet, and ask him which brands he'd start with for your foot.
- **Don't buy the tightest pair you can squeeze into,** especially if you're new to the sport. **Shoes don't need to be painful to perform.** If your toes are scrunched up and you're cramping

across your foot or arch, try a half-size larger until you have a snug fit. Many modern shoes, especially ones with synthetic (vs. leather) uppers, barely stretch, so you might never break in those foot-binding-torture shoes.

○ **Your big toe should reach the end of the toe box,** but it and your other toes shouldn't curl unless you're in an aggressively downturned shoe. Ideally, your toe and the shoe should become one; when standing on an edge (not a ledge), your foot shouldn't separate from the end of the shoe, which happens if the shoe's too loose.

○ **There should not be air pockets** where the shoe sags or bags, and **the heel cup shouldn't pop off** in heel hooks.

○ **Consider entry-level shoes when starting out.** With flat lasts and rounded, symmetrical toe boxes, these shoes are more comfortable and supportive than high-end rock shoes. They aren't as precise, but they get you up and running while your feet are still building the necessary flexibility and musculature.

○ **Upgrade to a shoe with an asymmetrical toe box and/or moderate downturn** for greater control and sensitivity if you progress to 5.10 and above. You need to *feel* those smaller footholds. Such genre-spanners are also great if you're an intermediate or advanced climber (5.10–5.13) looking for a single, all-around performance shoe. They fit precisely but, unlike a downcambered shoe, aren't so aggressive that you have to yank them off after one pitch.

○ **Shoes without laces or with laces that don't come low over the toe box are best for crack climbing;** all that twisting and torqueing will chew your laces up. Hard-crack master Rob Pizem recommends shoes with a high toe-box rand that extends back past the point where your toes meet your foot. Size them so that your feet sit flat in a natural way and aren't curled—"tight enough so you could wear a thin pair of socks if you wanted," says Pizem.

3

SHOE BUYER'S TERMiNOLOGY

Helpful terms for researching shoes:

- **Asymmetrical.** Instead of being laterally symmetrical across the toe box, the shoe follows the foot's natural, irregular curve. This design's good for performance climbing and for focusing power through your big toe.
- **Downcambered.** The shoe has a bananalike underfoot swoop shape, beveled high through the arch. This aggressive last is best for overhanging rock and redpoint climbing.
- **Downturned.** The shoe's forefoot droops in a hook or talon shape, driving the big toe hard into the tip. This design is best for overhanging climbing, where you need to dig and pull, but it can be painful on slabby or vertical rock.
- **Flat lasted.** A shoe that's flat along the sole from heel to toe is good for edging, trad climbing, cracks, slabs, and all-day wear.
- **Footbed.** The interior of the shoe, which your foot slides into, might be lined or unlined. A lining can reduce both odor and stretch.
- **Last.** This is the three-dimensional shape around which the shoe is constructed, i.e., the negative space contained by the shoe. Most modern shoes are slip lasted, with the shoe built around a slipperlike or socklike form.
- **Midsole.** The subsole made of cardboard, leather, plastic, etc., situated between the footbed and outsole, imparts form and edging stiffness.
- **Rand.** The band of sticky rubber wrapped around the shoe above the sole that links it to the upper. It provides contact for heel hooking and toe scumming, as well as grip and protection in cracks.
- **Symmetrical.** Lateral symmetry across the toe box produces a rounded look. Symmetrical shoes are comfortable and best for moderate or crack climbing.
- **Upper.** The upper part of the shoe enclosing the footbed is usually leather or a synthetic material. Shoes with leather uppers might stretch a half to a full size, while shoes with synthetic uppers stretch very little.

3

How to Place Your Foot

Every foot move (and every move, really) initiates with solid placement of the big toe, or the pinkie toe if you are outside edging. Begin by *slowly* making contact with the best part of the foothold to reduce readjustment, which is a strenuous waste of energy:

1. Study the foothold—really look at it!—and isolate the best part for your direction of travel.
2. Keep this sweet spot in view.
3. Bring your foot slowly and silently into contact with the wall's vertical plane and with the foothold's horizontal aspect simultaneously.
4. Push *into* the sweet spot, applying force deliberately and perpendicularly to the climbing surface. Your abs and core generate much of this inward force, a tension you can feel if you focus on it.

Voilá, you're standing precisely on a foothold! Whether you're edging, smearing, toeing down, or what have you, the keystone is *accuracy*. The trouble is, most of us don't naturally do this. We instead bring our foot to the wall, slide down to the foothold, and then weight it (see the "Bad Footwork" sidebar), which jams your big toe hard against the climbing surface instead of on the lip of the hold and locks your ankle and heel in place, limiting mobility. In a domino effect, it also limits how tall you can be on the foothold and how well you'll execute the next reach. Ideally, you want your toe to be a few millimeters from the wall so you can be playful over your ankle and heel, swiveling around to inform your direction of travel and standing tall to activate your calf.

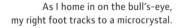

As I home in on the bull's-eye, my right foot tracks to a microcrystal.

Placing your foot precisely on the lip of the hold provides more play (and height) over your ankle.

Jamming your foot sloppily against the rock limits your heel and ankle mobility.

3

We'd all like to think we have laser-guided footwork, but the reality is that we could all stand to improve. To measure your footwork accuracy, try the hover-foot drill:

1. Look down at your foothold, confirm how you'll use it, and then hover your foot above it.
2. Stay there for two seconds.
3. Notice what happens. If your leg stays firm and solid, it signifies that you have advanced fine motor skills and that you are in the appropriate balance position. If your leg shakes, you either lack these

BAD FOOTWORK

We can easily recognize sloppy footwork in others, but how do you isolate these tendencies in yourself? The gym, with its thin, hollow walls that loudly and cruelly highlight every last shortcoming, makes a good test zone. Most of the following mistakes will create noise or leave skid marks. Jump on a climb just hard enough to push you, say a number grade below your limit, and look out for:

- **Carelessness.** Making hasty, inaccurate foot moves that result in slipping off.
- **Noise.** Bringing your feet into contact with the holds too aggressively, creating thumping or booming (aka "thunderfoot"). Noise can also indicate you're first contacting the wall around or above the hold or that you are dragging your toe along the wall because your ankle and heel are rigid.
- **Passivity.** Moving your feet the bare minimum, as a byproduct of having already reached for the next handhold.
- **Lack of coordination.** Choppy, flat-footed footwork without play or pivot over your heel or big toe.
- **Dragging.** Smearing your foot above a hold and then letting it ooze downward, settling where it will.
- **Blindness.** Either not looking down when you place your feet or looking at the foothold until you're almost on it and then closing or averting your eyes; this might involve popping your heel up and down to test the hold instead of verifying it visually. Keeping your eyes on the foothold until you're settled in ensures that your foot stays put and inspires confidence.
- **Readjustment.** Dithering on a foothold, which tires you out and introduces doubt.
- **Window shopping.** Trying your foot on a slew of different holds instead of picking one and commanding it, even if it might ultimately be the wrong choice.

fine motor skills (muscle control through your feet and calves) or are out of balance and have overtightened your core to compensate.

Now place your foot, confirming your placement with sight and feel. Recruiting your eyes trains you to focus, letting you zero in on the best part of the foothold (e.g., its grittiest facet or even individual crystals). It also lets you decide how much pressure to apply.

Hover on the bottom half of a route and then climb the top half normally, noticing the difference. Continue the practice day-to-day on your warm-ups to hone your eye-foot coordination.

Other Drills: Silent Feet and the Failure Threshold

Another great accuracy drill is silent feet, trying to climb as quietly as possible on a gym bouldering wall. Here are four fun silent-feet exercises:

1. Team up with a partner, who monitors your progress. If he hears any thunderfoot, you must repeat the problem until you've done it quietly, or undergo other punitive consequences like push-ups or traverse laps.
2. Wrap a strip of duct tape around your toe box about an inch from the point. This slippery tape will feel like glass underfoot if you use any part of the sole other than your big toe.
3. Pretend that the climbing wall is covered in wet paint and that you want to leave as few dots or dashes as possible around the holds.
4. Learn how much you can pivot around your big toe by locking it onto a hold and then "squishing ants" with your heels. You'll quickly see how much versatility this power point possesses when you place it precisely.

Yet another way to gain faith in poor footholds is to find their breaking point. This drill also shows you the technical limits of your rock shoes and can help refine model choice and sizing. To begin, pick a foothold that feels insecure. Now grab two good handholds, pull on them, stand precisely, relax your arms, and bounce up and down on the hold until your foot slips. Is the foothold really as insecure as you feared? And does it fail with more or less pressure than you thought?

SMEDGiNG:
AN ALTERNATiVE PoiNT OF ViEW

Has anyone ever yelled at you to stop smedging? *Smedging* combines "smearing" (pressing your toes and ball of the foot frontally into the rock) and "edging" (standing laterally, hip turned out, on your big toe on a crimp). When you smedge, you essentially smear on an edge, by placing your big toe frontally and then applying pressure until your shoe buckles into a creased smearing position. But is this technique really undesirable?

Professional climber Tommy Caldwell swears by smedging for certain tiny footholds, like the miniscule granite crystals, soap dishes, and micron-width edges on 5.14 face pitches on his project the *Dawn Wall* of El Capitan. "I tend to wear my rubber out about a half inch back from the transition to rand to sole," says Caldwell, "which means that I'm smedging a lot. Even if it's a small edge, I kind of roll my foot onto it as if I'm smearing."

Caldwell likens the process to grabbing a crimper, where you might initially use an open-handed grip but then close your fingers and bring your thumb over into the final crimped position. So too with your feet: When you first contact a hold, your ankle will naturally be extended back and down; then, as you stand in a frontal position, you lift your heel and flex your ankle to elevate and smedge, spreading the sole and increasing rubber-to-rock contact.

Caldwell also recommends stiffer shoes than you'd guess for smedgy footholds. "The whole idea of feeling the rock is way overstated," he says. "I'd rather not feel the rock as much and learn how the shoe works." The reason? "A rigid shoe forms on the footholds way better," says Caldwell, "whereas a soft shoe melts off of them."

3

Tommy Caldwell says that on the very worst footholds, he thinks about applying just a hair of pressure—that it *is* possible to overdo it. "People who are small and don't weigh that much stand on the smallest footholds the best," he says. "If you keep that in mind, it helps with being light on your feet. If you press too hard, the rubber will fail and you'll slip off."

Key Foot and Balance Foot

We're all born with two legs and two feet, yet we often climb as if we only have one foot—or at least, one at a time! We'll almost always cue into our *key foot* or *active foot,* the primary foot used to make the next reach. But we often neglect the *secondary foot* or *balance foot,* the one that trails below us, letting it end up where it may. I've often heard climbers lament that a move is "too reachy" when in reality the problem was that they'd failed to bring up their balance foot.

Let's examine the role of each foot:

- **Key foot.** This foot has to have a home, as it bears most of your weight. It's automatic to have a plan for this foot, as you're using it to initiate a move.
- **Balance foot.** This foot keeps your body in balance though it also bears some weight. Good technique involves finding a home for it too.

Now consider each foot in light of your desired type of move. There are four basic wrist positions (see photos on next pages), which in turn inform your body—and foot—position:

1. **Downpull.** Like climbing a ladder.
2. **Side pull.** A vertical lieback that activates your key foot in a backstep, the balance foot kicked (flagged) out to the side.
3. **Gaston.** A reverse, thumb-down side pull that activates your key foot in a frontal or edging position, with your balance foot placed laterally to create tension between your feet.
4. **Undercling.** An upside-down hold, like a waiter carrying a tray, that forces you to bring one or both feet up in opposition.

To work efficiently with each wrist position, you need to locate its neutral body position, the point at which you're in balance and not straining to remain there. It's here that you're strongest, can rest and decompress, and then steel yourself for the next pull. Hop onto a bouldering wall and monkey around. As you do so, notice how elevating your body over your heels or rotating around your ankles changes your balance point—even a change of a few degrees can restore or upset your equilibrium. As you progress, you'll see that balance comes from activating both your key foot and balance foot.

3

Jonathan Siegrist in a classic **downpull** position on *Horse Latitudes* (5.14a), Virgin River Gorge, Arizona

Heather Robinson works a **side pull** at the Secret 13 Wall, Red Rock Canyon, Nevada.

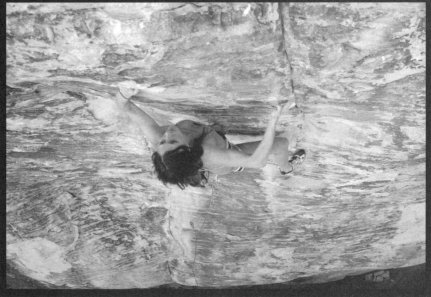

3

Jonathan Siegrist **gastoning** on the first 5.14 in the United States, *To Bolt or Not to Be,* Smith Rock, Oregon

Building the feet up on an **undercling**: Todd Perkins at the Cathedral, St. George, Utah

3

Posting and Flagging

Your balance foot has two main ways to actively extend reach and steady you: posting and flagging. Posting involves bringing your balance foot up below you, sometimes tick-tacking from lower to higher footholds, and pushing. It can even, counterintuitively, involve stepping *down* onto low footholds you've already used. In either case, your foot is engaged.

Lauren McCormick demonstrates **a standard flag** on the 5.13d *Porn Star,* Little Si, Washington.

Flagging, meanwhile, is more complex. To flag your foot, you bring it against the wall in opposition to your key foot or even kick it out in the air behind you. Think of your flagged leg like a rudder: As with a boat, if you leave the rudder unmanned, you'll wobble all over. There are four main flags:

1. **Standard flag.** When using a side pull, kick your balance foot out to the side for stability, either onto a hold or by pasting it against the rock.
2. **Inside flag.** Put your balance foot between your key foot and the climbing surface, and cam your pinkie toe against the wall to counterbalance, a static move useful for off-balance stances.

3

Working the **inside flag**, Capston Rock, Flagstaff Mountain, Boulder, Colorado

3. **Outside flag.** Bring your balance foot around behind your key foot, with the toe box (big toe or pinkie toe) kicked against the wall; this dynamic move allows you to pivot over your hips to generate momentum and create elongation.

4. **Rudder flag.** Move your balance foot through the air behind you, with your knee bent and toes pointing as for certain standing yoga poses like Warrior Three or Revolving Half Moon. Your balance foot acts as a rudder that you can manipulate by subtly articulating your knee, ankle, and toes. Think of it as "super flagging," actively kicking your foot into the air and playing with its position.

Jonathan Siegrist pushes hard with an **outside flag**, *The Heretic* (5.13b), City of Rocks, Idaho.

3

You have a universe of options for your balance foot. The key is to *always* have a plan for it. *For every move you make, have a plan for both feet!* To learn this principle, practice climbing with one foot: Pick a semihard gym route, and use only your key foot to make each move. You can place both feet on the footholds to set up, but then while making the move, only flag your balance foot against the wall—you may not place it on any footholds. You'll soon see a rapid decline in efficiency, if not a total roadblock on up to 10 percent of the movements.

3

The **rudder flag** as flown by Michael Fuselier, St. Ange, France

1

2

Drop and Drive

Now let's move on to the drop and drive (aka "popping"), which involves sagging into the negative space below your neutral position to create the controlled dynamic momentum that lets you extend through a reach. It's a playful, active, youthful way of climbing, an efficient way to capture energy that uses inertia to extend the deadpoint, that weightless, hovering moment atop a jump. The drop and drive also spares climbers the elbow tendonitis that comes from climbing too statically.

3

1. **Drop.** From your neutral body position, *drop* down into the negative space within that position. Going all the way to a straight arm (dead hang) might trap you at the bottom, so play with how far to sag. Picture the dead lift and how weightlifters crouch and sag at the very bottom, generating bounce to come back to standing and lock their knees.

2. **Drive.** Now *drive* your key foot down into its hold, with your knee bent to maximize muscular spring. Meanwhile activate your balance foot to *push* and *scoop* you into the wall, keeping your hips parallel with the rock. Gun for the next hold, pointing your balance toe, flicking off it, and *holding tension* along that leg, which might even come off the rock as you complete a move.

The drop and drive: (1) dropping into negative space to generate upward momentum, (2) driving off the key (right) foot and activating the balance (left) foot to align the hips with the rock, and (3) pointing and flicking off the balance foot's big toe to snag the target hold while cresting the deadpoint.

If the drop and drive still seems esoteric, try this experiment. Next time you fail on redpoint because you're pumped, notice what happens: A hold you reached easily after hangdogging and resting somehow felt miles away, right? Hang and recover, and then try the move again.

Chances are that when you start from the dog, your natural tendency is to drop and drive, which brings distant holds closer. However, when you are pumped, you get nervous, tighten up, don't drop and drive, and then fall because you come up short statically, correct? Or perhaps you slouch and drive halfheartedly *out* for the hold instead of *up*. These might be our two most common mistakes, errors caused almost solely by nervousness and exhaustion. The solution is to make dropping and driving your default mode, even when you are too pumped to think. To learn the pattern, try these three exercises:

Jumping Pull-Ups

Grab a pull-up bar, and do 30 to 90 seconds of jumping pull-ups, springing off your legs from the negative space to propel you up over the bar in the positive space. This exercise conditions you to think "legs, legs, legs!" instead of locking off when you are tired.

Box Jumps

Find a flat, solid surface as high as you're comfortable jumping onto repeatedly, and then face it. Leap onto and off of it continuously for 30 to 90 seconds, standing tall and proud with your shoulders back. Make the jump a single, solid movement driven by your legs: Drop into the negative space, bring your buttocks down, and swing your arms as you leap. When we get tired, we slouch; this drill conditions you to cultivate the confident on-the-rock posture that maximizes reach.

Sassy Ass (aka Wrecking Ball)

This fun warm-up cues playful, leg-driven motion. As you climb, swing your hips in an exaggerated fashion. Generate momentum with a flick of your balance foot's heel (as in the drop and drive); your knees tuck in, your hips follow, your shoulders follow, and with that comes a flick of your backside. This drill teaches you to loosen up, open your body, be tall, and make big moves. It is a useful skill to recall on a route that features tenuous "pole up the butt" climbing down low to a sassy big move up high.

Digging

Digging further conditions you to stand precisely on your big toe; you dig and pull with your toe to transition over onto a foothold, often to initiate a sideways or diagonal move. Your toe is pointing down and in like a ballerina, and your ankle is flexed to accentuate the pulling motion. Try this: On your gym floor, push down to dent the foam and then drag your foot back toward you. You'll feel this digging on the underside of your hamstring and in your glutes.

Digging with the right toe to transition up and rightward over it

Backstep, Egyptian, and Drop Knee

On overhanging rock it's often more efficient to bring the outside of either hip into the wall. This shift keeps you in line with the angle of the rock, unloading your arms and extending your reach. The most basic move is the classic backstep, which on a lieback uses the pinky toe of your key foot with your balance foot flagged or digging out to the side. Two more advanced moves initiate from your big toe: the Egyptian and the drop knee. Both use this pivot point to suck you into the rock, creating a wave of extension from your toe to your fingertips.

To move into an Egyptian, place your key foot laterally (edged position) on a low foothold, and then locate a comparable hold for your balance foot near the same level. Situate your balance foot frontally on its hold, and then rotate your hip in toward the rock and point your knee groundward to bring you onto your shoe's outside edge, which you press in opposition to your key foot. You'll look like an Egyptian hieroglyphic.

A drop knee is simply an exaggerated Egyptian on a higher foothold, often so radical that your calf contacts the back of your thigh.

David Hume in a classic backstep position while flashing *Hellion* (5.13c), Ten Sleep Canyon, Wyoming

3

Find a hold high and to the side for your balance foot, place your big toe frontally or in an edging position, and then bend your leg and point your knee groundward as you rotate your hip down and in. This position sucks you in hard and allows you to reach up and out for a high handhold. Radical drop knees have claimed more than a few knee ligaments, so use them cautiously.

Paige Claassen busts a rowdy Egyptian on *Ultra Perm* (5.13d), Red River Gorge, Kentucky.

Testing my 40-year-old ligaments on a radical drop knee, the Barrio, Boulder Canyon, Colorado

3

Hooking and Scumming

Lest you think all rock climbing takes place in the toe box, there are also the ninja tricks of heel hooking and toe scumming, used most often to hold your hips in on big features on overhanging rock. Both fairly obvious moves also come with infinite permutations. As always, have a plan for your balance foot (the one not hooked or scummed). Does it belong on the wall below you or in another heel hook or toe scum or dangling in the air? Finally, pull as hard as possible with your activated heel or toe. The more confident, stable, and forceful you are, the better your rand will bond with the rock.

To heel hook, you place the heel cup of your shoe on a hold and lock it in place by tensing your hamstring, creating opposition. There are four different heel hooks:

Michael Fuselier pulling hard with **a standard heel hook** on a 5.14d at St. Ange, France

1. **Standard heel hook.** Facing the rock frontally with your hip turned out, you drop your heel onto a hold and hook it.
2. **Reverse heel hook.** In a backstepped position, cam the heel of your balance foot backward into a hold, like a back heel kick in soccer. This position counters barn-door rotation over your key foot.
3. **Heel-toe.** Jam the top or side of your big toe up under a rooflet in opposition to your hooked heel, creating camming tension; you can also lever your toe against a flat surface to lock in a lateral heel-toe. This is a good position for resting.
4. **Reverse heel-toe.** For this backstepped heel-toe, you cam your pinky toe instead of your big toe against the rock. This good rest position might involve dropping your other leg into the air for counterbalance.

Tucking into a **reverse heel hook** to counter any barn-door rotation

3

A bomber **heel-toe**, slotted deep in a hueco

A **reverse heel-toe** in the same hueco with the balance foot posted below for counterbalance

Meanwhile, there are three types of toe scums:
1. **Standard toe scum.** Place your toe up under a feature like a roof or spike, or around an arête; press your upper toe box (rand rubber) into the rock and flex your toes back toward you, as if you are flicking a hacky sack, to empower the scum and lock it in place. This position helps you balance or move your hand up.
2. **Dragoning in.** This toe scum off to the side on a vertical hold involves rotating your knee and ankle toward your big toe (down and in) to lock them in place. Think of your foot as a dragon talon reaching out for a victim!
3. **Yoga toe scum or upside-down toe scum.** With your foot on a ledge or large, extruded hold, rotate your leg (turn your inner knee down and outward, as if you are sitting cross-legged) and ankle to bring your foot upside-down, slopping your toe rand on the lip. This is a good position for resting, bringing your other foot up, or for keeping your feet from ripping off a traverse as you bring your other leg along. I also use this as a step-through move, when I need to move my feet sideways but don't want to make a bunch of mincing little foot switches.

Paul Robinson working a **standard toe scum** on *Moostie Meisie* (V13), Rocklands, South Africa

As you get comfortable on overhanging terrain, you'll soon see that hooks and scums can also be combined in surprising but effective ways. You can double down on heel hooks and toe scums, using *both* limbs in concert to create oppositional forces (aka squeezing or compression), or you can mix and match hooks and scums. Remember, the more weight you can direct to your legs even in "weird" or nontraditional positions, the stronger you'll be when recruiting your arms.

Dragoning in on a vertical toe scum to suck over the foot, with the knee pointed down and in

3

Fancy footwork: the yoga toe scum

BONUS FOOT TRICKERY

Here are a couple other moves to incorporate into your steep-rock repertoire:

- **The bicycle.** This move creates and holds body tension below you or to the side; it works best on blobs like blocks, cobbles, or tufa drips. Push one foot against the top (or front) of the hold, and toe-scum your other foot beneath (or behind) it, creating opposition.
- **The hook.** This variant on rudder flagging helps check an unruly barn door, often when you have only one good foothold to work with. Intertwine your balance foot sideways around your key foot, camming the top of the former's toe box against the outside of your key foot's ankle. Play with your key foot's angle of articulation to find your balance point.

Bicycling on a granite spike at the Barrio, Boulder Canyon, Colorado

Staying in balance on steep rock with the hook, one foot intertwined around the other. *Matt Samet*

COMPOSURE

The next big concept is composure, or your ability to rest, relax, and stay focused. But first, let's start by acknowledging that climbing, even sport climbing, is intrinsically scary. We're high in the vertical plane, and our bodies and minds, under duress, will scream at us to come down. Thus, to perform as an athlete, you must learn to tune out fear when safety is less of an issue, like on a well-protected lead. You must learn *composure*. (Another key is learning why, how, when, and where to fall, which we'll examine in Chapter 5.)

Consider this: You're on a difficult onsight, breathing like a freight train, making bold, dynamic moves, and growing progressively more pumped. You reach a tough clip—it's all on the line now. Grab the draw and your efforts will have been wasted, yet you're also hesitant to pull up rope because you're approaching failure. You make a snap decision and quickly tag the clip, then lo and behold your body drops down, your arm straightens, the tension releases, you exhale audibly—*Whooo*—and suddenly that marginal clipping hold feels like a jug. Nothing has changed about the stance or your tiredness, but your mind has let go and is no longer alerting your body to peril. Your muscles relax, and you're in control. Your mind is again controlling your body.

We can condition ourselves to recall this state on command (as we're warming up, on redpoint, at rests, and in clutch situations). The key is to train and rest our brains like any other body part, cultivate awareness and focus, and anchor ourselves in the present, otherwise known as "getting in the zone."

PLAYFUL WARM-UP

Once you've done a composure warm-up, it's time to dance. For your second route, still at a moderate level, introduce playful elements like the Sassy Ass drill from the preceding section. You can also flick your legs behind you, flag wildly, or skip grips to jump to holds, just to lose your feet. Be "obnoxiously" playful; exaggerate your movements so much that it looks like you're clowning. Mindfulness combined with a sense of fun takes the pressure off and eases you into the zone.

Composure Warm-Up

Just as your morning breakfast ritual sets the tone for your day, so too does your climbing warm-up inform what follows. We all know (or are) that guy who charges headlong through his warm-ups. But this approach can set a negative, chaotic tone that leads to jumpy nerves and failure. You're better off starting slow, anchoring yourself in the present below the wall on the very first climb of the day.

Begin by looking at the route's first two starting holds; be mindful and study them as objects unto themselves, not just as rungs on the send ladder. Notice their colors, patterns, forms, flaws, and angles; note how chalk has built up and what it tells you about the optimum angle of utility. Is that thumbprint telling you where to pinch? Which two fingers best fit into that pocket? Now softly brush the holds to further acquaint yourself with them, and then grab them and sag down to stretch out your body.

Stare down at your first foothold, noticing its color, texture, best aspect, etc., and then do the same with the second foothold. Place your feet to confirm how you'll be using the two footholds, and then step down off the wall. This is above all a warm-up for your eyes that conditions you to study the holds in a precise, mindful way.

Now climb, moving slowly, deliberately, and thoughtfully up through the first bolt or two, cultivating this mindfulness. Revisit your composure warm-up throughout the day on the lower reaches of each climb, scanning right until you pull on. We often fall

SCANNING VS. DARTING

While in the zone, you *scan* for holds, your eye movements smooth, your pupils like laser beams, your head and neck relaxed. A climber deep in the zone might even have a stoned or lethargic look. However, when we get pumped, tired, or scared, our heads *dart* around like crazed chickens, following the lead of our helter-skelter eyes. Notice what happens next time you're redlined—how your eyes begin to dart right before you fall or how darting might even precipitate a fall by forcing hasty beta.

Now counter it: When your eyes get wild, make them scan even as your body screams at you to go. Sure, the few extra seconds of effort might send you airborne, but then again they might keep you from launching into a bad sequence, which will spit you off anyway.

into the trap of scanning and sequencing up until the final seconds, and then jumping on preoccupied by the crux. But the zone is all about being present, even at the base of the route.

The Power of Now and the Composure Rest

Buddhists know this adage like the back of their hands: The only moment we have is now, because it's the only one in which we ever truly exist. The past is gone, dead, and cannot be resurrected, while the future lies ahead and is similarly beyond our control. The same holds true in climbing: All you have is now, this sequence, this move, this foot crystal and the way in which you'll stand on it. Still, we often make the following two mistakes, trapped by our churning monkey minds:

1. **Obsessing over the past.** Say you botched a sequence down low but squeaked through. As you climb past the trouble spot, you castigate yourself for sloppiness. However, all you're doing is weighing yourself down with the anchor of the past. The move happened the way it did, you held on, and now it's gone, even if you had to expend a little extra effort. Stay focused—let the move vanish into the fog of time.

2. **Obsessing over the future.** On routes with high cruxes, we tend to fret over this key passage instead of focusing on the sequences that lead there. Being distracted rips you out of the present and causes you to climb poorly and distractedly, so that you're tired and scatterbrained when you do finally reach the crux.

Fortunately, there is a cure: the composure rest or decompression rest, a meditative moment that rockets you back into the present. This is above all a reset for the mind, the byproduct of which is a physical rest. Sheer sustained concentration can tire your mind. Once your mind wears out, your body responds with hasty sequencing, clunky coordination, darting eye and head movements, jitters, or loss of form. You climb poorly and now your mind has to deal with a fear of falling, further overwhelming you with negative emotion. As Justen Sjong puts it, "Emotion does not belong on the wall." Interrupt this downward spiral with a composure rest, which requires only *one* good handhold:

3

1. Grab the hold and move into a neutral position, straightening your arm.
2. Look down and *away* from the engaged hand. (If your left hand is on, look down and right, and vice versa.) Focus on the first thing you see that's meaningless, such as a bush below the cliff or grains of rock off to the side. Don't look down at the route below you, which is the past and can be stressful; and don't look up at the route above, which is the future and can create anxiety.
3. Count to four, and drift into nothingness for a beat. Keep your head and spine aligned and your throat open to reorder your thoughts.
4. Snap to, give a whooping power exhale, and continue climbing.

Resting and the Triple Breath

Use the triple breath either at a classic two-handed shakeout or in conjunction with the composure rest. The goal is to slow your breathing and heart rate, to calm your nervous system, and to stretch and elongate your body. As a rule, it takes three full breaths to decompress. For each, inhale through slightly pursed lips, and then exhale with a slow, controlled "Whoooooo" through an open mouth:

1. **The first breath.** The initial relaxing and recovery breath, during which you might still be gasping. Drop low on your heels, and let your upper body straighten, sagging onto your extended arm(s) so that you're hanging by your bones instead of your muscles.
2. **The second breath.** Gently close your eyes, hold your breath for a tick longer than is natural, and then breathe out with a forceful "Whoooooo." You'll feel your arms and shoulders relax even more.
3. **The third breath.** Do the same as for the second breath, but now tune your *ears* into the quality of the breath. *Fully* elongate onto your arms and shoulders, just shy of letting go. Hear the different sensations in the breath, noting how you've gone from gasping to breaths that grow progressively quieter and deeper. Take confidence from this change. You're officially in control again, so own it!

HOW TO SHAKE OUT

Most of us instinctively clear the pump (trapped blood flush with lactic acid) from our forearms by dangling them at our sides and shaking, rotating, or flicking our wrist and fingers. However, you might also try the "G-Tox" (G for gravity), in which you alternate every five or ten seconds between the dangling position and holding your arm up bent at your elbow above shoulder height. One study has shown it to be more effective at accelerating forearm recovery than our instinctual response, and I have found this to be true. The rub, however, is remembering to G-Tox. After shaking out in a dangling position, I'll often bring my mitt up and think as I look at it, "Oh, hello, what are you doing up here, you cheeky little bugger? Guess I'd better shake you out!"

On holds too poor for a dip and dangle, I'll often do a quick wrist flick or finger wave over a hold before I place my hand on the rock. I've even had some success with the "pseudo-shakeout": if the holds are too poor to release either hand, I'll alternate the amount of force with which I'm grabbing each to partially recover the arm I need most for an upcoming sequence.

As Sjong points out, climbers tend to close up and shrink (to become old and withered) as fatigue and tension accrue. Thus if you think about sagging farther with each breath, you will locate that point of maximum elongation, that point of barely hanging on. It's here that you become youthful, tall, and strong again.

Eyes, Facial Expression, and Emotions

We all have our battle face for the hardest moves, but we use it selectively, to cue maximum effort. Sjong also posits that we can cultivate two other climbing faces:

1. **Thinking face.** In this default face when deconstructing sequences, your mouth is shut; your eyes are stern, squinting, or even full of seeming hatred; and you grimace. Or you might

display other tics like gritting your teeth or wagging your tongue
like Michael Jordan.

2. **Open face.** In this mellow facial expression, your eyes are soft,
your mouth is open to facilitate breathing, and your facial muscles
are slack, smiling, or slightly smirking.

Now notice what happens next time you're on a challenging climb: Chances are you
sport a constant thinking face interrupted only by moments of battle face, but that
you rarely revert to your open face, even when you rest. And so you grind down mind
and body. Counter this by going to your open face at every opportunity (composure
rests or easier stretches) so that it stays with you as the difficulty increases. Even in
the heat of battle, you can force a smile or smirk ("Yeah, I got this, you bastard!") to
foster a self-assured mind-set.

Up-Shifting and Down-Shifting through the Four Different Breaths

You also have four climbing breaths you can call on to help influence your arousal
level. *Don't take breathing for granted, as something that follows movement. Breathing is
the transmission for your sending engine!* Getting pumped stems from having toxic (lactic acid), deoxygenated blood trapped in your extremities, in particular your forearms.
However, with aware, strategic breathing you can increase cardiovascular efficiency
and therefore your ability to recall trapped blood to the heart, as well as pump oxygen-rich blood throughout your body to stave off muscular failure.

Here are the breaths:

1. **Belly breath.** Deep, slow, relaxed breathing like you do on easy
terrain or at a rest.

2. **Power-endurance breath.** Heavy, labored breathing like you'd
experience running up a hill. It is common on sprinting-style
climbs (think gym routes) with consistent middling-hard difficulty.
This breath is connected to exertion or tension.

3. **Power breath.** A forceful, deliberate, whooping exhalation to rev
your engine when you leave a rest position. You can do about three
of these in succession.

4. **Scream breath.** A primal, "I'm giving it my all!" energy- and emotion-releasing shriek that tightens the abs and drives you up toward a hold. You get one of these at a time.

There is also **not breathing.** Your core is so tight that you're either holding your breath or barely breathing, as on a difficult boulder problem. Avoid this breath unless you enjoy feeling like your head is going to explode.

Now, think of each breath like the gears of your car: The belly breath is fourth or fifth gear for cruising down the open highway, the power-endurance breath is third gear for passing another car on a two-lane road, the power breath is second gear for gunning down a freeway on-ramp, and the scream breath is first gear for peeling out at a stoplight. Which breath is appropriate where on a climb, and how much can you wield it to your advantage?

Climbers make two common mistakes with the breath: We forget to move from the belly breath to a power breath when leaving a rest; we stay relaxed and lethargic instead of gunning the engine. And we forget to downshift from any of the three tensioned breaths to the belly breath after a hard sequence, thus expending precious energy. It's better to find your neutral body position, get over your feet, shake out or take a composure rest, and breathe from your belly.

While it's fine to work on a calming, circular yoga breath (in through the nose, out slowly through the mouth) on easy climbs, it's not necessarily applicable at your limit. Rock climbing is an anaerobic sport, with short bursts of activity rarely lasting more than a few minutes. Justen Sjong says that even when warming up your heart rate can be as high as 120 beats per minute, similar to where it would be with running, and when you're running at 120 beats per minute your mouth is certainly open. So don't be shy about being a mouth-breather. As Sjong says, "Your mouth needs to be open. End of story."

FLOW

The final component in improvement is flow, or how smoothly you link moves. Like a gymnastics routine, a rock climb is one continuous sequence. If you place your foot poorly on that traverse, you might juice yourself, becoming slow and jerky on the next crux. All moves are linked, with each sequence informing the next; thus good flow is an outgrowth of maintaining a consistent tempo and sequencing accurately.

Tempo

We all climb at different paces; there is no "correct" tempo. Some climbers are speed-demon dynamic hares, while others are static, methodical tortoises. What tempo really translates to is: Are you climbing at a consistent speed that's fast enough to optimize efficiency and at the appropriate speed in the appropriate sections?

Every climb has its unique cadence, its particular mixture of gallops (cruxes), canters (power-endurance sections), trots (middling-hard sections), walks (easy sections), and halts (rest stances). Analyze your project in terms of cadence: Where do you want to be efficient, where should you put your mind in neutral, where will you be playful, where will you calm your nerves, where will you fight for every last move, and so on? Draw a diagram or beta map showing the different speeds if it helps you to conceptualize these ideas.

The gym is a great place to work on cadence, because the routes are set with a consistent difficulty and thus flow best with consistent pacing. Try this drill to become quicker and smoother:

1. Recruit a buddy to watch and time you.
2. Have your friend time you as you climb a route un-self-consciously at your normal pace. This figure is your ballpark "normal" pace.
3. Now climb the same route at a deliberately faster pace with your friend timing you. Focus on moving quickly. Ask your buddy to let you know if you start to look harried so that you can then slow down.

Compare the two times: Did you get more or less pumped climbing quicker? Can you pick things up and still be smooth and efficient—or even more so? What should your new normal pace be? You can even have someone video each lap so that you can evaluate it later. If you notice jerky, choppy, or staccato movement in the video, you're *pausing* where you should be *flowing*. You're missing a beat, and that's poor, inefficient flow. You want to be like a metronome *(tock-tock-tock-tock-tock-tock)*, without any unnecessary pauses or hesitancy (hiccups).

Sequencing

Sequencing, namely precisely and confidently decoding, remembering, and executing discrete sets of moves, can be daunting. Newer climbers especially may struggle to recall an entire climb. Much of this comes from lacking mental stamina and experience and having a smaller repertoire of moves, such that new, unfamiliar moves are harder to recall. The solution to the latter issue, of course, is to climb, climb, and climb some more to expand your database of movements. But memory drills also improve move identification and recall. Try this:

1. Find a route near your limit; it's easiest if it's a bouldering traverse. If you use a roped climb, pantomime counting, complete with beta hand movements, on the ground.
2. Break the climb into blocks of 10 moves.
3. Start with the first hold (zero), and count aloud through the first 10 moves. Most of us make only four or five consecutive moves before pausing to regroup; your aim is to double this number. Focus on your sequence's accuracy. Your eyes should be like laser beams, homing in on each hold in its due time. If you're not sure where your right hand goes next, hang straight-armed (go to neutral) from your left arm until you've located your target grip.
4. Be authoritative. Make eye contact with the hold, see it, grab it, and control it. Watch how even when redlining on 5.14 onsights, a top climber like Adam Ondra reaches confidently as if he knows exactly what the next hold will be. Recite the move numbers in your head, and stick to this cadence.
5. Repeat the process for the next 10 moves, etc. up through the end of the climb.
6. Jump on and climb exactly as you have sequenced, even if your monkey mind hollers, "This beta is wrong!" Don't dither—if you must, fall off doing the sequence you set out to do.

Another skills exercise is reverse sequencing: Say that you're at a stance below a crux that culminates in an obvious jug eight moves higher. It's clear that you need the jug with your right hand, but how to get there? Start at the jug and reverse-engineer the sequence between where your hands are now and this target grip, mentally rehearsing each possibility until you settle on the most likely option. Like driving a car in reverse, reverse sequencing is tough, but it will train you to better evaluate cryptic cruxes.

3

Visualization

Visualization has long been part of all competitive sports, but it's particularly relevant in climbing given our up-close sensory interaction with the stone. I've long used visualization to wrap my head around a project—to make sure I've sequenced the moves correctly, to refine and imprint that beta, and even to help me fall asleep like counting sheep. Justen Sjong councils his clients to visualize, visualize, and visualize some more, be it during a down moment at home or in the nervous minutes before a redpoint. Try this:

- **Count the moves on your project as you climb.** Then on the way home mentally review the moves, and make sure they match the count. If you skipped any holds, rewind mentally to find the missing puzzle pieces. Use this instant replay to stay stoked about the route.
- **Create a visualization movie of a true, honest effort**, not just the glamorized Hollywood version where you float the route effortlessly. Sit or lie in a quiet place, close your eyes, and relive the moves as they actually happen while you're climbing: good, bad, and ugly. Feel yourself rolling into that kneebar and moving your hands to the correct location, visualize that big lunge and how you have to open up for it, picture that awkward section where you always have to thrutch and battle. Finally, when imagining the redpoint, picture a rousing, killer, all-out performance, one that has them cheering for you in the bleachers.
- **Use all your senses.** Hear the birds chirping in the trees, feel the wind flowing over the stone, smell the pine trees, and taste the sweat rolling into your mouth.
- **Visualize things going wrong and what you'll do to recover.** Picture that clip you have to skip and how you'll combat nerves on the runout. Imagine what would happen if your foot popped at the crux and you needed to stab it back on. Run through the hypotheticals so that you're prepared to address them.

Climbing Tall for Short People

Another impediment to good flow is stopper moves, usually cruxes we find ourselves unable to *reach* through. "This route is so reachy. I'll never do it!" is the excuse we most often hear, usually from our stature-challenged partners: But are the holds really too far apart, or are we failing to think creatively? One of the top US climbers, Jonathan Siegrist, stands five feet five inches, onsights 5.14a, and redpoints 5.14-plus. I've never once heard him utter the word "reachy." As Siegrist affirms, "It's rare to find two handholds so far apart that I can't reach between them. More often I find that the feet are lacking. It's the existence or nonexistence of feet that makes a route doable or impossible for me."

Siegrist says the number-one thing a short climber can do to extend his reach is to hone his footwork. His pointers:

- **Don't hog that jug.** "Short climbers sometimes run into issues exiting an undercling or a jug," says Siegrist, "but you'll get an additional three inches if you bump your jug hand out and use the edge of the jug or the undercling," even if this means moving off a smaller part of the hold. You can also use this technique to extend reach on iron-cross moves, by shuffling your hand to the side of the jug laterally closest to your target grip.
- **Don't develop tunnel vision about using only big footholds.** Newer climbers often become blinded to smaller footholds or ones that aren't also handholds, which precludes them from scanning for other options, limiting their available sequences and creating "reachy" scenarios.
- **Become comfortable building your feet high onto miniscule footholds.** "Having the ability to feel comfortable using smeary dishes and a not-very-defined

3

Jonathan Siegrist (at five feet five inches) standing tall on microfeet on *To Bolt or Not to Be,* Smith Rock, Oregon

145

edge is really beneficial to shorter climbers," says Siegrist. Scan for anything with definition, be it a crease, ripple, or microflake, sloping smear-dish, little mound, or the merest crystalline protrusion. Think about gym jibs, which stick out only millimeters but offer much better purchase than the wall itself. If you can stand on those and extend, then why not try it on the many natural jibs outside?

○ **Talk a foothold up.** Trick yourself into thinking that that tiny foothold is huge so that you use it with authority. The main reason we slip off poor feet is because we stand on them halfheartedly, scarcely pressing because we're scared of slipping, which of course causes us to slip. When Siegrist was working *Vogue,* a 5.14b near Boulder, Colorado, he had to use a wide stem onto a poor smear. When he first coached himself, "This foot is an inch-by-inch block," Siegrist would press into the hold with his full weight and could execute. But when he fell into pessimism, thinking, "This foothold sucks," he'd chicken-leg his foot out and dither around, only to fall. "Basically I convince myself that a foot is huge," says Siegrist. "And when I move over it, I'm good and my foot just stays."

○ **Wear stiff, new shoes.** Having good, crisp shoes vs. blown-out softies equals the difference between standing on tiptoes vs. the ball of your foot—a solid inch or two of height.

Also, as the central link between hands and feet, a strong core makes it easier to push off poor footholds and climb taller. Siegrist swears by two core exercises:

1. Find a severely overhanging gym route one or two number grades below your limit. Climb it first using only your left foot and then a second time using only your right foot. This will force you to repeatedly cut your feet and bring the one back on, developing not only your abs but also climbing-specific lateral stabilizing muscles like the hip flexors and obliques.

2. Do medicine-ball pull-ups in sets of 10. Hold the ball between your knees, and then pull your knees up until your thighs are perpendicular to your torso. Now, with the ball in place, do standard pull-ups, keeping your back straight and knees high, and applying good form.

Climbing Short for Tall People

On the flip side is another common refrain: Given the option, is it better to do one big, dynamic but strenuous move (tall-guy beta) or to tick-tack through, making more moves on smaller holds (short-guy beta)? Ace climber Beth Rodden, who has established 5.14 and tops out at five feet even, says that small moves can often be a good, if overlooked, option. "They might set your body up better, and might conserve energy in that you don't have to do one big, powerful move but can instead do three easy moves," she says, particularly on vertical rock where you can distribute your weight evenly over your feet.

DON'T YOU FORGET ABOUT ME

Climbing is the act of moving up. But take things too literally, neglecting holds below and around you, and you'll exclude countless potential sequences. A few reminders:

- **A hold doesn't vanish after you use it.** I've unlocked many cruxes by resetting on a handhold I used two or even three handmoves earlier, perhaps grabbing it in a new, different way.
- **Footholds don't vanish either.** A previously used foothold might have a new application higher into a sequence, perhaps even with your other foot. Think of Da Vinci's *Vitruvian Man* and the circle through which his limbs rotate. A similar circle accompanies you while you climb, so work *all* the holds within that circumference.
- **Sometimes you have to go down or sideways to go up.** Don't be afraid to lose ground in order to gain it back later.
- **Bring your clipping hand back to the rock.** We forget to do this and then rush into a sequence cranking a brutal one-armed lockoff. By replacing your rope (quickdraw) hand on the stone after clipping, you also give your other arm a breather and can optimally reposition yourself on the stone.

3

Progression, Review, and Repetition

There are three fundamental ways to evaluate what we've learned so far: a ladder of real-world progression, reviewing it later, and repeating a route to demonstrate ultimate control. (As any great coach will tell you, "It's not whether you reach the top or not; it's how you got there." Or as Jorgeson puts it, "OK, you got to the top, but it looked like hell. You could climb three grades harder if you cared about *how* you got there!") *Style equals progression.* Sjong thus proposes four rungs on the ladder to send enlightenment:

1. Apply the skill on an easy redpoint, one that takes you two to three tries. This practice gives you ample opportunity to review and reflect as you climb.
2. Next demonstrate the skill on an easy onsight, which still permits moments of calm when you're able to process the skill.
3. Now roll it out on a hard redpoint, where the climbing is so difficult you're not able to think logically about the skill while executing it but can still cue it on the ground before heading up.
4. Finally, use the skill on a hard onsight, where you're so far beyond rational thought that it must surface intuitively, on the fly, or not at all. Using it then shows that you have imprinted and ultimately mastered the skill.

The second tenet is review, or noting all the things you did right and wrong after coming down off a route. For example, you might have noticed that your second go on a route you barely missed onsighting is often poorer than your first. You're climbing worse, even though you now know the moves. You probably unconsciously applied a skill during the onsight, but then on your second try you failed to recall that skill. You were no longer in the zone, but instead you were climbing self-consciously, intruding into that sacred space between rock and reflex.

Interrupt this negative spiral by consciously reviewing each time after you are lowered. Sit quietly, and review the route while it's fresh in your mind. Visualize your sequencing, flow, and how and where you correctly applied each skill. Then analyze your mistakes: What went wrong, why did it go wrong, how did it go wrong, and how will you fix it the next time?

Finally, as Sjong puts it, "Sending a route does not mean you've mastered the route—it means you've mastered the *skill* you're working on. *Repeating* a climb is the first step in gaining true mastery." Think about that: Could you repeat your hardest redpoint given that you had to go all-out just to do it the once? If you're applying these teachings and holding yourself to the highest standards of technical excellence, then the answer theoretically is *yes*. On a favorable day you should be able to repeat the climb or at least come close.

In his Professional Climbers International (PCI) clinics, Jorgeson urges his students to repeat boulder problems and asks them to move more efficiently with each go. "As they progress through the attempts and it gets easier and easier, they'll understand that it's not because they're stronger at try five than on try two," says Jorgeson. "It's because they're using a lot less energy even though their body's more tired." To Jorgeson, cleaning up your moves embodies the difference between getting up the wall and doing so *thoughtfully and well*. "If you climb just to tick a route, you're not going to take everything away from that climb that it has to offer," he says. "Every climb will teach you if you're listening to it. If you go back and clean up that awkward, out-of-balance move, it demonstrates control."

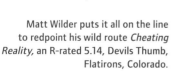

Matt Wilder puts it all on the line to redpoint his wild route *Cheating Reality,* an R-rated 5.14, Devils Thumb, Flatirons, Colorado.

3

Fall Doing Something Right

Finally, Sjong recommends that you *always fall doing something right.* Become mentally tough, and make this your mantra. Despite knowing the difference between correct and incorrect sequencing, when we are tired, we become lazy and often succumb to wrong or halfhearted beta to nab a new high point. But this is putting the cart before the horse. "If you need to get that foot up, you fall getting that foot up," says Sjong. "And if you need to shift your hips, you shift your hips. If you know what right is and wrong is, you'd better fall doing something right, even if you might fall. Because you will fall *for sure* doing the wrong beta!"

HANDWORK

You could write a book as big as the Milky Way is wide were you to sit down and describe every last handhold, so I won't even try. The main point is not to overgrab, which pumps you out. Treat handholds like light bulbs: Hold on enough not to drop them, but don't squeeze so hard that they shatter. To find this threshold, first try a difficult route on lead, and then try it again on top rope. On lead, chances are you'll find yourself stressing about certain holds, deeming them too small, slick, or slopey. As fear of falling crowds in, you'll then overgrab, clinging for dear life, making the holds feel even poorer. Now try the route on top rope, and notice the difference; marginal holds from before probably feel like mini-jugs, correct? Absent the pernicious influence of fear, you grab the holds like little light bulbs. Remember that feeling, and carry it with you the next time you lead.

One more thing about handholds: *Don't forget your thumb. It's your fifth finger!* Almost every hold has multiple thumb options: closing it against your index finger to crimp, opposing it against all four fingers in a pinch grip, locking it against the wall to activate an open-handed sloper, splaying (spragging) it off to the side on a nubbin, or deliberately leaving it off the rock on a slimper. You can use your thumbs in seams and thin finger cracks to stabilize yourself, or you can cam them against the crack wall opposite the one your fingers push or pull on.

FORGOTTEN BODY PARTS

"Body off the rock, Samet!" barked my instructor, an old-school mountain clubber in New Mexico back in the mid-1980s, as I was flapping my way up a 5.7 chimney with a convenient ledge midway. Not sure how to high step and rock or mantel over, I'd pressed a knee to the ledge lip and then fish-flopped over it.

"It's bad form!" he hollered. "You'll embarrass us all."

I took the lesson to heart: Scumming is bad form. But my teacher did me a real disservice because I've since learned that not falling is better than scoring style points. Sometimes climbing is ugly, and that's just how it has to be: The rock permits no other solution than fleshy, scummy wrestling.

The Head

Traverses under roofs can be strenuous and awkward: Your head bumps the ceiling, your butt stinkbugs out, and the footholds all seem to be at the wrong elevation. However, you can sometimes unweight your arms by scumming the back or top of your head and your neck and shoulder blades up under the ceiling and pressing in opposition to your feet. Climbers also use head scums and jams in offwidths.

"I used a head jam and face smear combo to rest on *Maxilash,* a 5.11a at Vedauwoo [Wyoming]," admits Colorado traddie Chris Weidner. "I first wore my helmet, but at one point was nearly hanging from my chinstrap with the helmet firmly wedged in the crack." Weidner subsequently ditched the helmet, estimating that the resultant head jam lightened his load 50 pounds.

The Shoulder

Herman "the German" Gollner was a Rifle, Colorado, fixture in the 1990s and 2000s, redpointing hard climbs wearing special knee-barring pants with Stealth-rubber pads, as well as a shoulder-scum shirt with rubber epaulets. On Rifle's corners, grooves, and hanging

Tommy Caldwell scums his shoulder and back on the 5.13 crux pitch of *El Corazon,* El Capitan, Yosemite National Park, California. *Corey Rich / Aurora Photos*

NINJA GRABS

Here are a few nonstandard handholds for your ninja grab bag:

1. **The wrist-pull.** If you have only one good handhold but need to generate two-handed momentum, grab your engaged arm around your wrist with your free hand, pulling on the wrist as if it were a handhold. This movement imparts a minor hydraulic boost.
2. **The false grip.** For big, beefy, cross-body reaches off horns or buckets, place your hand in an undercling position, and then rotate it inward 90 degrees, back toward you; hook your palm and fingers over the horn, and "beast a lever" to your target hold.
3. **The thumbdercling.** To stand into scoops, bowls, or depressions, or to stabilize on slabby terrain, engage an undercling with your thumb pressing up

A helpful wrist-pull, good for when you have only one handhold

Pushing up into a thumbdercling

"Beasting a lever" off a false grip

against a small downward-pointing overlap in opposition to your feet.

4. **The fishhook.** To use your thumb as if it were a finger, floss it into a pocket, seam, or fissure and curl or cam it; also permits you to place your fingers outside the thumbhole on deformities in the rock.

5. **The slimp-to-crimp.** When you go hard and high for a crimp, you can't always close the grip. Try to grab the crimper as you would a sloper (in the sloping-crimp position), and then turn on the crimp as you bring your feet up or catch a helper hold with your other hand.

Thumb engaged deep in a pocket in a fishhook

The slimp-to-crimp. (a) Contact the edge in an open-handed position without your thumb engaged, bring your feet and hips up and start to close the grip, and (b) end in a fully crimped position, with your thumb locked against your index finger.

3

stemboxes, Gollner would press his shoulders against the stone. With a declivity for your shoulder and a good foothold in opposition, you can lean hard against the muscle or bony point. The basic move is the dihedral lean, but you can cop shoulder rests under roofs too. Think *opposition:* "Look around for a wall close to your back, tufas hanging behind you, or footholds opposite a blank wall you can lean against," says Weidner.

The Elbow

In blank corners, your elbow might be your only manual point of contact. Think of the 5.14a Changing Corners pitch of the *Nose*, a granite version of a building's inside corner. Here, the El Cap free maestros Lynn Hill, Scott Burke, Tommy Caldwell, and Beth Rodden chicken-winged a wedge, elbow first, into the right angle. Hill has also devised a yoga-inspired move with the elbow: with her hand locked off and elbow pointing toward earth, Hill drives the elbow into her thigh, allowing her to shake out her other hand.

You can also cam your elbow sideways into large huecos in a chicken-wing position. One hueco at New Mexico's Enchanted Tower, the Jack Daniels Pit Stop, is so big

and incut you can free up both hands to swig off a whiskey bottle!

There is also another top-secret elbow move: levering it against the rock and bracing your forearm parallel with the stone. Caldwell swears by this (as well as pressing off his knees) for climbs ranging from just less than to slightly past vertical. "On that angle, I'm constantly pressing my knees and elbows to have more balance points as I move up," says Caldwell. "It allows you to climb smoother." He contrasts this to the style of dynamically thrutching, ootching, or tick-tacking your foot up to a high foothold, which can be awkward and tiring.

Tommy Caldwell drives in a chicken-wing (articulated elbow scum) on the 5.14a Changing Corners pitch of the *Nose* of El Capitan, Yosemite National Park, California. *Corey Rich / Aurora Photos*

3

Extend your reach and stay flush to the rock with a forearm lever.

3

Jonathan Siegrist busting an elbow-to-thigh "Lynn Hill yoga rest" on *The Heretic* (5.13b), City of Rocks, Idaho

The Palm

Your palms are also quite useful for levering off the rock. In blank stemming corners, bridging, pushing, and palming past blank sections comes naturally. More counterintuitive is simply using your palm to push off a face or even a random hold, to get away from the rock, open up your body, and gain a bird's-eye view of the foothold landscape. A good place to experiment is the gym, with its monolithic surface.

The Hip

A hip-scum or dynamic check ("ketch") against the rock helps counter barn-door swings, when you are elevating your core up and over a ledge or when you are leaning deep into a dihedral. You can smedge your hip many different ways, from digging into the hip bone, to using the outside of your quad, to pressing the side of your buttock. Caldwell says that in dihedrals you can scum your hip much like you use your back chimney climbing. "Say you're in a hybrid-chimney position in a left-facing dihedral," says Caldwell. "I put a foot on the wall to the left of me, press against that to scum my right hip into the right side of the dihedral, and it lets me get in balance and move my hands up."

Palm off a flat surface to get a bird's-eye view of your foothold options.

DRESS FOR SUCCESS

Clothing that creates friction, not slick materials like spandex that reduce it, is the key to a good scumfest:

- **Pants.** Trad climber Chris Weidner recommends burly canvas pants to protect your knees, ankles, butt, and thighs in wide cracks or on rough rock. Professsional climber Tommy Caldwell similarly favors canvas pants or corduroys for trad and for steep (cave) bouldering, with all its scumming and kneebarring. He says the ridges on cords stick well to the rock. Caldwell also uses synthetic insulated pants on long free climbs since they have good friction and are quick to dry.
- **Shirt.** Caldwell recommends wearing a thin fleece. He also wears a midlayer hoody as an outer layer; it keeps your head warm and fits well under helmets.

The Butt

In chimneys and off-sized fissures, when you move into heel-toe mode, your posterior is your friend. I've also seen climbers cop a butt rest on overhanging terrain, when they find small ledges large enough to drape one or both buttocks over. The hardest part can be turning around to sit—though you can sometimes lock a heel or heel-toe against the wall below for balance.

The Knee

The knee is perhaps the most misunderstood and belittled body part in climbing, a sad reality when you consider how useful it is in unweighting your arms. By ushering in kneebar technology, modern cave climbing has shifted this mind-set somewhat, but first, let's examine kneecapping as another way to use your knees.

Kneecapping

I had to tear my LCL (lateral collateral ligament) to figure this out, but you can use your kneecap to climb. As I wore a constricting knee brace, I found that I couldn't jack my injured leg high and sit on it—my typical short-guy MO. I started placing my padded kneecap on holds to raise my hips and move my hands up. Then I would turn the knee into a toe on the same hold. Voilà: a kneecap high step! This technique works especially well on extruded gym holds and ledgelike features.

Any hold big enough to slap your forefoot onto is also big enough for your knee. To kneecap:

1. Place your toe below or beside the target knee hold such that your kneecap hovers above the hold. If you can't find a decent toehold, find a temporary smear.
2. Turn your leg slightly inward, as if you are initiating a drop knee. Now drive your patella (kneecap) or tibial tuberosity (the bump below your kneecap)—whichever fits better and hurts less—onto the hold.
3. Weight the knee, taking this opportunity to reposition your appendages or move your hips up. Knee braces are optional; you could also use athletic tape in strips or a square over the bone. Now bring your toe onto the hold, perhaps manteling onto it.

1 Locate your desired knee hold. Place your kneecap against it, and drop your knee toward you.

2 Weight your knee and reach to the next handhold.

3 Stand up, placing your toe on the former knee hold.

Kneebarring and Knee Scumming

Kneebarring and knee scumming (camming your knee or lower thigh against the rock in opposition to your foot) falls into the sometimes-derided category of jessery, or technical trickery—including toe scums, hip scums, etc.—that takes the sting out of powerful cruxes. And so some climbers avoid kneebarring, often to their own detriment. "I see people who are willing to try a powerful sequence over and over," says kneebar aficionado Chris Weidner, "but if you give people kneebar beta, some of them seem reluctant to try it. They'll just keep banging their heads against the power wall."

Modern kneebar technology was refined in the 1990s, mostly at blocky, overhanging areas like Cave Rock, Nevada; Jailhouse Rock, California; and Rifle, Colorado. Climbers quickly figured out that they could rest in kneebars, sometimes taking both hands off the rock, and that knee scums, no matter how marginal, made fiercely powerful, low-percentage cruxes more doable.

You can *kneebar* in any place where you can obviously throw your leg and cam your knee against the rock in opposition to a toehold. It might be a big block, roof, undercling arch, offwidth, or similar feature. If you are wearing a thick pair of pants, you might not require pads. You engage the front of the thigh above the knee and may even be able to release both hands.

Chris Sharma recovering with a stealthy kneebar rest on *La Dura Dura* (5.15c), Oliana, Spain

Knee scums are useful on subtler features like an offset layback, rooflet, undercling, scoop, or pinch. To milk a knee scum, it helps to use a sticky-rubber kneepad (see the "Pads Done Right" section below): Weidner says that using pads on technical scums has let him take off 20 pounds. As opposed to a kneebar, a scum might also use the inside (not just front) of the thigh and a squeezing or flexing motion.

By keeping an open mind and scrutinizing the stone, you can find bars and scums everywhere, including granite flares, sandstone pod cracks, offset laybacks, underneath cobbles, and up against gym holds. Whichever you are doing, the drill is the same: The placement needs to stick, which means big-time *pressure*.

1. As a rule, you place your toe or foot before slotting your knee, so start with a designated foothold. Lacking an obvious foothold, smear forcefully in the desired locale with the goal of quickly getting your knee in before your foot skates off.
2. Slot and set the kneebar or scum, flexing your calf to create opposition. You may need to articulate your ankle, standing on tiptoe like a ballerina to drive your knee in.
3. Continue pressing as you shake out, resituate your hands, etc. The most common mistake is being intimidated by technical placements and only half-weighting your knee, which makes you slip. One trick Weidner employs is flagging his nonkneebarring foot in the air, which works particularly well for bolstering insecure knee scums or flaring kneebars.
4. To exit a kneebar, come out *slowly* so that you don't fly off. A well-placed kneebar can turn your body into a coiled spring. Tommy Caldwell focuses on lowering his ankle to release pressure on his calf, all the while clenching his stomach muscles and easing out of the kneebar.

Some other guidelines:

-   Don't forget your balance foot when you are setting a kneebar. Putting it in just the right place to allow you to micro-refine your hip position can help more than you realize.
-   Kneebarring is strenuous for your calves. Wear a slightly stiffer shoe than you usually would for steep terrain (an edging as opposed to a grabbing shoe).

CALVES OF POWER, ABS OF STEEL

Cultivate kneebar endurance by training your calves and core. Calf fatigue is often the "limiting factor" between resting and not resting on a kneebar-intensive route. Try these exercises:
- Standing calf raises, which you can do on a rock, step, or any elevated lip (with one or both legs)
- Calf raises on a gym machine or tip-toe calf exercises on a leg-press machine
- Exercises on a balance board like a Bongo Board (the most fun option)

Having a generally strong core helps you both kneebar and get your feet back on if they rip off. According to Tony Yao, a climbing coach at Boulder Rock Club, Colorado, staple core exercises include:
- Crunches
- Front levers off a hanging bar: Either hold a single lever as long as you can, or do three sets of three levers with a dead hang between each set.
- Straight-legged leg raises on a machine or lying on the floor: Do three sets of 10 to 15 with minimal swing on the raise. These will help you bring your penduluming feet back to the rock.

- If your calf is getting pumped, try switching legs in the kneebar. Sure, this takes energy, but the extra minute or two of rest will depump your forearms.
- Look all around you for kneebars, not just in the vertical strip of rock before you or at your knee, thigh, or waist level. I once watched Caldwell, on his 5.15 *Flex Luthor,* throw a wild drop knee at almost head level and then turn it into a kneebar. Crazy!

Pads Done Right

The two basic components of proper kneepadding are constructing a good, reliable pad and getting it to stay put. You could buy a commercial pad, or make one yourself. The ingredients are a Neoprene kneepad and climbing shoe rand rubber:

3

1. At a sporting goods store, buy a long Neoprene pad (12 inches or so) that slides over your leg. You want to maximize the surface area, as it's harder to get shorter pads to stick. Also, make sure your pad doesn't have velcro closures or buckle straps; they do little to anchor the pad and can get in the way.
2. Size the pad fairly tightly but not extremely so, because once you add rubber the pad loses elasticity and will fit more snugly.
3. Machine-sew on a patch of rand rubber (two millimeters thick), or have a cobbler glue it on. The rubber should run up the bottom two-thirds of the pad, starting flush with its bottom (downhill) side. Use a wide swath that covers the front of the thigh and wraps around the sides.

To get the pad to stay put, you will need a razor, some shaving cream, adhesive spray, duct tape, and spray remover:

1. Shave your legs anywhere the pad will go (from your kneecap to your bikini line). This is mostly to prevent pain when you remove the pad.
2. Pull your kneepad on, with the rubber patch rotated slightly toward your inner thigh for knee scums.
3. Fold or roll up the bottom half of the pad.
4. Coat your knee and thigh with spray-on sports or medical adhesive. Rifle local Weidner recommends Mueller Tuffner Pre-Tape Spray, while Dave Pegg, another Rifle local, uses Mueller Stickum. (To keep dried-spray-and-sweat gunk from coagulating inside his pads, Pegg first puts the self-adhering compression bandage Sensi Wrap around his thigh then sprays atop that.) Weidner "sprays like a beast" in a 270-degree arc around his leg (excluding the back of his thigh), but for demanding, super-technical scumming, he'll also spray the exposed, rolled-back inside of the pad.
5. Let the spray dry for 45 seconds, and then carefully roll the pad back into place, smoothing out any ripples.
6. Repeat the process with the top half of the pad.

7. Compression-wrap the pad with duct tape, generally a single or double wrap one to two inches below the top. Weidner wraps nearly to discomfort; "I can't straighten my legs when I'm walking," he jokes. You'll want to prep just below the route. You can also add a supplementary strip of tape partway down the rubber. The tape is merely to keep the pad oriented—Weidner says that the holding power is mostly in the spray.

8. Climb your route. To remove the pads, roll them off inside out, and then set them out to dry this way.

9. Use tape or spray remover or wet wipes to clean your legs, or put on pants to keep dirt off your gummy skin.

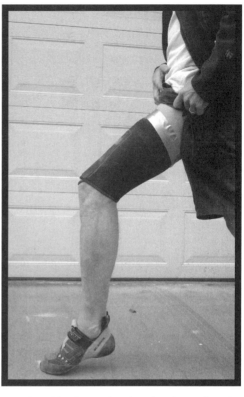

A sticky-rubber kneepad anchored in place and "ready to scum." *Chris Weidner*

ONE GIANT HAND

To wrap up, living master Tommy Caldwell shares a metaphor that may help your climbing technique overall: "Think of your hand—your fingers all operate separately to control the hand," he says. "In climbing, your body is like one giant hand. The limbs are your fingers, and you want to coordinate them to work together."

Caldwell says he transforms himself into a hand by activating his core and by using footholds differently depending on where his hands are—but that he's always just one big hand. Caldwell then uses this "hand" to squeeze the rock, recruiting every last body part in every imaginable permutation. Concludes Caldwell, "That's one of the things I love in climbing, these really complicated, improbable-seeming things you can figure out with your mind instead of brute strength."

4
BODY SHOP

Self-Care at the Crags and Beyond

CAUGHT UP IN ATHLETICISM, our surroundings, sheer animal panic, or some mixture of the above, we become singularly focused on getting up the rock. It's wonderful to be in the zone, to feel the chaos of the world fade away. Yet if you neglect secondary, logistical details like atmospheric conditions, the condition of your skin or tendons, or bodily needs like food and water, climbing, paradoxically, becomes harder, and brute, cold reality slaps you in the face when your performance takes a nosedive. Investing in common-sense self-care, including tips geared toward our sport's unique demands, means that you won't *have* to leave the zone.

CONDITIONS, CONDITIONS, CONDITIONS

In rock climbing, conditions are king. Stack them in your favor, and you increase your odds of sending. Ignore them and plow through anyway, and you will probably fail. It's a Goldilocks thing: On a too-hot day your hands sweat, reducing skin-to-rock friction; your shoe rubber turns gummy, rolling and sliming off holds; and in wet, humid climates condensation even builds up on the rock. On a too-cold day, your skin gets slick, hard, and unfeeling; your fingers and toes go numb and you flash pump from overgripping; your shoe rubber hardens until it feels like it's coated in verglas; and your core gets so cold that all your mojo goes into shivering. On a perfect day, however, none of this happens and it's like you're velcroed to the rock.

Everyone has his or her ideal conditions. For most climbers it's somewhere between 60 and 75 degrees Fahrenheit (in the shade) with low humidity and a light breeze. (For hard bouldering, it's more like 40 to 60 degrees Fahrenheit.) In this mythical sweet spot, the rock is cool but not numbing; the holds are tacky and your skin sticks easily; your shoe rubber is working around its optimal range; and you're thermically comfortable in an overall way that facilitates high energy and optimum flexibility. Sadly, these perfect conditions exist only a few months a year, generally in spring and autumn; your job the rest of the time is to make existing conditions work for *you*.

SKIN, RUBBER, AND THE COEFFICIENT OF FRICTION— WHY ARE IDEAL TEMPS "IDEAL"?

To understand what makes temps ideal, it helps to first understand a principle from physics called the coefficient of friction (symbolized by the Greek letter μ—pronounced "mu"), which describes the ratio of the frictional force between two bodies (an object and a surface) and the force pressing them together. In climbing, the object is either shoe rubber or skin, and the surface is the rock; μ would therefore be the ratio describing the bond between your shoes or your skin and the rock, and the force holding you there as you resist gravity.

Our fingertips are endowed with friction ridges (fingerprints) designed to increase μ, allowing us to grip and hold objects. Add intervening moisture like sweat, humidity, or dew or wear your fingertips smooth, however, and μ decreases. That's why sweaty, hot-day climbing or climbing on thin tips is so much harder. A dry, cool day offers ideal μ between skin and rock because, as per David Flanagan in an article at www.theshortspan.com, the cooler air reduces not only sweating but also "the fluidity of the liquids that constitute our cellular membranes." Your skin becomes harder and drier, bonding better to the stone. A breeze also further dries sweat. Get your hands too cold, with frozen tips, hard skin, or poor circulation, and μ decreases as your skin fails to deform to the rock's porosities.

4

4

With shoes, every type of rubber has its proprietary temperature range, but most work best between 70 and 72 degrees Fahrenheit—with some exceptions on the cooler side. As Jonathan Lantz of La Sportiva USA puts it, "As temps increase or decrease from that target temp, the breakaway friction decreases, causing poor performance." If you're thinking, "Wait a minute, most of the time it's *hotter* or *colder* than 70 degrees Fahrenheit," consider that, as per Flanagan's article, rubber generates friction three ways: deformation (foot pressure causing rock crystals to penetrate the sole and deform the rubber); adhesion; and wear (think of the black polish on well-loved footholds, where our soles have worn off on them). Thus climbing-rubber compounds are designed, as a compromise, to perform well in all three arenas at a mean ambient temperature: to not be so hard they consistently slip off or so soft they deform and gloop off or wear out after a week of use.

So we arrive at our ideal temperature for both skin and rubber: around 70 degrees Fahrenheit, with some personal and environmental (wind, humidity, etc.) variance to either side. It's not so cold that our shoes skitter off and we can't keep our circulation going, yet not so warm that our shoes become unreliable slosh-monsters and our hands unctuous sweat-mitts.

To learn more about this subject, read "Friction," by David Flanagan, www .thesportspan.com/features/friction/htm.

The Cold

Beyond the obvious need to stave off hypothermia, step one in cold weather is to first keep your hands and feet from freezing, which unless done deliberately and methodically—at least with your hands—to habituate yourself to cold rock as per the "Freeze-Thaw" section that follows, can compromise your climbing day. The saying "The best defense is a good offense" holds true for cold-day climbing. To defend against your body's hypothermic response of shunting blood from your extremities to your core, proactively maintain a warm core before your hands and feet become numb.

Dress for Success

Wear heat-trapping, easily layered synthetic clothing, including a warm hat and gloves that you wear on the approach or put on *immediately* at the cliff. Also, bring a puffy parka: Look around at a cold sport crag, and you'll see all the old-timers wearing big, puffy belay jackets that they won't remove until starting up a route. You and your partner can share a single jacket, with the added bonus that the jacket is always warm when you put it on.

Also bring a designated warm layer for climbing: one that stretches and moves well. Justin Roth, who used to put in arctic bouldering sessions at the Shawangunks in New York, swears by synthetic hoodies and fleece jackets with thumbhole cuffs and pockets. Hoods trap head heat, thumbholes let you retract your hands like turtle heads, and pockets let you warm your hand at a rest stance.

Get Your Blood Moving

To get or stay warm before jumping on the rock, do a short burst of aerobic activity:

- Jumping jacks
- Deep-knee bends or marching in place
- Running up and down a hill, talus field, or section of trail
- Windmilling your arms, elbows, and wrists and doing the same with your feet and ankles
- Completing a series of mellow warm-up climbs

4

Hydrate

A thermos of hot tea or coffee brings warmth into your stomach and out through your core. Holding a hot mug in your hands can also be comforting.

Roast Your Delicates

Use this loin-warming technique from Red River Gorge expert Hugh Loeffler: Sit in front of a propane heater with your legs spread, and let the radiant heat hit you in the groin. (Ignore lewd comments from your climbing partners.) The reasoning behind this is that the majority of your blood volume is stored in capacitance veins in the pelvis; heat the blood here and the warm blood will quickly circulate throughout your body, including hands and feet.

You can also heat liquid, put it in a thick plastic water bottle, and put the bottle between your thighs to warm up these veins and consequently your body.

COLD-WEATHER TOOL KIT

Bring these or you will freeze:
- Wool or synthetic cap and gloves
- Down parka
- Down booties or a second parka
- Easily layered synthetic clothing, including a fleece jacket or hoodie
- Propane heater or stove
- Chemical hand-warmer packets
- Thermos of hot drinks (tea, coffee, and so on)
- A plastic tarp and a grocery tote bag for carrying it
- Forearm warmers and stirrup socks or old socks with the feet cut off

Cold Hands

The first appendages to freeze are usually your fingers and hands since they come into direct contact with the stone. This exposure and letting your core get too cold trigger vasoconstriction (the narrowing of blood vessels), leading to numb, clumsy digits. Again, as with your core, stay one step ahead of the cold.

Freeze-Thaw

Professional climber Tommy Caldwell theorizes that the longer you climb, the more vascular and muscle-clad your hands become, and thus the better your circulation and insulation become. He recommends exposing yourself to cold rock to become habituated to it. But he and others consistently preach one overarching trick: start the session by *deliberately* freezing your hands, rewarming them, and then jumping on the rock. This conditioning helps your hands maintain a consistent threshold that should keep them from becoming numb.

Freeze your hands:
- Plunge them into snow, grab an icicle or a cold rock, or stick them in cold water.
- Climb a warm-up or the bottom of your project until your hands

168

CONSTRICTORS AND RESTRICTERS

Anything that restricts blood flow to your hands and feet makes it harder to climb on cold days. Beware:
- Pocket climbs where tight solution holes impinge the fingers
- Cracks, which do the same to fingers, hands, and toes and often have cold air issuing from them
- Taping your fingers too tightly
- Super-tight rock shoes

4

(and feet) go numb, and then have your partner lower you. Alternatively, hang on the rope to warm yourself back up, and then continue climbing.
- Grab the starting holds of your route and hold on, rocking back and forth until your fingers become numb (this can take five minutes or more). Beth Rodden did this on her 5.14 tips-crack *Meltdown,* which she sent in winter in Yosemite in 2008, and she says that the added pressure on her fingers worked better than simply freezing them in snow.

Rewarm your hands:
- Stick them in your pockets or inside your jacket, skin-to-skin against your stomach or in your armpits.
- Hold chemical hand warmers, or put the warmers into your pockets with your hands.
- Warm your hands with a propane heater.
- Use a stove to heat pebbles to hold onto (be careful not to burn yourself) or to drop into your chalk bag or pockets.

Warm your hands until you feel the "screaming barfies" (that cringe-inducing threshold at which the blood rushes back in, creating an electrical, nauseating

Cold rock never deterred Beth Rodden on her Yosemite, California, 5.14 crack *Meltdown. Corey Rich / Aurora Photos*

tingling), and sensation has returned to your fingers. Congrats: You're officially ready to climb!

Get going:

- Spend a couple more minutes prepping; windmill your arms around a final few times, and clap your hands together.
- Then pull on and start climbing.

While you might rest 45 minutes between attempts on a warm day, cold weather rarely affords such luxury, which means you'll have to make do with less rest between burns.

The Penguin

If the Freeze-Thaw is too brutal for you, try the Penguin, as suggested by alpine rock master Kelly Cordes. Start with your arms extended by your sides, hands eight to ten inches from your body and palms facing out (supinated). Shrug your shoulders up to your ears and back down rapidly, using David Blaine voodoo-magic to increase blood flow to your hands.

Hand Warmers, Hot Stove, and Fires—Oh, My!

Hand warmers and stoves will warm your fingers and toes, but are they really worth dragging to the cliffs? Both impart soothing localized heat, but they also cause your hands to sweat, which then freezes in the cold! Still, I have had some success with the following:

- Drop a hand warmer in your chalk bag, and then alternate hands in the bag at rest stances.
- Keep hand warmers in your pockets, so you can shove your hand in when possible.
- Tape a hand warmer to the inside of your wristband or to a forearm warmer to heat your blood as it pumps to your hands.
- Heat up rocks on a stove, and then drop them into your chalk bag or pockets.

Never build a fire to get warm or to heat the rock you are climbing. Not only do fires leave soot and cause spalling (surface plating), they also piss off land managers.

Warmth on the Go

On longer pitches you may still freeze even after leaving the ground in fighting form. Use these tips to warm yourself back up at a rest stance:

- Cup your free hand over your mouth, or make a fist, and exhale repeatedly into it hard, as if you are panting.
- Place your free hand against your belly or the nape of your neck, or jam it up into your armpit.
- Thwack your inactive hand lightly against your belly or thigh, and then open and close it rapidly, flicking your fingers with exaggeration.
- Keep a hot rock or hand warmer in your pocket or chalk bag.

4

Cold Feet

While they aren't in direct contact with the stone like your fingers, your feet can freeze just as easily thanks to tight, constricting rock shoes. Prevention is key.

Up Above It

For snowy, muddy staging areas, bring a crash pad, towel, swath of carpet, or tarp to cover the ground. Winter-bouldering aficionado Justin Roth recommends bringing a grocery-style tote bag for the tarp to contain the mud and muck. If you can't put your shoes on directly below a climb, wear approach shoes or down booties over your rock shoes to keep your soles clean.

Warm Your Shoes, Warm Your Feet

Cold shoes lead to cold feet, and vice versa. Some ideas:

- Keep your crag pack in your house the night before you climb so that your shoes *start out* warm. You can even keep them in your jacket pockets on the approach.
- Blow into your shoes, or put hand warmers in them before you put them on.
- Wear stirrup socks, which heat up the blood in your calves as it flows to your feet but won't compromise rock-shoe sensitivity.
- When you're not climbing, immediately remove your shoes, and shove them in your pockets or inside your jacket until your next burn. Wearing tight rock shoes around on the ground will only increase vasoconstriction.
- With your rock shoes off, keep your bare feet warm by wrapping them in a down jacket or putting on down booties. This tip works best when you are bouldering.

The Heat

Intense heat and strong sun can not only cause medical issues like sunburn, dehydration, heat exhaustion, and heatstroke; they also affect your performance more than the cold does. The reason, in a word, is *sweat*. Like that rainwater on the highway that makes a car hydroplane, sweat reduces the coefficient of friction between you and the rock, and you quickly lose purchase—and probably skin!

Your shoes, meanwhile, face a similar fate. That old urban legend about rubber working better in the heat because it conforms more readily to the rock is pure BS—on a hot day your sole deforms well past its performance point, resulting in goopy footwork and reduced adhesion. Don't believe me? Try a difficult slab on a cool day in the shade, and then come back to it on a hot day in the sun. Let me know how it goes.

Don't Be a Sweathog

You can't keep from sweating, though you can mitigate its effects:

- Wear a headband or bandanna to keep sweat out of your eyes.
- Wear wristbands to keep sweat from running onto your hands.
- Bring towels to dry yourself between climbs, as Red River Gorge climbers do on the infamous "two-towel days" of the Kentucky summer.
- Bring extra chalk, and rock a full chalk bag.

NIGHT CLIMBING

Zombies, vampires, boulderers, and other temp-obsessives climb at night, when it's coolest. Pro climber Tommy Caldwell, who's climbed 5.13 traditional pitches on El Capitan by headlamp, shares these pointers:

- Wear a single, bright, full-strength headlamp, and seek out climbs that you know well and that are relatively straightforward, or tackle flat surfaces like faces or dihedrals (three-dimensional rock will cast confusing shadows). If one headlamp isn't cutting it, wear multiple microheadlamps around your ankles and wrists like bracelets.
- Practice until night climbing no longer feels scary and you can push yourself harder: Let your mind go quiet as you focus only on the area lit up before you—for the moment, your entire world. Harder climbing is sometimes easier than moderate terrain because there are fewer holds to track, and also because headlamp shadows make tiny footholds look bigger, a psychological leg up.
- Bring a lantern out bouldering. Add flameproof reflective tape over half the inside of the globe; like the reflector in a car headlight, the tape will effectively double the lamp's light output.

4

- Bring a thermos full of iced tea, coffee, fruit juice, or the beverage of your choice.
- Coat your hands in liquid chalk before you start. Commercial brands are available, or you can mix block or powdered chalk with rubbing alcohol (the higher the alcohol content, the faster the chalk will dry). Stir the ingredients in a bowl, with a ratio of about 3:1 alcohol to chalk, until you have a thin paste the consistency of yogurt. Liquid chalk provides a base layer for regular chalk, and it coats and protects your skin.
- Try Antihydral cream, especially if you're an extreme sweater. Use it sparingly until you figure out your threshold, as this powerful desiccant can cause peeling, splits, and fissuring and needs a few days to take effect. Put a light layer on your fingers or fingertips, avoiding the creases, two nights before climbing or over a few consecutive nights beforehand, and then wash it off come morning. (Be careful also not to touch your eyes, mouth, etc., after putting it on.) You can buy it online through foosball supply outlets.

4

The Damp

There's not much help for rock that's fully soaked, but rock with damp spots or a humid veneer *might* still be climbable with these workarounds:

- For a seepy hold or water streak, especially when you are bouldering, check up top for snow or ice you can remove.
- For seepy pockets or huecos, stuff an athletic sock, chalk-filled sock, or chalk ball in the hold, and then pull it out when you're done. You can also use a towel to spot-dry wet rock—or at least attempt to!
- Wear pants so that you can wipe your shoes on your opposite leg, and wipe your hands dry on your shirt each time *before* you chalk up.
- Stay off wet sandstone for at least a day, to let it dry, as this porous rock becomes fragile, causing moist key holds to snap.

Never use a blowtorch to dry a hold. It can lead to cracking, spalling, and scarring.

SKIN AND FINGER CARE

When it comes to climbing on rock, skin is *everything*: "It's your primary contact point with the rock other than your rock shoes," says Chris Schulte, a Colorado boulderer known for his difficult compression problems and hair-raising highballs. "You want to be able to feel really small holds, but also have your skin be tough enough and well-trimmed enough that nothing's going to snag on a sharp little crystal, and flapper." Or as Herman Feissner, another hardcore Colorado boulderer, puts it, "Skin is like the tires on an F1 race car: Compound, tread pattern, temperature, and pressure are all important. Much the same, the skin on my fingertips and hands connects me to the rock. Having good skin is more or less equal to racing on fresh rubber."

Self-care starts with making good choices. Tear up your dermis, and you might be benched for days, watching *Bad Girls Club* reruns, weeping, and slathering on lotion while your friends are at the rocks having epic fun. The key is to climb smart. Don't chew up your skin in bad conditions, end a session before your tips are worn to the quick or bleeding, and always stop before you're climbing so tired that you're making sloppy, uncontrolled moves to holds and sliding off them.

As Schulte warns, "Know when to say when. Always stop, be in tune to the whole thing, and pay attention, especially with small holds. Once you split a tip and there's blood on it, you're out. You won't climb on that hold again for five days at best, unless it's with tape on." Schulte himself knocks off as soon as his skin tears even a little or if he sees the telltale eye or half-moon shape of a scalloping tip—or a mere pinpoint of blood.

Schulte and Feissner recommend that you pack a skin-care kit for maintenance and field repairs:

- **Nail clippers.** A quiver of three or four different-sized clippers for every situation, some with flat blades, others with curved ones. If you bring only one pair, make it the oversized (toenail-clipper) ones with a curved blade, which lets you snip closer to the skin. The big ones also let you trim both your finger- and toenails.
- **Sanding block.** A dual-textured drywall sanding sponge (one side with heavy grit, the other with a finer grain) or a 3M medium-grit sanding sponge.
- **Nail file or emery board.** An oversized emery board or a black, professional nail file.

4

175

Chris Schulte walking the skin-care talk on the
undone *Dreamtime Project,* Mount Evans, Colorado

Herman Feissner babying his tips on *Full Throttle*
(V13), Hardman Rock, Hueco Tanks, Texas

4

- **Razor blade.** For trimming calluses, fissures, or split tips.
- **Antibiotic cream.**
- **Band-aids.**
- **Athletic tape.** Both boulderers specifically recommend Johnson and Johnson Consumer Coach Porous Athletic Tape, which is ideal for climbing because it's thin enough to let you feel the rock but also anchors well to skin.
- **Hockey tape.** Its rubber content gives it extra friction. It's harder to tear into strips compared to athletic tape, so use nail clippers or a small knife.
- **Liquid bandage.** Use it to fill in cracks and splits, instead of the overly hardening superglue that climbers applied back in the day (Schulte recommends Skin Shield). You can also paint liquid-bandage compound onto thin fingertips to anchor the tape.

Each type of hand wound requires a different approach:

- **Calluses.** Over time, rock and gym holds build up yellow callus ridges on your fingers and palms. Once a ridge sits too high, it can catch on holds and tear, leaving you with a gaping wound. Or it can dry out and fissure, causing painful splits. Use your sanding block or emery board to file these ridges down flush. Start with the grittier side of the board or block, and then move to the finer-grained side. You could also moisturize your callused hands with lotion to keep them supple (see the "Lotions and Salves" sidebar).
- **Splits.** A split callus is excruciating and slow to heal. If you bust a split that's painful enough to end your climbing day, clean it out and cover it up with a band-aid. (If you think you can keep climbing, protect the wound with tape as per the "Skin-Taping Tips" that follow.) Once back home, sand the callus flush, and pack the split with antibacterial ointment or moisturizer.
- **Flappers.** Flappers occur when a callus tears off or when you catch any part of your hand on a sharp hold and peel back a flap of skin. Reduce your chances of flapping by sanding or using an

4

LOTiONS AND SALVES

Try these lotions and salves to soothe your hands after climbing. (Note: Never put salve or lotion on *before* climbing, as it makes your mitts greasy and gunks up the holds.)

- Climb On! products
- Sierra Salve
- Burt's Bees Hand Salve
- Metolius Climbing Climber's Hand Repair Balm
- Joshua Tree Climbing Salve
- Eucerin cream
- Vitamin E oil (great for thin tips)
- Vermont's Original Bag Balm

4

emery board to remove all burrs, callus ridges, and so on. "I'll sand my tips and anything that looks like it could hang up on a crystal or edge until it's flush," says Schulte. "The goal is low drag, low resistance. I'll also sand my cuticles, where the skin can get really hard, and the edges of my fingertips on either side of the nail." For bad flappers, clean them, pack them with antibacterial ointment, and bandage them.

- **Hangnails.** Chalk can cause hangnails. Use nail clippers to cut them.
- **Thin tips.** Worn tips sting and turn pink or purple, sport eye-shaped or half-moon indentations, and sparkle with sweat. Your best bet is to rest and let the skin regrow, but if you must keep climbing, you can bolster your tips with liquid-bandage compound or tape. A thin tip is also much more likely to split or flap.
- **Split tips.** Use a razor blade to clean the edges of the split down to a layer of smoother skin. The wound will heal quicker if it's uniform. To keep climbing, apply liquid-bandage compound to the split, and then tape it (see the "Skin-Taping Tips" sidebar).
- **Fingernail separation:** Thwacking the rock while going for a

hold can pull your fingernail away from your finger. Cram the gap between your nail and finger with antibacterial ointment or climbing salve, and keep it moist. Then take rest days until the throbbing subsides.

○ **Gobies.** These wounds incurred on the backs of your hands and fingers while crack climbing are some of bloodiest, scabbiest, nastiest dings around. Keep them clean with diligent hand-washing, and apply climbing salve or lotion.

TAPING TENDONS

Blowing a finger (injuring a pulley tendon, ligament, or capsule) sucks. Decades of hapless flailing have turned my already large digits into Jimmy Deans too clumsy and bloated for most technical pocket climbs, but my middle fingers have suffered the most. Both remain cranky on bidoigts and especially monos. As a teenager I had the footwork of a Mack truck careering off an icy mountain road; my feet once slipped while I was plugged into a left-hand monodoigt, and then a year later, again while my right hand was in a monodoigt at Cochiti Mesa, New Mexico. A solid 150 pounds shock-loaded each finger. To this day, I almost always do preventive, supportive taping on either finger. There are three ways to support a tweaked finger, all using a standard 1.5-inch roll of athletic tape:

4

The Old Fashioned

Separate your roll into three parallel strands, each roughly a half-inch wide, so that you can pull tape from each strand alternately and use the roll up at the same rate. Use a penknife or your teeth to start the slits.

Unspool and rip off about nine inches (enough tape for roughly three revolutions around your finger) from one strand. Wrap the tape tightly (but not absurdly so) below your middle knuckle. Beware of swelling or any purple or white discoloration; you don't want to occlude circulation.

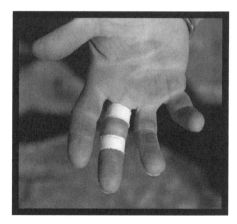

A tweaked middle finger supported by old-fashioned tape rings

Now press the end down firmly to secure it. Tear off another strip and repeat the process just above the knuckle. When you're finished, you should be able to bend your finger, still feel the blood circulating, and feel support from the tape.

Buddy Taping

Peel off a foot of tape that is roughly three-quarters of an inch wide, and then bind your injured finger to its neighbor at the base, and above the middle knuckles, so that you can bend your knuckles freely. Pair your index and middle fingers or your middle and ring fingers. You can also combine buddy taping with the old fashioned for a particularly compromised digit. The main disadvantage to buddy taping is that the paired fingers must bend in tandem, limiting how you grab certain holds, especially pockets.

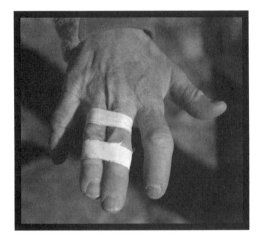

Buddy taping

H-Taping

A third method, H-taping, was created by the five authors of the study "Impact after Finger Flexor Tendon Pulley Ruptures in Rock Climbers," as published in *Journal of Applied Biomechanics* in 2007. Their thesis held that a flexor tendon needs the most tape support where it's farthest from the bone, to "effectively change the course of the flexor tendon and therefore reduce the tendon-bone distance."

The old-fashioned ring of tape doesn't do this, argued the study, because of all the intervening soft tissue. (The study found that H-taping decreased the tendon-bone distance by 16 percent—other methods had no effect—and imparted 13 percent more strength in the crimp position.) Although H-taping is more time intensive than the other methods, it might well be worth the effort:

  ○ Pull a four-inch strip off a roll split into thirds. (More exactly, a
    strip 10 centimeters long by 1.5 centimeters wide.)

180

First cut the legs of the H,
leaving a crossbar in the middle.

Now place the crossbar on
the palm side of your middle knuckle.

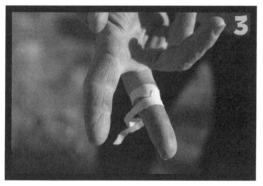

With your finger straight, secure the lower
legs of the H below your knuckle.

To finish, bend your finger and secure the
upper legs of the H above your knuckle.

- Cut lengthwise from each end of the strip toward the center with a small pair of scissors or a penknife, leaving a 1-centimeter bridge in the middle (the crossbar of the H).
- Keeping the injured finger straight, place the crossbar on the palm side of its second (middle) knuckle.
- Tightly secure the legs of the H below the knuckle.
- Bend your finger, and secure the legs of the H above the knuckle.

Replace after each climb, as the tape will stretch.

SKiN-TAPiNG TiPS

Despite proactively caring for our skin, we can still split, flapper, or wear our tips down to sparkly meat. If you want to keep climbing with a wound, you usually need to tape it. Mummy taping and X-taping are the least intrusive and most reliable methods.

To mummy tape:

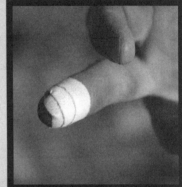

A mummy-taped tip, ready to jump back into action

- Apply a spray, such as the climbers' staple Mueller Tuffner PreTape, to your fingertip, to hold the tape in place.
- Split a thin strip off a roll of athletic tape, about one-quarter or one-third the roll's width.
- Wrap the strip around your finger, starting at the tip and overlapping half the width of the tape across itself with each pass (the mummy wrap).
- Tape clear down to the first crease on the palm-side of your finger. On the final wrap, bring the tape back below that knuckle (back of the hand) and anchor it lengthwise down your finger.

To X-tape, which is Schulte's preferred method (one he likens to Chinese fingercuffs):

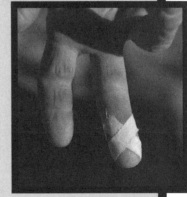

An X-taped tip: good as new!

- Apply liquid-bandage compound to your tip to supplement your skin and anchor the tape.
- Tear off a thin strip of tape, one-third the width of the roll.
- Start at the base (palm-side first-knuckle crease) of your tip with the strip, wrap it diagonally up across the tip, circle your fingernail, and then come down at a crisscross angle back to the palm-side crease. Configure the tape such that both legs of the X cover your wound.
- Use a daub of liquid-bandage compound along the nail to glue the tape in place and keep glue residue off the rock.
- Apply more crisscrossed layers as needed.

FLASH PUMP

There's perhaps no climbing malady worse than the flash pump, that painful, lingering forearm swelling that happens when you're either climbing in the cold and/or warm up too quickly. It's basically a mild version of compartment syndrome, an increase in pressure in one of the body's muscular compartments. These few home remedies can get you back on track after you become flash pumped so that your climbing day isn't over:

- **Stretch your forearms:** Use one hand to pull down on the other, with the palm of the latter perpendicular to the ground and those fingers pointing downward. Now rotate your wrist 180 degrees, with your fingers pointing skyward, and pull back on your hand. You can also stand next to the cliff with your arm outstretched and palm flat on the rock; with your wrist flexed and your fingers pointing behind you, turn slowly away from the rock and feel the stretch opening your shoulder, biceps, forearm, and fingers.
- **Massage:** Massage your forearms crosswise, kneading and pinching the muscles and rubbing the heel of your hand back and forth over the meat.
- **Warm back up slowly:** Start your day anew, and warm up twice as slowly as usual. Climb laps on routes three or four number grades below your limit, shaking out and stretching your forearms against the rock as you go.
- **Hydrate:** Drink extra water to increase your blood volume and help your heart flush the trapped blood from your forearms.

CRAG NUTRITION AND HYDRATION

We take so much for granted in the throes of climbing, including basic needs like nutrition and hydration. I've noticed a tendency among my partners and myself to skimp on eating and drinking at the cliff, whether out of laziness, distraction, constant motion (going from pitch to pitch), or a lack of preparedness. I'll often sketch by on a half bottle of water and an energy bar all day and have climbed with 5.14 shredders who survive purely on coffee and miniature donuts. However, in

4

demanding the utmost from our bodies, we should also pay better attention to how we fuel them. Eating and drinking well are as important as wearing a good pair of rock shoes.

Crag Food

Before we delve into nutrition, a brief note on climbing, body weight, and eating disorders: It's probably our sport's biggest "secret" that in order to climb your hardest, you want to be lean. One look at top climbers shows incredibly honed athletes with body-fat percentages well below 10 percent, and we all either know or are that climber who drops an extra five or ten pounds for a redpoint. However, it's a fine line between healthy eating, selective dieting, and a full-blown eating disorder. Whether they cop to it or not, more than a few climbers (myself included) have succumbed to anorexia, bulimia, and bulimarexia, diseases with long-term ramifications like slowing one's metabolism, osteoporosis in women, and emotional issues like anxiety and depression. If you're serious about wanting to lose a few pounds, be smart. Consult a nutritionist, and devise a balanced, sustainable meal plan that gets you to a realistic target weight over a comfortable span of time.

Now to the big question: What should I eat while climbing? The answer might surprise you. According to Neely Quinn, a longtime climber and nutrition therapist (www.paleoplan.com, coauthor of *The Complete Idiot's Guide to Eating Paleo*) in Boulder, Colorado, you should eat what you would at home. In other words, follow the same common-sense habits of eating well and avoiding junk food and the carbo or sugar loading that leads to blood-sugar spikes and crashes. Your goal is to maintain a sustained energy level throughout the day so you don't go into a deep, dark, hard-to-recover-from blood-sugar hole. By indulging in the typical lazy-climber diet (granola bars, energy bars, and bags of cookies), you're taking a ride on the nefarious blood-sugar roller coaster.

"If you're just feeding your body sugar, you need a constant supply of sugar," says Quinn. "But if you had fat and protein, it would be much more of a sustained energy, and you wouldn't need to feed it every hour. Think of a hearty dinner—that's what people should be eating every meal of the day, and that's what gives you sustained energy." Coming at it from a Paleo-perspective, Quinn recommends that you calculate 80 percent of your body weight in pounds and eat that amount of protein in grams per

4

day. In other words, if you weigh 150 pounds, you would aim for 120 grams of protein each day. Some staple, quality sources include:

- Organic poultry, organic beef, smoked salmon, tuna, etc.
- Vegetarian deli slices
- Soy (tofu, tempeh, etc.)
- Milk, cheese, and Greek yogurt
- Legumes
- Eggs

You also want a healthy dose of fat, particularly fats high in omega-3s, which combat inflammation, and not omega-6s, which contribute to inflammation (i.e., disease, including climbing-specific problems like tendonitis). Americans and especially climbers are fat phobic, but fat is crucial for hormone productions and the health of your skin, nails, hair, and immune system; without fat, you can't process fat-soluble vitamins like A, D, E, and K. In the 1990s, when many top sport climbers adhered to radical fat-free diets, they often experienced skin problems like splits, gobies, and thin tips. Eating a little lard could have healed their skin! Staple sources of good fats include:

- Avocados
- Nuts (almonds and macadamia nuts)
- Olive oil and coconut oil
- Fish (salmon)
- Pastured butter
- Fat from pasture-raised meats

At the same time, don't discount carbs. When they come from a solid whole-grain source (e.g., whole wheat bread), they also form part of a balanced diet. Being carb-phobic has never helped anyone.

Pack a nice, regular, hearty lunch to bring to the cliffs and a supply of healthy snacks, and throw in some fresh fruits and vegetables. Examples include a turkey sandwich with avocado and tomato or a quinoa, spinach, feta, and tempeh salad. Quinn likes to bring leftovers (meat and veggies) with plenty of fat and protein, along with fruit for carbohydrate energy. Most food will keep in a cooler or a plastic container with a cooling pack. The small risk of food poisoning is no excuse for bringing only bars.

4

BLOATiNG AND CLiMBiNG

We all want to feel light, flexible, and mobile, but a full belly pressing against your harness has the opposite effect. Nutritionist and climber Neely Quinn says that taking an hour break midday to eat a healthy lunch often eliminates this problem, as does studying which foods make you feel bloated on a nonclimbing day and eliminating them from your crag diet.

"Some people are affected by dairy, some by grains, and some by soy," she says. "It makes them bloated and fatigued." If you eat pizza and notice that you feel like taking a nap an hour later, pizza probably isn't a good food for you to bring to the crag.

4

What you eat before and after climbing matters as well. "It's super important that people eat breakfast on climbing days," says Quinn. "It's been proven that people who don't eat breakfast generally have more cravings throughout the day. If you don't eat breakfast, you'll crash and then it will be harder to catch up from that crash." Neely recommends a high-protein breakfast, such as one heavy on eggs. Eat a high-protein meal with whole-grain carbs, fresh fruits and vegetables, and healthy fats like olive oil after you climb to give your body the building blocks it needs to repair your muscles.

Crag Hydration

It has taken me decades to figure out that most of my worst, low-performing days have been because of dehydration. Barely remembering to drink water or being too lazy to bring enough along, I would feel heavy, get logy, lethargic, and clumsy, and my muscles, especially the fine ones in my forearms, would cramp. In the throes of thirst, I also felt more irritable when I inevitably failed. Telltale signs of dehydration include:

- Dry lips and mouth
- Thirst
- Sleepiness or lethargy
- Infrequent urination (going hours without peeing) and dark-yellow or brown urine

- Headaches, especially at higher altitudes
- Confusion and irritability
- Lightheadedness or dizziness

According to Quinn, drinking less water than you need hammers your performance three ways:

1. You become fatigued more easily since your desiccated body has to work that much harder to keep up.
2. You become more brittle and injury prone because water lubricates joints, tendons, and muscles.
3. It's more difficult to recover the next day, as you might still be trying to make up for your water deficit.

It's easy to get wrapped up in climbing and forget to drink, especially on chilly days when we're experiencing cold-weather diuresis and not receiving clear thirst signals. But dehydration and its negative effects are real and insidious, in any climate. As a rough guideline, multiply your body weight by 0.6 or 0.7 to get the amount in ounces you need on an average day. So if you weigh 150 pounds, multiply 150 pounds by 0.7, and you get 105 ounces (a little more than 3 liters).

On a day that you're climbing dozens of pitches or going on an outing that incorporates a strenuous hike, drink more. Because we come in all shapes and sizes, the old doctors' adage that we need eight glasses of water a day doesn't necessarily hold true. However, as a rule of thumb you should be downing one to four liters at the cliffs. Pay attention to your body's signals, and stay ahead of dehydration before your climbing goes to hell.

Water vs. Sports Drinks

Sports drinks have become all the rage, with the preconception that anyone working out (climbers included) somehow "needs" them. You can thank marketing for this myth, because the fact is such drinks aren't entirely necessary, especially in an anaerobic sport like climbing. If you enjoy them, fine, but you don't always *need* them!

According to Quinn, sports drinks are overconsumed these days. They were originally devised for endurance athletes—recall Gatorade's origin story of University of Florida football players sweating their butts off during practice and needing electrolyte

QUINN'S HONEY-LEMON THIRST QUENCHER

If water's not your thing and you want a natural electrolyte replacement, try this homemade drink that nutritionist and climber Neely Quinn recommends:

- ○ 1/2 cup raw honey
- ○ 1/2 teaspoon sea salt
- ○ 1/4 cup fresh lemon juice
- ○ 7 1/2 cups filtered water (lukewarm to dissolve the honey)

Combine the ingredients in a container that holds eight cups (two liters), mix or shake it, and then chill it in the refrigerator. In terms of electrolytes and calories, it's similar to Gatorade but without all the processed sugar.

The Thirst Quencher has (per cup) 60 calories, 17 grams of carbs, no fat or protein, 119 milligrams of sodium, and 85 milligrams of potassium. For comparison, Gatorade has (per cup) 63 calories, 16 grams of carbs, no fat or protein, 110 milligrams of sodium, and 37 milligrams of potassium.

4

replacement—and tasted fairly nasty. However, they've since been punched up with sugar, including high-fructose corn syrup, and chemical color and flavor additives. "Now people think that they need them every time they exercise, and that's a huge misconception," says Quinn. If you're hitting up a sport crag like Rifle, with no approach and where you spend most of the day hanging out, you probably don't need a sports drink. Moreover, if you're mostly inactive, the drinks' high sugar content contributes to blood-sugar spikes and crashes.

Quinn says that most climbers need drink only water or water mixed with natural fruit juice. She recommends sports drinks only for athletes undertaking true endurance activities like long runs or bike rides, and then she recommends that they consume the drink 10 minutes before starting and at specific intervals thereafter so that their body recruits the sugar directly.

Coffee

Because it's legal, widely available, and sanctioned by society, many climbers pound caffeine without questioning this stimulant's impact on their health. There are plenty of studies showing its benefits in athletic performance, yet caffeine is a diuretic that contributes to dehydration. Don't discount its effect on your climbing or on exacerbating overuse injuries like tendonosis, tendonitis, and tweaked knee and shoulder ligaments.

According to Quinn, caffeine has effects that are often incompatible with climbing well:

- **Dehydration.** You'll need even more water than usual; I drink eight ounces of water to compensate for every cup of coffee.
- **Blood-sugar spiking.** Caffeine affects your blood sugar similar to the way sports drinks do, especially without food. You'll feel big spikes followed by epic crashes, because by stimulating stress hormones like cortisol and adrenaline, caffeine tells your body to release glucose from the liver. (Long term, all that cortisol creates constant stress on the body, negatively affecting everything from your immune system to your reproductive system, muscle tone, ability to lose weight, and digestion.) The same thing happens in a traumatic event like a car crash: Your body cues your liver to dump sugar into your bloodstream so that you have immediate, available energy for survival. However, what you really want out climbing is level blood sugar and sustained, balanced energy.
- **Jitters and sleeplessness.** Some people feel fine after drinking coffee, while others have a more anxious reaction. Even a moderate amount of caffeine makes some of us, perhaps unknowingly, shaky and sweaty, speeds up our heartbeat and breathing, and has all the other effects our bodies feel under duress. None of these effects are ideal in a heady sport like climbing, where we want calm. Caffeine also causes insomnia, and a lack of sleep certainly hampers athletic performance.

Like all things in life, it's a matter of degree. The sky won't fall if you drink a moderate amount of coffee and do well with it. However, if you suspect that caffeine is causing issues, consider a trial detox period and see if you don't feel better after a few weeks.

4

5 BECOME A ROCK NINJA
Tricks of the Cragger's Trade

LIKE SURGEONS PLAYING WITH the newest microsurgery machine, we climbers love fiddling with our widgets and the tricky techniques that make them work. Most of this select handful of unique, cragging-specific tools and tricks have a sport-climbing focus, and many will also improve your game as a redpointer. Couple them with the movement and mental tips presented in Chapter 3, and you too will become a rock ninja.

REDPOINT ROPE, QUICKDRAW, AND PSYCHE MANAGEMENT

Redpointing is an art, a performance, a blizzard of sequences linked at your limit with little margin for error. Nothing is more fascinating than learning every last nuance of timing, resting, and foot and hand placement on a route that initially feels impossible, and then putting it all together. Putting your gear to work for *you* frees you up to focus on the movement and on cultivating a positive, process-based mind-set.

PINKPOINTING KERFUFFLE

I often chuckle at the endless threads on climbing sites debating the merits of redpointing vs. pinkpointing, which reveal more about the anti-pinkpointers' n00b status than some core ethical truth. *Pinkpointing* was coined in the 1990s to describe redpointing a climb with either the gear or quickdraws already hanging to distinguish such ascents from "proper" redpoints. This distinction mattered, sort of, for a few years, to a few people, and still has some merit when discussing traditional climbs. But in sport climbing, the focus should be on athletic performance, not on how the safety gear came to be there. The bolts are in place anyway, so what does it matter if the draws are too . . . or if a few clips have extendo slings . . . or if you start with the rope preclipped? I doubt Chris Sharma lost any sleep over pinkpointing his 250-foot 5.15b *Jumbo Love*, a wildly futuristic cave climb that took him months to complete.

5

Seamless Redpointing

These logistical pointers will help you redpoint seamlessly. The first six will help you minimize rope drag so that the weight and friction of the rope aren't pulling you earthward at the 15th bolt. Drag is often overlooked, but it's a legitimate limiting factor. Sixty- and seventy-meter dynamic ropes weigh anywhere from 7 to 13 pounds, so even on a perfect plumb line, at the 30-meter mark where most climbs finish you're still hauling around four to six pounds of nylon. Now envision super-routes that go much farther and the inevitable drag our protection systems introduce: *Ugh!*

Extendo Draws

Long or "extendo" draws are helpful for two reasons:

1. They reduce drag in key spots like doglegs, below roofs, etc.
2. They take the sting out of high, strenuous clips by requiring you to lock off less and pull up less rope.

Some routes, because they have hollow rock, sharp edges, or sustained crux sections, are even expressly bolted for extendo draws. I've equipped an extendo and a regular draw on the same bolt (the extendo to clip low; the regular draw to clip when I am higher) so that I can clip into both draws if I'm concerned about taking a longer fall onto the extendo.

The best extendo options include:

- **Metolius Climbing Long Draws.** They come in 12-inch, 16-inch, and 20-inch lengths.
- **Trad draws.** A sewn runner with two carabiners. To keep it tidy on your harness, clip both carabiners to the sling. Now take one

1
To make a trad draw, begin with a sewn sling that has a biner clipped to either end.

2
Feed one biner through the other.

biner, feed it *through* the other, bring the first biner back down, and clip it into the tripled webbing strands. To undo the draw, simply unclip two of the strands from either biner. If your trad draw will be hanging for a while, tape the bottom (rope-side) biner in place so that it doesn't flip upside-down.

○ **Draw-and-a-half.** Remove the bottom biner from a normal quick-draw, and clip a full draw into the webbing loop, making sure all three biners orient the same direction.

5

3

Clip the "fed" biner through the tripled strands of webbing.

4

You now have a trad draw!

Revolver Carabiners

DMM's drag-reducing Revolver biner has a revolving wheel in the rope cradle to cut drag. As with extendo draws, use them on low bolts, in places where a route zigs or zags, snakes up under roofs, and so on.

Lightweight Rope

Lightweight, thin-diameter cords are killer (see "The Redpoint Quiver" sidebar) both for weight savings and drag reduction; they mean less rope material runs over the carabiners. Typically, lightweight single ropes range from 9.2 to 10.2 millimeters in diameter.

Preclipping

There is no shame in preclipping the first or even higher draws if it will prevent an injurious ground fall or reduce drag. Many climbs that are cruxy right off the deck have high first bolts that are meant to be stick-clipped. And other climbs are so long and wandering that clipping into low bolts will cause horrendous drag when you move higher. Rifle, Colorado, maven Chris Weidner put up a 31-bolt pitch in Rifle in 2012; he started with the fourth bolt preclipped, to a Revolver on a long draw, to avoid being pinned by drag on the route's upper headwall.

Unclipping on the Fly

Unclipping a bolt or bolts below you once you're connected to a higher clip can reduce drag.

Stancing and Sequencing for Drag

Despite your best efforts, you might in certain cases still face heavy drag, so work out stable sequences and clipping stances. Weidner had to devise a different clipping stance for his Rifle route on lead versus on top rope, because when he was on lead, the weight of the rope pulled him off balance.

Skipping Clips

Some climbs have "dogger" bolts, meant to be clipped while working the route but that you can't tag on the go. Plan to bypass them, and look at how that affects the clips above and below, watching out for the resulting whipper potential. For the sake of efficiency, you might also bypass a bolt you could clip if doing so isn't dangerous.

Chest or Waist Clipping

Certain clips are best made while you're level with or slightly above them, where you can hang straight-armed and pull up less rope. Clipping high with one arm cocked drains your energy, and with all that extra rope out, you risk taking just as big a fall as you would if clipping the bolt at your chest, waist, or even shin. Moreover, falling with armloads of clipping slack out challenges your belayer more than catching a straight-forward whipper does.

Sequencing a Hard Clip

Crux clips are often tough, strenuous clips amid a crux section. Part of climbing your hardest is figuring out how to make these. Jonathan Siegrist, a 5.14-plus redpointer, advises that you first evaluate a clip to see if you can extend the draw or skip it. If you cannot, then play on top rope with the different handholds and body positions, and find the stance that suits you. You might have to go off-sequence, tweak your sequence subtly, or reverse-engineer the moves above and below to arrive with the correct hand. Once you have figured out the sequence, face the gate in the direction in which you're best (quickest) at clipping, as long as it won't affect safe ropework up higher.

5

THE REDPOINT QUIVER

Just like you dress to impress on a first date, so too should you dress up for a redpoint, bringing your A-list gear. While working a climb, you might use a good but broken-in pair of shoes and an older but reliable rope. However, when you're close to sending, bring:

- **Redpoint shoes:** A just-broken-in, usually nonresoled pair of performance shoes kept in reserve, and maybe worn once while working the climb so that you know how they feel. You want solid midsole form and stiffness, and square (not rounded off) toe rubber, for maximum bite on tiny footholds.
- **Redpoint rope:** A new or nearly new lightweight dynamic rope around 10 millimeters in diameter, with a nice, slick dry coating so that it runs well.

- **A new brush and your favorite chalk bag** loaded with plenty of chalk.
- **One lucky article of clothing:** A T-shirt, hat, shorts, or pants that have brought you luck in the past.

When redpointing, onsighting, or even climbing recreationally, consider which accoutrements you have clipped to your harness and how much they weigh you down. Some climbers head up sport and gym routes with pounds of unnecessary weight clipped to their harness and slings: belay devices, belay gloves, cordelettes, belay knives, extra draws, prusiks, and so on. Worse yet, instead of using a waist belt, they've clipped their chalk bag to their haul loop with a locking carabiner, where it dangles awkwardly. *You are not Batman, and your harness isn't the Bat Belt; pare it down.* On a redpoint burn with the draws already hanging, you only need a single quickdraw to fifi in with. Stow the rest of your kit where it belongs—safely in your crag pack until you need it.

"Not sure—but maybe I could clip a few more things on here . . ."

Putting a Route Together

We climbers spend a lot of time failing. Some days our fingers are tired, some days our head's kaput, some days the conditions are execrable, and on the worst days *nothing* clicks. And so you become frustrated, and then climb even worse. It's a vicious cycle and might even get you so wound up that you pitch a fit, which only revs up your nervous system and fosters your worst, most childish emotions. Any longtime climber will confirm that you must instead "fail upward" to put a climb together.

Consider Beth Rodden's February 2008 first ascent of the 5.14 crack *Meltdown* in Yosemite Valley. If Rodden hadn't learned to embrace failure, the route never would have happened. It took her 40 days of effort to unlock this 70-foot crack, barely wide enough for fingertips. At first, Rodden struggled to do the hardest moves, so she bouldered to increase her power. She soon began to put sequences together, but then the Sierra's winter storms raged through, dumping feet of snow. At one point, Rodden and her then husband, Tommy Caldwell, headed up with shovels. She excavated the base of the crack, while he did the same up top so that the rock wouldn't course with meltwater.

Rodden came painfully close to sending around New Year's 2008, but then she was sidelined by more storms, a ligament injury in her right hand from trying the crux repeatedly, and ongoing wintry conditions. Still she persevered, falling and failing and dealing with the cold, training on her home wall, and heading to *Meltdown* when conditions permitted. On Valentine's Day 2008, after 40 days of heartbreak, Rodden redpointed *Meltdown,* the culmination of one of the most heroic efforts in US climbing history.

While we're not all going to have Rodden's perseverance, her redpoint campaign offers lessons we can apply to our own projects.

Savor the Little Victories

Instead of focusing on failure, notice any advent, no matter how small, that smacks of progress. "On *Meltdown,* if I made a slight amount of progress, like pulling an inch higher on the crux holds or I was able to take my foot off a foothold and think about moving it up, that was a victory," says Rodden. "These always kept me coming back for more." Each time you reach a new high point, that's a victory. Each time climbing through a crux feels a little easier, that's a victory. Each time you do the route with one less rest, that's a victory. Each time you grab that crux crimper and it feels a little bigger, that's a victory, too.

Don't Develop Crux Blinders

We tend to focus on a climb's hardest section and figure that, if we can't do it right off—or do so reliably—then there's no point in trying the route. This thinking, however, is backward because often you'll become stronger and more comfortable with a route's style while working it, until eventually you *can* do the crux. Or you might incorporate specific training to prepare for that crux. In the earliest phase, don't be shy about pulling past cruxes to work the rest of the climb. "On *Meltdown* I would go up, try the crux for a bit, get frustrated, get a little victory on another move somewhere, and that would keep me coming back," says Rodden. "The crux didn't come for a long time, so I tried to take in the rest of the route. I figured, if the rest is doable, then maybe I should focus on that for now instead of beating my head against the crux forever."

Go Bouldering

If you're unable to crank on or hang those piss-poor crux grips, boulder for a few weeks to build focus, finger strength, and power. With its emphasis on distilled

Abbey Smith and her bouldering-honed fingers of steel on the first ascent of *Breathless* (V11), Cordillera Blanca, Peru

difficulty, bouldering teaches you to zero in on minutiae: fine details like conditions, your skin, and nuances of the rock and movement. "Mentally learning how to dissect parts of a problem is really helpful," says Rodden; it's a skill set you can apply to ruthlessly deconstruct the crux of your project, as if it were just another boulder problem.

Meanwhile, the boulders' often miserly holds strengthen your fingers, and bouldering teaches you to be aggressive, hence powerful. "Out bouldering, I'd be forced to do things I would avoid on a route," says Rodden. "Like jumping for something or bearing down as hard as I could."

Link and Overlap Critical Sections

Build endurance on and for your project by linking its various sections. For instance, a Flatirons route I redpointed in autumn 2012 breaks down naturally into thirds; the first two-thirds is a pumpy sprint to a decent rest, and the top third is a sustained, extended boulder problem. I worked on getting the first two-thirds down, as a "redpoint" unto itself, to build my endurance. Then, if I was too pumped to continue, I'd hang at the bolt for a few minutes and then push for the top, focusing on how the final third felt with a pump on. I approached each section as a mini-route and endeavored to link each in its entirety before I strung them together.

The next step is linkage: If you fall off the crux, lower to a logical starting point one or two bolts down, and then climb back up through the crux again while torched. This concept teaches your muscles to fire when they are tired, and might even help refine beta by forcing you to find the most efficient sequences. Each time you overlap linkage, lower a little farther so you're that much more pumped at the crux. Eventually, you will be starting on the ground.

Don't Get Angry

Monster fits not only perturb others, they also hold you back by teaching you to associate failure with negative emotions. Screaming isn't cathartic—it only increases anger. Instead, fall off, give a whoop of fear or exhaustion to release any tension, vent a little in a regular voice, and then immediately channel your energy into acceptance. As you hang, think about what went right; next, consider what went wrong and how you'll fix it the next time.

Cultivating Endurance

It's a standard lament: "I can do all the moves on my route, but I can't put them together because I get so pumped. How do I build up my endurance?" Well, we're all endowed with a roughly 50-50 blend of fast-twitch muscle fibers, great for snap and power (anaerobic recruitment), and slow-twitch muscle fibers, which contract more slowly and over greater time, hence help with hanging on or enduring (aerobic recruitment). But we also all lean one way or the other in this ratio; thus climbers blessed with more fast-twitch fibers might be "power junkies," while those, like myself, with a preponderance of slow-twitch fibers are "enduro pigs." We enduro pigs naturally have good route endurance, but we can all always improve our baseline staying power. First, however, let's examine what "endurance" really is.

It's a common misconception that endurance equates to not getting pumped, and we even get it in our heads that the very best climbers *never* pump out, that they just keep hanging on effortlessly, even on 5.15. But 5.15 climbers might feel fatigue even on lowly 5.13s—simply because hard climbing is, well, hard. However, they keep climbing anyway. Thus endurance equates to the ability to recover and continue through difficult sequences *despite* being pumped. As Bill Ramsey, an enduro fiend who has put up 5.14s at the Red River Gorge's Motherlode cave, frames it, "Endurance is getting used to that feeling of doing very hard moves when you're a little bit fatigued." *In other words, endurance equals fatigue management.*

As a counterpoint, the sensation of being totally pumped, gasping, and useless, with lactic acid jacking through your system and your hands about to open, is more of an indicator that you're in poor shape—not just pumped. If you're fit, even on a route at your limit you might feel fatigue, but it will be a manageable, predictable condition.

Ramsey has five suggestions for building endurance: become comfortable climbing pumped, train for and master resting, increase your failure threshold, build your stamina, and play games on a climbing wall.

Become Comfortable Climbing Pumped

Expand your comfort zone such that you become used to always being *a little* tired while climbing. Boulderers in particular aren't accustomed to this sensation (their comfort zone is much smaller). They might go up a bolt or two, doing moves that are easy for them, then jump off pleading that they're "pumped" when they're really only mildly fatigued. Through repetition, you can habituate yourself to doing fairly hard moves with only 50 or 60 percent of your energy reserve or even less. Power-endurance gym climbs are good for this—go until you fall.

Train for and Master Resting

Ramsey doesn't train for endurance per se but instead focuses on learning how to rest when he is pumped, and then continue. "The really good route climbers know how to rest," he says. "They can get a hold that's not that great and still get a ton back, getting their heart rate down, breathing under control, flushing out the lactic acid, and hanging on with one hand and shaking out the other."

At the gym, Ramsey will climb to near-failure and then, at a rest stance, gradually build his reserves back up, taking first one hand off for a half-second shake, then his other hand off for a two-second shake, back to the original hand for a five-second shake, and so on, the shakeouts getting longer and longer until he's recovered. This tactic most accurately simulates resting on a hard rock climb where you'll crank a hard section, nearly blow out, perhaps encounter a decent hold above and feel so wiped you can barely take one hand off at first, but then you gradually recover. If you're simulating a rest on an artificial wall, use a technical or semisloping jug (a hold you have to work for), not some mindless handlebar.

To master resting:

- **Improve your hip flexibility and turnout.** The more you can suck into the wall and distribute your weight over your feet, the less your hands must bear: Ramsey estimates that each inch you can get closer to the stone makes you feel 10 pounds lighter. Try yoga and stretching, with an emphasis on frontal hip turnout. One good exercise is the butterfly (frog stretch).
- **Experiment with different footholds and body positions.** Hang straight on your bones, don't bend your elbows, and stand as low as possible. Play with less obvious holds like thumb catches and jams, and experiment, while shaking out, with pairing each hand up with a foot, not necessarily on the same side. Also, be aware that some rests improve when you have only one foot on the rock.
- **Strengthen your core.** Do 4x4s (see "Increase Your Failure Threshold" below), as well as standard exercises like crunches, leg

5

Nina Caprez settles into a creative heel-hook rest on the limestone of Siurana, Spain.

lifts, and front levers. A strong core lets you connect your feet to your torso, and take weight off your arms.

○ **Be in tune with your whole body.** Don't focus solely on recovering your forearms, even though they're screaming the loudest. Pay attention also to your heart rate, breathing, and nuances such as "Is my butt sagging out too far?" or "Is my calf getting pumped in this kneebar?" Don't be shy about shaking out or alternately resting every last body part.

○ **Learn how to rest actively.** We don't always get a two-handed bucket for rest stances, so practice recovery at one-handed stances as well as on the go. Sometimes a quick flick of the wrist is all it takes, or you can rest actively through easier sections by focusing on doing the moves efficiently, to slow your breathing and pulse rate.

Increase Your Failure Threshold

The goal with endurance is to become more resistant to failure, to extend your threshold of collapse. Rock climbing is one of the few sports that asks us to exert ourselves until we fail, so you should demand the same of your training. In the "climbing dojo," Ramsey seeks to create constant effort, constant motion, and constant exertion. Many of us try to cultivate endurance by doing multiple gym routes back to back, but Ramsey posits that even having a brief rest while lowering doesn't faithfully recreate the failure experience. His punishing tactics instead include 4x4s, building the burn, and Treadwalling.

4x4s

Identify four challenging yet doable eight- or nine-move boulder problems at your local gym. Do one problem, jump down, immediately do a slightly easier problem, jump down, do an easier one, jump down, and then finish on the easiest. If possible, downclimb the wall so that your core remains engaged, quickly shake out at the bottom, and then head up the next problem. To challenge yourself even more, wear a weight belt.

Building the Burn

After finishing your 4x4s (or a pumpy route or traverse), exploit the beneficial fatigue window you are feeling and jump on a campus board or system board with footholds. Hang off decent-but-challenging holds (at least a full finger pad), and bleed it all back, hand-by-hand, just like you would on rock. "The experience I'm trying to replicate is getting to a rest so wasted you can barely take one hand off at first," says Ramsey. "This builds recovery back while you're still on the wall."

Treadwalling

Ramsey also swears by the Treadwall, which he used diligently while living in rock-free South Bend, Indiana. Ramsey's tips:

- Set up routes that are all crimps, all pockets, all pinches, etc., to train specific grip strengths, and then tilt the wall one or two degrees steeper every week as you wire out the routes and get stronger. "It's all about gradually increasing the difficulty of what you're doing," he says.
- Play with linking the routes to stay on as long as possible. Put somewhat large rest holds out left near the Treadwall's start/stop button, so that you can pause the wall and shake out between climbs without stepping off.
- Play a laser-pointing game with a friend two to three times per session. Point out handholds (any feet) to your partner for a single, extended climb, say, around six minutes. A good pointer can take a climber right to the edge, then put her on better holds so that she gradually recovers.
- Do interval training with a partner to work on your power-endurance. The first person does one minute on the machine with laser pointing, one minute off, then two on, two off, and so on, up to four or five minutes, and then back down. You can swap out climbing and pointing duties during the off minutes if you prefer.

Alternatively, a method I often use at the gym is bouldering for an hour, and then climbing routes for an hour. Climbing routes while your power is already drained emphasizes efficiency, smart sequencing, and recovery.

Build Your Stamina

Having stamina (overall fitness or the ability to still climb after a long day of climbing) will bolster your endurance. Instead of squandering your session lapping easier routes, push yourself on redpoint, and then finish yourself off near the end. *Doing laps on a 5.12a won't make you stronger for a 5.13a; trying a 5.13a until you're blasted and then doing laps on a 5.12a will!* Pumping laps on easier climbs becomes beneficial only when you're already cooked.

Play Games on a Climbing Wall

Ramsey suggests that you play endurance games with friends, using friendly competitiveness to help push everyone. He likes to play add-on with four or five people. On a bouldering wall each person adds two moves per turn to an increasingly longer problem, using a laser pointer or stick to help with move recall. Toward the end, you might wind up doing a long route several times, totally working yourself.

5

THE STIFFIE QUICKDRAW

Sometimes when you are hanging draws, a bolt may be just out of reach. While the caveman approach is to tape a quickdraw to a short stick to make a "stiffie" (a rigid, supported quickdraw you ootch high to extend your reach), there is a better solution, one that won't become a spear in a fall. Veteran Colorado climber Tod Anderson, who climbs often with his son, Gordie, devised this draw so that Gordie wouldn't stress on reachy clips:

1. Procure a carabiner that uses a gate-latch system to stay open until it is clipped, such as the Mad Rock Trigger Wire. This will be your stiffie's top (bolt-side) biner.
2. Cut either supertape or one-inch tubular webbing in a strand long enough that, when looped and tied off in a water knot, it becomes standard dogbone length (about four to six inches). If you're up for carrying a longer stiffie, you can make the dogbone up to two feet long.
3. Use malleable wire to stiffen the dogbone. Anderson recommends home electrical wiring, specifically three-wire Romex NM-B W/G yellow cable; this jacketed copper wire is stiff enough to support your draw but also bends well, and the insulation adds protection between wire and webbing.
4. Snip off a section of wire about a half inch shorter than the looped webbing, and then tape its ends to prevent it from poking through the webbing.

5. Insert the wire into the looped webbing, and then complete your water knot so that the loop still runs slightly longer than the wire. Use duct or athletic tape to burrito both the dogbone and wire together, leaving adequate clipping eyes on either end of the tape wrap.

The legendary "Gordwah" (Gordie Anderson) demonstrates the stiffie draw. *Tod Anderson*

6. Slap your Trigger Wire on one end of the dogbone, and tape a short circlet of wire around the base of the biner, where it meets the draw.
7. Clip your bent-gate (rope-side) biner onto the other end of the dobgone, and use a rubber band to secure it. Now you too have a stiffie of grand proportions!
8. Cock the top biner with one hand, and press it up to your target bolt. The gate will automatically snap shut as it connects with the hanger.

Be careful when cocking the Trigger Wire, as it's a hungry mouth that will happily grab the rope or that clip you just passed—wait until you really need it. After using it and then reaching that bolt placed by the six-foot-five-inch first-ascent party, swap it out for a regular draw, and save the stiffie for the next stretcher clip. The easiest way to remove the stiffie from the bolt hanger is usually to push the replacement draw up from below.

A commercially available quickdraw called the Kong Frog also lets you push a connector up to bolt hangers and extend your reach. Or you can slap a Mad Rock Trigger Wire on the rope-side (rubberized, tight-looped) end of a draw to similarly gain a few inches.

RACK FOR SUCCESS

Over-the-shoulder padded gear slings and harness gear loops are great for racking trad protection, but there is no one-size-fits-all solution. It's better to be flexible and adaptable, depending on the route. Some thoughts on the advantages of each system, culled from multidiscipline master Tommy Caldwell:

- A gear sling is great for easier or slabby-to-vertical multipitch trad climbs, where you can keep your gear organized and centralized, and it's handy for handing off the rack at belay stations. In dihedral and flare climbs, harness-racked gear might pinch between your hips and the wall. To lighten the load on harder routes, you can even shoulder-rack on a thin Spectra or Dyneema sling instead of the standard padded sling.
- Racking your gear on your harness is great for overhanging climbs, where a sling would dangle low off your shoulder, out behind you in space; it's also great for face climbs, where a sling might feel awkward or cumbersome. And having your gear on your harness allows you to reach for a piece with either hand, which is great for splitter cracks, such as you find at Indian Creek, Utah.

On long pitches that eat gear, Caldwell recommends clipping the same pieces together. Say a route requires three No. 1 Camalots: You clip each piece on its own single biner, clip the first No. 1 off to your harness or gear sling, and then clip the other two No. 1s into the first piece's biner for easy access.

Colored tape lets you easily sort biners and pro, but it falls off over time. The most surefire method I've seen to mark your gear is to use nail polish. Only apply it to the metal components (stems or trigger pulls) of slung items like cams, to keep the chemicals from affecting the nylon.

SOLO TOP-ROPE IN STYLE: THE MINI TRAXION

Life being what it is—busy, chaotic, filled with less free time than we might like—it's often impossible to get out climbing with a partner. Fortunately, modern equipment permits climbers to top-rope alone. It's the staple of parents, misanthropes, and the self-employed everywhere—in only two hours, you can fire off a dozen pitches and get thoroughly pumped. Aficionados typically go with Petzl Mini Traxions or Micro Traxions, lightweight progress-capture pulleys that can be used in redundant pairs. The Traxions have become a go-to tool for big-wall free climbs, where it's often more efficient to work a route solo on top rope than with a partner. Mini Traxions are reliable, easy to use, and versatile. (Note: The following is not meant to replace Petzl's official product literature.)

Ten Easy Steps to Mini Traxioning

How to go about safely setting yourself up for a solo top-roping session, in 10 simple start-to-finish steps:

1. Anchor a beefy static rope to a bombproof anchor *below* the lip of the crag. (A static line limits stretch and will stand up to the toothed cams of the Mini Traxion better than a dynamic rope.) Running your rope from an anchor back over the lip and then down the face can abrade or cut the rope when it's weighted. You might have to rappel in to a bolted sport or trad anchor first and fix your rope from there. Use rope protectors as needed. You could even add a second fixed rope and run each Mini on a separate line.
2. Rap down or walk around—whatever's easiest.
3. Rig your top, primary Mini Traxion first. This is the first one to catch in a fall, while the lower one serves as backup.
4. Build a "chest harness" out of two sewn shoulder-length runners; put one over each shoulder, and cross them across your breastbone. This harness doesn't bear weight; it keeps the locking biner for the top Mini Traxion upright so that the pulley slides freely and you reduce the risk of cross-loading. For further safety, you could also use a real chest harness.
5. Thread your rope through the Mini Traxion as per Petzl's instructions (the device has a handy diagram), close it, and engage the trigger cam. Clip it into your belay loop with a locking biner, and lock the locker. *Always* use a locker designed to prevent cross-loading, like the DMM Belay Master 2. If you fall and cross-load

your Mini Traxion biner, the force might spring or bend the device open, which could be catastrophic.

6. Thread a small cinch strap through the X on your chest harness and then through the Mini Traxion's clipping eye. Tidy the strap up and tighten it; it attaches the pulley to your chest harness and keeps the locking biner upright and Mini Traxion oriented properly. Again, since this part of the system has no holding power, use any old cinch strap.

7. Rig your bottom Mini Traxion by threading it, closing it, and engaging the trigger cam; clip it into your belay loop with a locking biner below the upper Mini Traxion, and lock the locker. Use a screwgate oval (and not D) to minimize cross-loading. You may

Two Mini Traxions, cammed, rigged, sitting parallel on the rope, and ready to roll for solo top-roping

need to disengage the cams on either or both Mini Traxions to feed enough slack through to clip them in, but once you've done so, immediately reengage the cams. If they are rigged correctly, your Mini Traxions will sit parallel on the rope.

8. Double-check that the trigger cams on both Mini Traxions are engaged. Now climb up a little so that you can sit back, test your system, and remove any slack. My first day using these tools I didn't engage the cams or double-check them; it's a good thing that the route I was on was below my limit. The pulleys will slide much the same whether they are engaged or not; when cammed, they'll make a reassuring raspy or mechanical sound you'll soon learn to recognize.

9. Finally, attach something weighing a few pounds to the rope just off the ground, so that the Mini Traxions have resistance down low and you don't have to manually pull slack through. (They will slide better the higher you climb because of the rope's increased weight.) I usually clove-hitch in my crag pack or a rack of draws or trad gear.

10. Climb to the top, and clip into the anchor directly. Now introduce slack into the line to uncam or derig your Mini Traxions, which you can do by pulling up a length of rope and clove-hitching it to your harness. Rappel down for another lap, move your rope to another climb, etc.

5

MiNi TRAXiON NiNJA SKiLLS

These pointers will make your Mini-ing smooth like butter:

- In lieu of the "chest harness," try girth-hitching the thin band of a microheadlamp band through the top Mini Traxion's clipping hole, and then slip the band over your head like a necklace. Bonus: You're now carrying an extra headlamp.
- If you wish, back up your belay loop with an anchor tether, tied-off sling, or small sewn sling girth-hitched through your leg loops and waist belt to which you also clip the Mini Traxion lockers.
- Solo top-roping works best on routes that run straight up and down and aren't much more than gently overhanging. However, if you are trying a super-steep or traversing climb on which you might end up dangling in space, carry a jumar with etriers to ascend the rope or get free of the Traxions; or at a minimum carry a lightweight alpine etrier, Petzl Tibloc, shoulder sling, and a pear-shaped locking biner to jury-rig a quick ascender. You should also clip your rope into any and all directional gear, to keep it close to the rock; and should you fall, be prepared to "auto-batman" for short distances with the Mini Traxions, though clearly you wouldn't want to travel more than a few feet this way. I also carry a couple of draws or shoulder slings to clip into fixed pro and rest.
- Because the pulleys only travel in one direction, you can't try crux moves repeatedly. If a hard section's coming and you're already flamed, consider

hanging before you get there so you have a better crack at doing it straight through your first (and only) time.

○ Avoid climbing clear to your anchor knot before you clip in, as the Mini Traxions will be harder to uncam after they are locked up at the knot. (It's like jumaring, when you get too close to a piece and then have a nightmare of a time unclipping it.) Hang two trad or extendo draws slightly lower than the anchor knot as clip-in points, and clip in directly to them and then pull up slack to uncam the Mini Traxions.

○ Because setting up the top Mini Traxion is time-consuming, you could uncam it at the anchor but leave it rigged on the rope and your "chest harness" if you're doing laps off the same anchor. That way you can rappel with the device sliding along with you below your Grigri or rappel device, recam it once you're back on the ground, slap your lower Mini back on, and head up again without futzing around. Beware potential logjamming or cross-loading between your top Traxion and your rappel device.

5

Multipitch Mini Traxioning

The Mini Traxion also lets you scope out multipitch routes without a partner. The basic rigging is the same with multipitch Mini Traxioning, but there are a few subtle differences.

Seven Tips for Rope, Anchor, and Multipitch Mini Traxion Management

On a multipitch climb, you'll likely be using a longer (80- or 100-meter) static line, which can be an unruly beast. You'll also need extra carabiners, slings, and pro for rigging. To keep things streamlined:

James Lucas uses his Mini Traxions to figure out *Father Time* (VI 5.13b), Middle Cathedral Rock, Yosemite National Park, California. *Mikey Schaeffer*

1. **Learn the "rabbit ears" figure 8.** This useful knot for top and intermediary anchors lets you equalize the load on a static line with only two locking carabiners, assuming you have a double-bolt anchor. It's also easy to untie after it has been weighted.

   a. Make a big bight (about three to four feet) in your rope.

   b. Tie a standard figure 8 on a bight, leaving a two-foot bight (loop) emerging from the hole.

   c. Feed this bight back into the hole the same way it exits.

   d. Girth-hitch the end of this bight up and around the *entire knot,* including the two rabbit ears now protruding from the hole.

   e. Hold onto the ears and adjust the knot to equalize these two clip-in points. When the knot is properly dressed, the two ears will emerge cleanly and separately from the hole.

2. **Don't huck the rope.** Bigger cliffs have bigger features and bigger weather (read: winds), meaning your rope can snarl or hang up if you cast it off blindly. Keep your rope with you, letting it unfurl as you descend. Either butterfly coil it in long bights, and stack it across your shoulders; or better, stack a butterfly coil on a Metolius Rope Hook clipped off to a gear loop. The rope should always feed off the top of the stack.

How to tie a "rabbit ears" figure 8.

3. **Beware the bulge:** Single lines running over lips, ledges, or bulges are subject to abrasion and even cutting, especially when they are loaded. As you rappel, scope for and avoid these features, or mitigate accordingly. Rope-protector sleeves are good for edges, ledges, and arêtes that you can't easily circumnavigate. For bulges, fix your rope to a point below them so that your weighted rope won't rub against the rock. Carry quickdraws and a rack for this purpose.

4. **Anchors, anchors, anchors.** Fix your rope to intermediate anchors as you descend so that it's aligned with the rock and into multiple load-bearing points; use either the rabbit ears or a clove hitch, which is easy to untie. Also, clove-hitch into single points of protection where useful.

5. **The switchover.** Say you're rappeling down 400 feet from the top of a 2000-foot cliff, to a hanging stance. What's the easiest way to escape your Grigri and get into the Mini Traxions? Chris Weidner, Mini master extraordinaire, keeps an anchor tether girth-hitched to his harness. At the switchover, he can fifi into a quick anchor, feed a few feet of slack through his Grigri (keeping it on the rope), rig his Mini Traxions, test and weight them, and then remove his Grigri. Having been backed up by his anchor the whole time, Weidner then unclips his anchor tether, removes the anchor (if need be), and sets off climbing.

6. **To weight or not to weight?** On a multipitch route, the rope will quickly weigh enough to keep the Minis sliding, though feeding will still be tricky on the bottom 40-odd feet. You can either pull the rope through manually, use whatever is handy for weighting the rope (like your approach shoes or rack), or coil up the rope's extra tail and let it hang below.

7. **Knots, knots, knots.** Back up your Minis by tying knots in the rope below you as you climb. A rough guideline is every 30 or 40 feet, but you can also do this whenever you get scared, each time you reach a stance, or any time you're already hanging. Clipping quickdraws back in under the Minis also backs you up to some degree and keeps the rope out of your crotch.

5

To learn more about belaying yourself on top rope, consult Petzl's official literature (specifically www.petzl.com/us/outdoor/product-experience/self-belay-solo-climbing /introduction-us) or explore their website in general (www.petzl.com).

MULTiPiTCH MiNi TRAXiON TOOLS

One nice thing about the Mini Traxion is that it also lets you scope out multipitch routes without a partner. Here are some key tools:

- Assisted-braking belay or rappel device, such as a Grigri, to facilitate rope and anchor maneuvers
- Rope protectors
- Multiple locking carabiners
- Quickdraws and extendable trad draws
- Trad rack
- Anchor tether
- Jumar and an etrier
- Helmet

AIRBORNE: WHY, HOW, WHEN, AND WHERE TO FALL

On a primal level, dropping into space, whether you are tied into a 10-millimeter rope or on the Devil's Drop at the amusement park, is scary. Humans are hardwired to equate being airborne with dying. It's likewise natural to want to avoid the void, an instinct that's prevented our stumbling off cliff edges through the eons. Unfortunately, as much as fear of falling and exposure contributes to self-preservation, it also prevents you from climbing your best by introducing the undesirable element of terror.

Think of how visceral your first lead fall felt. Gravity pulled with heretofore-unthinkable force, air whistled past your ears, the rock flashed by in a blur of color, and the ground rushed up at impossible speed. Then, miraculously, you slowed to a halt as your belayer caught you. Depending on your temperament, you either loved the adrenaline and craved more, felt somewhat neutral and realized that in the future

Dan Mirsky logs monster air off *Omaha Beach* (5.14a), Red River Gorge, Kentucky.

falling would probably be no big deal, or abhorred the sensation and wanted never to whip again—or some combination of all three. Perhaps subsequent falls provoked different responses, or maybe you later took an injurious fall and formed a more tentative relationship with gravity. Or perhaps, like me, your fear ebbs and flows, and is strongest early in the season.

To make falling a tool that works for you, it helps to know why, how, when, and where to fall—to fall as needed to habituate yourself so that fear isn't holding you back, but also to recognize when it's best not to fall and to seek other solutions. More and more I see gym-bred climbers whipping outside with impunity because they have learned to do so indoors: The padded floor will eventually stop you even if your belayer cannot, goes the reasoning. Well, yes, but outside you can crater into rock or the ground, which aren't nearly as soft. The real world is more complex and riskier.

Why to Fall

I tend to climb tight, like an overly wound watch, when I'm preoccupied with whipping. My movements become staccato, I overgrip, my arms or legs might quiver, and I inevitably come that much closer to falling—or do fall. It's a devilish paradox. Becoming comfortable with dropping through the void, especially with repeated falls on a project, frees you to climb your smoothest.

First try leading a climb with fall potential that is safe but mildly intimidating: say, 10-plus-footers. It doesn't matter if you hang or lob—just get to the anchors. Now leave the rope up and run the climb again on top rope, noticing how it feels the second time. That smooth, devil-may-care playfulness is what you want to cultivate on lead. You do so by becoming comfortable falling until you realize that the crux whipper is no big deal and you have pushed the anxiety from your mind, which leaves you free to just climb. (Pioneering Southeast climber and rock philosopher Arno Ilgner explores this topic in greater depth in two great books: *The Rock Warrior's Way* and *Espresso Lessons*. I encourage you to read them.)

Watch videos of the best climbers trying their hardest climbs and notice which direction they're looking when they hit the end of the rope. They're not looking down, freaking out about their belayer catching them or the ground rushing up. They're staring up at the holds that just spat them off, puzzling through what went wrong. While they were climbing, they were focused only on making the moves, not on their potential to fall off those moves. Even as they became airborne, they're still thinking about the sequence—falling becomes an afterthought, an accepted and logical consequence of realizing their physical potential.

How to Fall

If you master falling just like any skill, it starts to feel second nature instead of foreign or frightening. The best place to practice is on overhanging sport climbs with no landing obstacles (ledges, spikes, or large protruding holds). Indoors, pick a gently to severely overhanging panel without big volumes, top ropes, or auto-belays. Whether indoors or out, you want a clean drop, with nothing to distract you or to get hung up on.

Grab a trusted belayer and try this drill:

- ○ Climb to a high bolt (at least four or five clips up), tag the clip, and then have your belayer pay out an extra foot or so of slack. Let go and sag onto the rope, taking this top-rope mini-whipper to build trust in the system. Repeat until you no longer feel trepidation or a startle response when falling.
- ○ Now climb until your last clipped bolt is just below your waist and then let go, ensuring that the rope is always either between your legs or coming off the hip opposite your direction of travel. As you take a four- or five-footer, be conscious of your hands. If you're volleying into the air, grab the rope above your knot, and focus on staying upright. If the wall is slabby, keep your feet and hands out in front with your toes or soles activated and your palms flat (like a mime in a box), ready to push off. Have your belayer give a soft catch so that you gradually stop. If your belayer weighs less than you, this, coupled with rope stretch, should happen naturally. If he weighs the same or more, however, he'll need to feed a little extra rope or jump up and in. (Hard, short, abrupt catches, aka "short roping," can swing your climber into the rock. You're not doing her any favors, unless you're trying to keep her from smacking the ground or some other obstacle.) Take three or more baby whippers until they no longer provoke fear.

5

- Climb until your last clipped bolt is at your feet, and log a few proper double-body-length falls, the kind that deposit you one bolt down. Do this until it's boring.

Other factors:
- On giant whippers, coils of rope may fall along with you. Keep your hands on the rope above your knot as you drop to "throw" the slack upward, away from your person.
- Bigger falls can be better than small ones if they drop you past a dangerous obstacle like a block, ledge, ramp, roof lip, etc. In these cases, coach your belayer to give you extra slack or jump high, halting you below the hazard.
- Belayers should be extra attentive down low, in general on the first three pieces or bolts. Also, at the first clip on very over-hanging climbs, a hard catch or a falling climber outweighing his belayer can cause a climber and belayer to collide midair. Mitigate such "clacking" by anchoring the belayer or preclipping higher up the climb.

This falling clinic can help whenever your head needs a tune-up. Just like you honk into a handkerchief to clear your nose, so too can you honk fear cobwebs out of your melon.

When to Fall

Often, unforeseen falls (those sudden slips when your foot skates or a hold breaks) can be more frightening than the ones you can predict. However, deliberate falling will make you better at surviving and preparing for those unforeseen whippers; you'll become more like the proverbial cat, ready to land on its feet.

Controlled falling is not only good practice but also a useful escape hatch in the following situations:
- When you are too pumped to make the next clip, you could jump off beforehand to avoid an even bigger whipper, especially if you're so nuked you won't be able to hang onto the quickdraw.

- When your head or body isn't ready for a runout, you could take a deliberate fall low into the runout while you are still safe to rest and regroup.
- When you've climbed off-route, it can be safer to jump than to continue or traverse out of there.
- When you encounter dangerous loose rock, with no way around it, and don't want to risk grabbing it, a whipper is preferable to prying off that guillotine death block.
- When you want to reverse out of a situation but are too tired to downclimb or cannot downclimb a difficult sequence, you could fall instead.
- When something on the ground needs your immediate attention, such as a dogfight or an accident, a controlled fall could let you escape quickly.

5

Where to Fall

It's not always appropriate to fall outside, especially when you're trad climbing or are on loose rock, on moderate or ledgy terrain, or on dodgy fixed gear. Some years ago at a sport crag called the Palace in northern Colorado, my wife, Kristin, and I were climbing across a gulch from a young woman (part of a big college group), who was attempting an overhanging 5.11 prow while her friends cheered her on. Hearing the commotion, we looked up to see the woman taking whipper upon gleeful whipper. The catch? She was going for the chains on a mild runout 20 feet over a giant, jutting ledge and would stop only a foot or so off the ledge each time. What seemed like a rad adventure to this crew was in reality a series of near double-leg-breakers barely averted thanks to benevolent rock gods and, one would assume, a relatively attentive belayer. She could have just as easily needed to be rescued.

Before you start any new climb outdoors, evaluate the terrain, risk level, and fall potential every step of the way, and make sure you're up for it. That's right: Stand below the climb and assess what a fall in each section means, just like you run through the rest of the beta. You can't rewind gravity. Let's consider the fall-potential safety spectrum from the good to the bad to the ugly:

Good Falls

There are several situations in which falling might be considered relatively safe:

- **Clean air.** The wall is so overhanging that you'll drop into space, or it's monolithic or has no protrusions, such as ledges, ramps, sharp arêtes, roof lips, dihedrals, or big blocks.
- **Bomber gear.** The route has well-placed new or modern bolts and well-seated, bombproof (A1–A2) nut and cam placements, ideally doubled down in crux situations.
- **Good ropework.** The rope runs smoothly and cleanly, out away from the stone, and will not abrade over bulges or rub across sharp features, such as roof lips, flakes, or arêtes.
- **Good fall line.** The fall line is more or less directly in line with the rope, or if the route traverses, the sequence doesn't move so far from your protection that the gear becomes meaningless and could cause you to pendulum into some obstacle.

Bad Falls

There are situations in which falling is not the greatest idea:

- **Slabby or broken terrain.** The rock below you is less than vertical, broken up, or has dangerous features, such as ledges, ramps, sharp arêtes, roof lips, dihedrals, or big blocks. Such features are unfortunately common on moderate (5.9 or easier) terrain. Thus even on mellow ground, don't preload a big fall if you don't have to; protect well and often, even when you are climbing below your limit. Another hazard is falling off a bulge or roof with protection under the lip; a soft, extra-slack, dynamic catch should gradually halt you, but a harder belay might slap you against the stone below after you arc through space.
- **Iffy gear.** The route has sketchy old bolts, such as quarter-inchers, bolts with profoundly rusty hangers, and spinners; traditional gear placed in loose, wet, hollow, dirt-covered, or friable rock; or marginal traditional placements (A3–A4) such as flared-out cams or wobbly, tipped-out nuts that are better suited to body weight (hanging, not falling).

Matt Wilder in a "no-fall" position on the first ascent of
Viceroy (5.14a/b X), Castle Rock, Boulder Canyon, Colorado

5

AVOID THE VOID

Here are a few alternatives to taking an undesirable fall:

- **Grab the draw.** Some people are ashamed to grab a draw instead of taking the ride, but this is silly thinking. Falls wear your rope out over time, so if you can avoid a pointless fall, do so. When you go for a quickdraw, either grab it by the top biner or dogbone, and then clip your rope in, or first grab the bottom biner before moving your hand higher to clip. *Never try to clip the rope in with your hand still in the bottom biner; doing so can crush or sever your fingers.*
- **Bail.** If you are uncertain about continuing, leave a bail biner or quick link on a bolt or sacrifice some trad gear, and rappel or have your belayer lower you. Gear is replaceable—you aren't! As with all things in climbing, double down when possible: Put a biner or quick link on the bolt below you, or nest two or more pieces instead of one.
- **Aid through.** On sport climbs, you can sometimes fifi directly into a bolt and walk your feet up, reaching high to rig a top rope on the next clip. You can also bring a trad draw (with its handy shoulder sling) to fashion an impromptu etrier, clipping it directly into the bolt to stand tall on tension and reach high for better holds or the next clip. On trad climbs, especially cracks, you can aid or employ hybrid "fraid" (free-aid) climbing, placing pieces and pulling or fifing as needed.
- **Set up a top rope.** Lower off, and then walk around or do an adjacent climb to set up a top rope. Out of the gate you can also aid up, moving from bolt to bolt with an extendo stick-clip, to rig a top rope.
- **Jump before you fall.** If a controlled jump seems preferable to climbing up into an out-of-control-whipper scenario, then prepare your belayer, let go, and jump.
- **Downclimb.** Back in the trad days, climbers were skilled at downclimbing, which is now somewhat of a lost art. The best way to become proficient is to just do it: Practice at the boulders or on your warm-ups. Focus on straightening your arms, creating visual space between your torso and the rock, and scanning for footholds before you step down onto them.

○ **Subpar ropework.** The rope is running around or across sharp features like roof lips, flakes, or arêtes, or is otherwise pinned against the rock by zigzagging or too-short quickdraws, creating friction, abrasion, and drag. Ropes have sliced in such falls.

○ **Sketchy fall line.** If you are well to the side of the gear, you risk taking a massive, slamming pendulum. This scenario most classically occurs when a leader traverses out of a dihedral but does not protect adequately near the edge, risking a gnarly, pancaking lob back into the opposite wall.

Ugly Falls

And then there are those situations in which you really must not fall at all—these ugly falls are the same as bad falls, except with a runout, say 10 feet or higher above your gear. As forces multiply because of greater airtime, so too does the strain on each point in the system and the potential for catastrophe.

5

GEAR

Keep the Nylon Burly, the Metal Shiny, and the Shoes Sticky

CLIMBING IS A PUNISHING SPORT, and we wear out gear in short order—we need to maintain and eventually replace it, both for performance and safety reasons. Fortunately, caring for gear is not rocket science, and almost everything you need to know about a specific product will be covered in its hangtags and manufacturer literature. *(Note: None of the information presented herein is meant to replace official product literature. When in doubt, check manufacturer specifications and recommendations.)*

Our safety equipment is made out of nylon, metal, or plastic. Since nylon and metal have all the holding power, we'll examine these two categories and the subcategories within each before finishing with that most critical of items, the rock shoe.

NYLON

The synthetic fiber nylon has revolutionized climbing, giving us reliable ropes, slings, cordelettes, sit harnesses, and quickdraw dogbones. But before we go into the specific categories of nylon gear, we'll cover a few universal nylon inspection points. (Note: I use the generic term *nylon* to describe all subtypes and brand names like nylon, polyethylene, perlon, Spectra, Dyneema, Dynex, etc.)

WHERE SHOULD I STORE CLiMBiNG GEAR?

6

Store your gear in a dry, dark place away from chemicals, solvents, and heat and light sources (including sunlight and powerful indoor lamps, which can also produce nylon-damaging ultraviolet-light radiation). Some climbers have dedicated gear closets, while others use plastic bins or milk crates. If you use containers, make sure they've never held a chemical agent like cleaning supplies or gasoline, and clean them with water and dishwashing soap to remove any contaminants. Also, never put your gear away wet or it will molder; if you're caught in a rainstorm and your rack gets soaked let it dry before you cache it back home. Keep ropes either in their factory bag or a dedicated rope bag.

Also, be careful about where you store your gear during transport to the cliffs. Keep it in your crag pack, don't drop your precious rack and rope atop some random parking lot when jumping into your buddy's car, and don't huck your rack, draws, and rope into the dirt at the cliff. Keep your gear clean to extend its life span and to protect it from contaminants, many of which are invisible.

MARiNE ENViRONMENTS

Because of the peculiar corrosive effect the salts in the air, water, and on the rock near the sea can have on metal and nylon, thoroughly rinse your gear (rope, harness, biners, draws, rack, etc.) in fresh water and air-dry it each time after you climb by the sea. This precaution will also keep sand from gunking up the small moving parts on your carabiners, belay devices, and cams. Metolius Climbing even recommends spraying their cam heads with Cam Lube or WD-40 prior to seaside climbing, and then wiping off the excess lube with a rag. Rinse and dry them, and then reapply lubricant to the cam heads again before putting them away.

○ **Exposure to ultraviolet-light radiation.** Ropes, cordelettes, slings, dogbones, and anchor webbing left in the sun for extended periods bleach, dry, crack, and weaken profoundly. One study found that the major drop (approximately 16 percent)

6

in strength with slings came in the first 10 weeks of sun exposure, with incremental drops after that. Nylon deteriorates quickly in the sun. So be wary of any in situ gear you encounter. *Even a seemingly new-looking fixed sling or quickdraw might be weak—you never know how long it's been there.* Red flags include stiff or crispy material and discoloration (bleaching). Climbers have perished from trusting "white" rappel slings that turned out to be ancient, blanched slings that were formerly of some other, darker color. If you encounter white nylon, feel its texture, and make sure it was indeed white in the first place before you consider using it. Better yet, carry a belay knife to cut away old slings, and add new, reliable ones at commonly used rappel anchors. Your life is surely worth that eight dollars in new webbing and rappel rings.

- **Exposure to the elements.** The elements include the sun, wind, rain, snow, ice, etc., all of which contribute to rotting and deterioration.
- **Exposure to chemical agents.** Contaminated slings and even ropes have failed in real-world and testing scenarios. Keep your gear away from petroleum products, cleaning supplies, solvents, caustics, car batteries, and the like. Jim Karn of Metolius Climbing cites one or two ropes that climbers at the Shawangunks in New York had which failed after exposure to fumes from car batteries, an insidious invisible contaminant. The ropes had been stored on the back shelf of a Volkswagen van over the van battery, and this airborne exposure compromised the fibers.
- **Abrasion.** Rope or slings running over or against edges can fray or cut; if you see substantial abrasion or multiple broken fibers, retire the equipment.
- **Cyclic loading.** Repeated falls (such as on fixed quickdraws) and nylon-on-nylon rubbing (e.g., jumaring with a daisy chain girth-hitched to your belay loop) cause repeated stress to nylon fibers and can deform or weaken them.

Ropes

As ropes are costly, it's nice to prolong a beloved cord's life span as long as you safely can. Try these three pointers:

1. **Clean your rope.** Keep dirt, grit, and gravel particles from grinding into and abrading your rope by flaking it in a rope bag and not stepping on it when it's on the ground. Not only does keeping it clean protect the nylon fibers, but a dirty, gritty, or even wet rope becomes like a serrated blade sawing through metal, such as carabiners, belay devices, and anchor hardware. To clean a rope, hand-wash it in lukewarm water in a contaminant-free container using a mild household face or body soap—and *never* use bleach. You could also use a commercial soap called ReviveX Climbing Rope Cleaner Concentrate. Regardless of the soap you use, rinse your rope thoroughly, and hang it to dry out of direct sunlight. Petzl also states that you can clean their ropes in a washing machine on the 30-degree Celsius delicate synthetic setting, without the spin cycle, though manufacturer recommendations may vary. A good time to clean your rope is before it obtains that dreaded black coating (dirt plus aluminum oxide, from running through metal).

2. **Switch rope ends after every pitch.** This tactic prevents twists from the tie-in knot and gives each side of the rope time to recover its elasticity, especially after a whipper session. "Ropes attenuate force by stretching," says Karn. "It's the only part of the system that relies on elasticity to work. When you fall, you stretch the rope out, and it takes awhile to recover." Thus the older the rope or the more falls it's held, the more it will have lost elasticity because of that stretching. Slow the aging process by switching rope ends after you lower, especially after repeated whippers, in which the impact forces on the fibers mount with every fall.

3. **Store your rope *uncoiled* in a rope bag.** This practice limits twisting, keeps the rope out of ultraviolet light, and protects it against contaminants.

6

A few common rope questions, answered:

How do I undo the factory coil without making my rope kinky?
- Put your hand through the eye of the coiled roped and unspool it off your forearm, coil by coil. According to Randy Leavitt of Maxim Ropes, "The most important thing is to proceed slowly, then slow it down again. Never assume you are close enough to the end to just drop the remaining coil and start pulling—the rope will get tangled." Once you've unspooled the cord, flake it five or six times for good measure.
- In a big room, say at the gym, unspool your rope out straight end to end or with as few bends as possible, and then do the same starting from the opposite side. Repeat as necessary.
- Pull your rope through anchors the long way the first few days using it (see below). Also, be aware that belaying your second through an upper redirect on multipitch climbs can kink a new rope—that is, the tension caused by having your second top-roped above you through a higher biner on the anchor will snarl the rope. Instead, belay your second directly off your belay loop the first few times out.

What do I do if my rope pigtails after lowering?
This usually happens to new ropes and/or ropes threaded through sport anchors that have an uneven number of chain links (and no rings) or anchors with two widely spaced bolts, introducing double 90-degree bends. The quickest fix is to pull the rope through the long way, from the side you lowered on, getting the other tail up off the ground so that it can unwind freely; this approach also reduces the chance of any kinks logjamming at the chains.

When should I retire my rope?
So much depends on usage, the type of climbing you do, abrasion, wear, how much you fall, and so on. Kolin Powick, director of global quality at Black Diamond Equipment, says that you should start with manufacturer's recommendations. For example, Sterling's guidelines are:
- Extensive and daily use: three to six months

- Weekly use: two to three years
- Occasional use: three to five years

However, these are just recommendations—you're responsible for inspecting your rope for wear every time you climb. "The part of ropes that wears the most is typically the 10 to 15 feet near both ends," says Powick. "This is where you typically fall, and then pull back up to the highest draw. The constant falling and dogging back up causes the end sections to get beat up more quickly than, say, the midsection." Hence when the rope ends become fat, soft, or badly frayed, it's time for either retirement or judicious trimming (see below).

6

Other red flags include:
- **Thin or flat spots or a damaged (fuzzy) sheath.**
- **Exposed core (aka core shot).** When the sheath has been worn or cut such that you can see the rope's white inner core, which can happen from dropped rocks, abrasion, wear over an edge, etc.
- **Fat ropes.** When a rope gets worn, it usually expands and its sheath becomes fuzzier. When it becomes difficult to belay (to feed and suck slack through the device), it's probably time to retire the rope.
- **Soft ropes.** An old rule of thumb holds that if you can find a soft spot such that you can fold the rope back on itself, pinch it, and *not* see any light through the bend, then the rope has a significant soft or weak spot and should likely be retired.
- **Degradation from ultraviolet light.** If you can use your fingernail to scratch off sheath material, it's time for a new cord.

How do I trim a fuzzy or core-shot rope?
- With middle-marked ropes, always cut equal lengths from both ends, keeping the middle marker squarely *in the middle* to avoid accidents.
- Wrap the fuzzy, core-shot, or cutting site in athletic tape, and then slice it under tension with a sharp blade. (If you have access to a hot knife gun use that, as it will automatically seal the ends.)
- Melt the ends to avoid fraying and sheath slippage. You can use a cigarette lighter and then tamp down and roll the gooey mess on a flat, hard surface such as concrete to seal it.

6

○ Affix a piece of tape to the end noting the rope's new length to remind you that your 70 meter cord is now a 65 meter, then a 60 meter, etc.

How do I mark the middle of my rope?

BlueWater Ropes' literature says it's fine to use a marker as long as you use a water-based laundry marker. However, Powick says that you never know what chemicals are in any marker, so if you're concerned, use a dedicated rope marker from a rope manufacturer. Years ago there was much furor over markers and marking after International Mountaineering and Climbing Federation (UIAA) testing showed that the middle marker weakens a rope, in particular fibers in the sheath, though the fall forces generated in the tests vastly exceeded normal real-world scenarios (i.e., if you're falling half a rope length onto that middle marker, chances are something's gone horribly wrong anyway). If you must mark your rope, avoid solvent-based markers and don't mark it near the end, where it's more likely to load in a fall. You should only be marking the middle anyway, to avoid confusion with multiple marks on long pitches and rappels.

My rope came into contact with sunscreen, bug juice, and/or gasoline. Is it still safe?

As Powick puts it, incidental contact (you had one of these agents on your hands and then touched the rope) is probably OK, but if your rope is saturated for whatever reason, then it's a real concern. Basically, anything you can safely apply to your hands shouldn't be particularly dangerous, though it might affect the rope's feel and handling. Meanwhile, gas, oil, and other petroleum products shouldn't necessarily compromise strength but will certainly change the feel and reduce confidence in your rope's strength. Moreover, some petroleum products could have nasty, potentially dangerous additives—you never know. *When in doubt, retire the rope.*

I've had a brand-new, in-the-factory-bag rope in my closet for 10 years. Can I still use it?

First consult the manufacturer's recommendations for help deciding. If you're sure the rope saw no dampness, chemicals, rodents, etc., it might be as good as new. Powick says Black Diamond tested a 20-year-old properly stored rope, and it had no reduction in strength. However, if in doubt, buy a new rope: Why feel skeptical about your very lifeline?

Slings and Cordelettes

Whatever name they go by, slings and cordelettes are subject to the same basic principles affecting all nylon. Inspect them for general signs of abrasion, including frayed strands and worn stitching or bar tacks. Also look for damage from ultraviolet light in the form of bleaching, stiffness, or crispness.

6

Harnesses

Like your rope, your harness simply must not fail. Inspect your harness regularly for wear, especially if you climb often or use it for burly tasks like wall climbing or equipping routes. Begin by keeping a watchful eye on your tie-in points, often the first things to degrade. (Many harnesses have handy wear indicators on the belay loops or tie-in points.) "If you've worn out the rope guards, it's time to get a new harness," says Karn. "Once you're starting to wear into the structural part it's stupid to keep climbing on it." Also monitor your buckles, looking for deformation, pitting, grooving, corrosion (especially if you climb near saltwater), and other signs of wear. As Powick puts it, "Badly pitted or flakey aluminum buckles can be weaker." And a weak harness is a deadly harness.

Of particular concern is the belay loop, especially following the 2006 death of free-climbing legend Todd Skinner in Yosemite Valley (California) when his worn-out belay loop failed while he was rappeling. This all-important, hyperstrong component (the belay loop on my current harness is good to 25 kilonewtons) is intended for clipping into anchors and for attaching belay and rappel devices. As Powick writes, "Guides teach that the belay loop is for metal," a good rule of thumb. However, some climbers also girth-hitch daisy chains, slings, or an anchor tether to it to clean anchors, to jumar, and so on, *which is a bad idea*. To preserve the loop's integrity, and to prevent nylon-on-nylon friction or sawing and cyclic loading as happens when you jumar, instead girth-hitch your daisy or anchor tether through your tie-in points. Inspect your belay loop regularly for deformation or fraying, rotating it through your leg loops and waist belt to review every last segment. "Many harness manufacturers put a protective layer of webbing on the belay loop (intended to protect the bar tacks), so you don't necessarily need to panic at the first sign of fraying," says Powick. However, if you note excessive fraying that makes you feel uneasy, it's time for a new harness. Don't just duct-tape the problem spot and keep climbing.

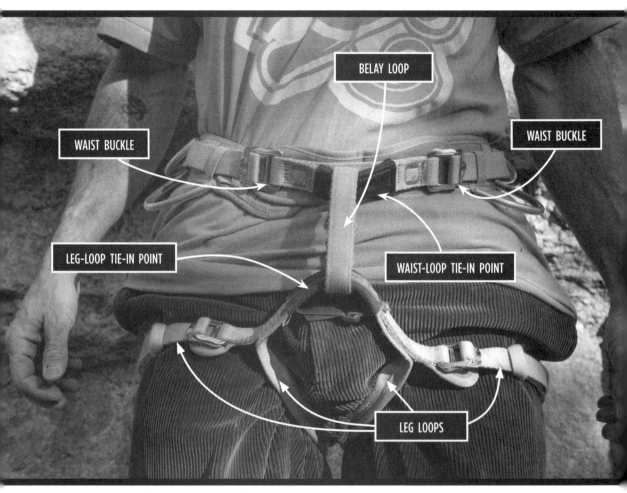

Inspect these parts of your harness regularly.

In terms of cleaning, Black Diamond Equipment recommends that you machine-wash their harnesses in warm water on the gentle cycle using mild soap (never use bleach!), though manufacturer recommendations may vary. As with all things nylon, air-dry it away from ultraviolet light and sunlight.

Quickdraw Dogbones

Inspect your dogbones regularly for obvious signs of abrasion, degradation from ultraviolet light, and general wear. Pay particular attention to fixed draws, standard quickdraw or sling setups left in place for a season or more. These are subject not only to the elements but to cyclic loading: catching the same falls repeatedly, which both hammers the nylon and abrades the draws across a singular spot if they're rubbing the rock. In one illuminating test Black Diamond Equipment ran on 15 former-fixed-draw samples from Rifle, Colorado, two Spectra (nylon) dogbones failed at only 790 and 810 foot-pounds, "well into the conceivable load range, even for a soft-catch sport climbing fall," wrote Powick. Even scarier, he added, "I've definitely heard of several quickdraw or sling failures in the field (even in a few gyms) where the nylon draws are continually rubbing against the abrasive texture of the wall." If that old fixed draw looks sketchy, remove or replace it so that others aren't tempted to trust it.

To clean your dogbones, hand-wash with warm water and a mild detergent (never use bleach!), then air-dry them away from direct sunlight.

METAL

We all expect that nylon will wear out, but we tend not to think the same of metal perhaps because of its heavy, elemental, and seemingly permanent nature. And so climbers abuse their racks, draws, and biners for years with only cursory inspections, then they act shocked when it's finally revealed—usually by a horrified partner—to be lethal garbage. It could also be that metal products are expensive, and so we stupidly push them well past their expiration date.

Inspect for certain universals, be it on an all-metal item like a carabiner or wired nut, or the metal components of a belay device or cam. Obvious deformation, grooving (one millimeter or larger), gouges, pitting, cracking, deep dings, corrosion, and so on are clear signs it's time to retire a piece, but there are also more subtle markers. We'll look at specific care for the major categories of carabiners, wired nuts, cams, and belay devices. *(Note: When in doubt, refer to manufacturer literature.)*

Carabiners

Inspect your biners regularly for wear, especially irregularities in the rope-bearing surface (sometimes called the cradle or crotch), such as burrs, nicks, pits, gouges, etc., that can damage your rope's sheath. To keep rope-bearing biners smooth, separate them from biners that you use to clip fixed hardware like bolts and pitons. Because of metal-on-metal wear, bolt-side biners can pit, gouge, and nick against hangers in falls. Mark each biner type differently, or tape your rope-side biners in place on trad draws so you know which is which.

Now check the gate action: It should be silky smooth, without your having to force the gate open. Any change in action, such as stickiness or the gate hanging up on the sides of the nose, usually indicates an issue. Check also that the gate spring isn't weak

THE FIXED-DRAW DILEMMA

As we discussed in Chapter 2, fixed draws, or permadraws, are becoming more prevalent at popular sport crags, especially overhanging ones. If the local ethics and land managers allow for it, permadraws can be a welcome advent. The mega-steep Arsenal cave at Rifle, for example, became a handy training venue after chain-and-quick-link permadraws were affixed in the mid-1990s. On the flip side, a fixed draw will see concentrated use and, just like a bolt, should not be trusted implicitly just because it's "permanent." Because such draws see heavy use, they become potential safety hazards.

From best to worst, the fixed draws you'll encounter today run the gamut from the steel Climb Tech PermaDraws (think: gym draws), which have quick links for a bolt hanger, chain or cable dogbones, and a zinc-plated steel-alloy bent-gate carabiner; to chain draws pieced together at the hardware store; to sling setups or standard quickdraws that have simply been left in place. In all cases, they should be inspected regularly and replaced or updated as needed. To consider:

How grooved is the rope-side carabiner, especially if it's aluminum?
According to an Access Fund blog post, today's lightweight aluminum biners like our beloved wiregate biners wear more than 10 times quicker than steel biners. Meanwhile, certain microbiners' T-profile (sometimes called an I-beam) can become

by making sure the gate fully closes on its own, and inspect for bent or loose gate rivets that might likewise compromise clipping.

The main wear hazard with rope-side biners is grooving caused by the rope, especially dirty ropes. Under tension, a groove that's deep enough and sharp enough can skin your rope's sheath like a potato peeler or even sever your rope entirely (see "The Fixed-Draw Dilemma" sidebar). As Karn puts it, "Once you have a noticeable rope groove, retire the biner." Even if a groove looks shallow, feel it to see how sharp the lip is, and retire the biner if you note even the slightest edge.

To maintain your biners:

- Clean dirty or grimy biners in warm water and mild dishwashing soap. Swish them back and forth to remove dirt and grime, rinse them, and then air-dry them completely.

a dangerous, rope-cutting blade after only two millimeters of wear vs. ovals, which are hazardous after five millimeters. In October 2012, a climber died in a fall sport climbing when his rope cut on a sharply grooved biner—*this is serious stuff!*

Beware any spot where the rope is forced through a carabiner at a sharp angle, especially below a roof or at the first clip.

Any sharp bend in the rope, such as between the belayer and the first draw, can exacerbate wear, eroding that biner faster than the others. A climber decked at a gym in the Czech Republic after his rope severed on an extremely worn first draw, and the same thing happened at Muir Valley in the Red River Gorge (Kentucky). Both climbers survived, but had this happened higher on the routes, it could have been much worse.

How well is the permadraw attached to the bolt hanger, and how does the bolt look?

Clipping our own quickdraws to bolts forces us to inspect them; we'll realize if the hanger is mangled or the bolt is a spinner. But clipping a permadraw somehow makes us complacent. Take a second to scan a permadraw's bolt, nut, hanger, and quick link. Check whether the quick link is tightened and in good condition, and whether everything else is kosher.

6

○ Lubricate the gate hinge with a non-oil-based lubricant as oil-based lubes will attract dirt and grime. Don't use WD-40. Instead, use a graphite- or Teflon-based spray or a wax-based formula like Metolius Cam Lube. After you apply it, wipe away excess lube with a cloth to avoid contaminating other gear, and then recheck the gate for springiness.

Wired Nuts

Consisting entirely of metal save the plastic color-coding on their clipping loop, wired nuts can be inspected and cleaned much like carabiners. Look for deformation or pitting in the nut itself, especially after a big fall, and keep an eye on the cable for corrosion or fraying, as well as the swage (if it's visible; many are enclosed in a plastic sheath). Monitor the solder points of micronuts with soldered heads, especially after a significant whipper, though the cable would likely break first.

Cams

Cams, those works of high-tech art, have myriad moving parts, and almost all incorporate some blend of metal, plastic, and nylon (for slings and trigger wires). Inspect your cams regularly, especially after a significant fall. Pay special attention to:

○ **Main body cable.** The main cable can bend over an edge in a fall, though it can be worked back into shape manually. However, each time you do this it weakens the cable a little—don't make a habit of it. If a cable's so bent that you can't straighten it by hand, retire the cam. Also, if any individual cable strands are broken, frayed, or kinked, retire the cam.

○ **Trigger wires.** These nonstructural components don't pose a safety issue when busted, but a broken trigger wire will make it hard if not impossible to retrieve a stuck cam. Don't let it reach that point. The Cam Doctor (www.thecamdoctor.com) sells trigger-wire repair kits, or you can send them back to the manufacturer for repair as soon as the wires look hinky.

○ **Cam lobes.** Lobes can deform or even partially shear in a fall, or the teeth can wear down. Says Karn, "If the teeth are wearing out (worn unevenly or flattened by a fall) or the lobe's lost its shape, it's time for that thing to go." Dings and small gouges in the face of the lobe are usually no big deal, and you can often smooth them over with a file.

- **Axle hole.** Big whippers can ovalize the lobes' axle holes, imparting extra play between lobe and axle. If you suspect this issue, compare the cam to a new one of the same size. With a new cam, there should be a little play but not too much laterally, whereas one with ovalized holes will feel downright sloppy, making it a good candidate for retirement.
- **Springs.** A broken spring will be obvious—the lobe won't stay open. In this case, return the cam to the manufacturer for inspection and repair.
- **Cam stop.** The only way to break a cam stop is to fall and expand the head past the stops, inverting the lobes (aka umbrella-ing the cam). While this doesn't pose a safety issue, it will make the cam harder to use in the future and thus a good candidate for retirement.
- **Axle.** You can bend a small cam's axle in a hard fall; if this happens, retire the cam.
- **Sling.** Inspect the sling as you would any nylon, looking for aging, bleaching, fraying, etc., to the body and stitching. Some people suggest that you resling your cams every five years. You can send the cam back to the manufacturer for repair or to Mountain Tools (www.mtntools.com), which will resling any brand of cam. Also, if you suspect sling contamination, resling your cams.

It's important to keep cams clean, not only for function but also for safety—namely, holding power. "In that moment before the cam actually engages and you get all that outward force, the only thing that's holding the cam in is the friction between the lobes and the rock," says Karn. "And the only thing that's giving you any outward force is the spring tension. If you have dirty, sticky cams, you're giving

6

them a way higher chance to skate out at that critical instant." To keep your cams firing well:

- Soak them in warm or hot tap water. Metolius suggests heating water in a pan until it's near the boiling point for their cams, while being careful to keep the sling away from the heat source.
- Swish the cams around in the water, and work the trigger while you do so.
- Add liquid dishwashing detergent directly to the cam heads, and scrub them with a stiff-bristled toothbrush, especially the springs and lobes.
- Rinse and air-dry them. Cams may require multiple cleanings and dryings. If you have access to a compressor, blast them with compressed air while they're still wet to remove particulate matter.
- Add a non-oil-based lubricant to the head's moving parts: either a graphite- or Teflon-based dry lubricant like Lock-Ease, or a wax-based lubricant like Cam Lube. Keep the lube off the sling to reduce the risk of contamination.
- If a cam is still locked up, squirt a penetrating lube (such as WD-40 or Triflow) deep into the head, but be extra careful to keep it off the sling. Use paper towels to blot up excess lubricant.

Belay Devices

Regularly inspect the rope-bearing surfaces of your belay device for grooving, and consider retiring a device if you wear these surfaces down one millimeter or more, especially if the grooves have sharp edges. Look also at the keeper loop on an ATC-style device to make sure it's in good shape: Nothing is worse than losing your precious belay or rappel rig 600 feet up a wall. Finally, make sure that the device is clean so it's not introducing sand, gravel, or other gunk into your rope: Submerge it in warm, soapy water, agitate it and wipe or brush the grime away, then rinse well and air-dry.

Grigri Love

As the go-to assisted-braking belay device and the one that's been around the longest (introduced in 1991 in the United States), Petzl's Grigri has become a staple tool for

DO CAMS WORK iN WET ROCK?

Bottom line: *Cams are not trustworthy in wet rock.* You're better off using passive gear like a hex or nut, because in wet stone a cam can skate before it has a chance to press outward. "Anything, like a layer of water, dust, loose rock, lichen, or ice, that interferes with frictional force between the cam lobes and rock wall reduces your chance of holding," says Karn. "Moreover, wet rock is weaker—the cam pulverizes the outer layer and skates out." Karn likens the phenomenon to bald tires losing traction on a wet highway, and adds that the harder and more compact the rock (e.g, quartzite or granite), the slicker that surface layer of water will make it. If you have to place a cam in wet rock, be aware that it might not hold.

Finally, never store your cams wet—hang them up to dry, and relube them immediately. Use steel wool or a scrubbing sponge to remove surface oxidation.

6

sport climbing's extended belay sessions. With proper care and inspection, you can make a Grigri last for years—I have one I've been using since the 1990s. Rick Vance, the technical information manager at Petzl America, says that you should vet your Grigri with a regular three-point inspection:

1. Ensure that all the moving parts (the handle, cam, and side plate) move freely, and that the cam and handle-return springs function properly. If the handle-return spring doesn't return the handle to its closed position, it might accidentally open the cam. Any malfunction of the cam may also prevent the Grigri from locking up during a fall, while a worn-out cam spring will cause the Grigri to lock up while feeding slack.

2. Check for wear to all friction-bearing surfaces, including the rope channel and the clip-in point. You're looking for deformation or wear of one millimeter or more (Petzl's guideline for all its metal products). This one-millimeter change may not significantly reduce strength, but it can reduce the Grigri's performance or affect its compatibility with other pieces of gear. Meanwhile, a worn cam

won't provide as much braking friction as a new one, and a sharp, worn edge on the side plate may increase wear on your rope.

3. Do a quick function test: Put the Grigri on a rope and ensure that it feeds, locks, and releases properly.

If the device fails the above inspection, retire it.

6

Inspect these parts of your Grigri assisted-braking belay device regularly.

A few final tips:

- **Keep your Grigri clean.** Several key components need to be kept clean. Dirt in the handle or cam can prevent them from rotating freely. Also keep the rope channel clean. Clean your Grigri by submerging it in warm, soapy water and agitating it. Rinse if off well afterward, and be extremely careful about lubricating these parts since you don't want to cross-contaminate your rope.
- **Keep your rope clean.** Rocking a clean cord will help extend the life of your Grigri or any other belay device. A dirty rope is like a 70-meter piece of sandpaper, and significantly accelerates wear to rope-bearing surfaces.

To learn more about how to care for your gear, including your Grigri, read Petzl's handy guide to gear care on their website (www.petzl.com).

Bolts

Countless articles have been written about how to place bolts, what to beware of with aging clippers, and how to upgrade and replace rusting hardware. The American Safe Climbing Association (ASCA, www.safeclimbing.org) is the number-one resource for this information and for anyone looking to do or donate toward anchor-replacement work. For our purposes, let's look at bolts in terms of lay safety assessment and making minor field repairs. First, however, a caveat: Always be skeptical of bolts. Even though we tend to think of them as permanent or bomber, bolts can and do fail. The hardware can be defective (almost impossible to detect until the bolt's placed) or improperly placed, or it can succumb to the elements and wear. *Inspect bolts just like you would any other protection, and back them up. Never entrust your life to a single bolt!* If doing so means preclipping the second bolt on a climb with a death-pit landing, then do so unabashedly.

Newer sport climbs usually have one of three types of bolts. First are glue-ins, titanium or stainless-steel rods epoxied into place generally in wet, soft, or maritime rock. Second are sleeve bolts, such as the classic hex-headed five-piece Powers bolts; when these are tightened, a tapered end cone sucks up into the sleeve, creating expansion pressure between the bolt and the hole. And third are wedge bolts,

6

HOW SAFE IS DROPPED GEAR?

It happens to the best of us: We're unclipping a draw or cleaning a piece, and we fumble it. It falls 20, 50, 100 feet and pings off talus, coming to rest far below, claimed by the rock gods. Carabiners, in particular, seem to meet this fate.

Back in the day, climbers worried about stress fractures, invisible cracks within the metal said to weaken it, but this theory has largely been discredited. Powick says that Black Diamond Equipment has over the years tested several dropped biners, cams, and belay devices, with a fall range from 50 feet to the entirety of El Capitan (2800 feet). He calls these tests "unofficial" in that Black Diamond Equipment had no way to verify if the product was fit for use, since they did not know its history other than that the piece had been dropped. In any case, using a single destructive test, "in all of the carabiners and cams we tested, the strength did not appear to be compromised," says Powick. He adds, "I've also seen carabiners, belay devices, and cams dropped from El Cap that were so mangled you couldn't use them if you tried." It's thus more likely that dropping a piece will render it structurally nonfunctional than reduce its strength.

If a piece isn't obviously unusable or so manked up you wouldn't want to use it, try this two-point inspection:

1. Check whether the biner gate closes properly, the cam action is smooth, its lobes aren't wobbly, and everything appears to function correctly.
2. Check whether the biner is free of significant dents or cracks; the cam trigger wires are still intact; its axles aren't bent; the webbing isn't frayed; the cam lobes have no significant dents, cracks, or flat spots; and its stem is still straight. Check whether your belay device is compressed or bent, or has cracks or dents.

Note that there are no absolutes. If gear functions well and looks fine, it could very well be OK. But, says Powick, "As with all things climbing, ultimately the final decision is up to the climber. If you're unsure about a piece, it may be best to retire it, because the last thing you want to think when you're 30 feet runout above that pro is, 'I sure hope that's not the piece I dropped a few weeks ago . . .'"

which also work by expansion, and activate via an expansion clip over the cone. With glue-ins, there's no real maintenance other than visually inspecting the clipping eye's integrity, but with the two expansion bolts, you can be proactive. It's helpful to carry an adjustable crescent wrench for minor fixes, as you never know what size bolt or nut you'll encounter.

6

1. **Sleeve bolts.** Hangers on sleeve bolts can start to spin, especially with sideways falls, or if the bolt wasn't fully tightened at installation. First check to see if it's just the hanger or the entire assembly that rotates: Clip a draw to the hanger, pull it side to side and up and down, and see if the bolt feels loose in its hole. If it's only the hanger, though such spinners aren't ideal (the hanger can bite or saw into the stud over time), they aren't necessarily an immediate safety hazard. But if the whole bolt wobbles, it's likely not tightened down all the way or the hole has been compromised—a hazard, as the bolt could pull.

   Now use a wrench to tighten the hex head and see what happens: Does the hanger tighten down, or do both the hanger and bolt still spin? If the hanger tightens, great! If not, the bolt might either be defective or not properly expanded and is a likely candidate for replacement—proceed with caution.

A five-piece sleeve bolt. *FIXEhardware Inc.*

A glue-in bolt. *FIXEhardware Inc.*

HOW BOLTS GET THERE

To understand what makes a bolt placement good vs. sketchy, it helps to know how bolts end up in the rock. I've bolted dozens of climbs myself and also talked to Tod Anderson, who since 1988 has established hundreds of new routes, most notably on the granite of Colorado's Devil's Head. Here's what we "drill sergeants" do:

1. Once the climber has ascertained where the clip will go, marking it with a chalk dot (usually on top rope), he taps the rock with a wall hammer to hunt for competent stone, avoiding flakes, hollow plates, or any overlaid or semiattached shield (with fracture lines going partway or clear around) that's likely to shatter. With bad rock, you can hear a booming or hollow noise, or perhaps see vibrations translating through the stone a foot or two away. Good rock will have a high-pitched ring just like pitons driven into a bomber crack. The ideal placement is a flat mini-panel where both bolt and hanger can sit flush and where quickdraws and carabiners won't hang up on any features.

2. **Wedge bolts.** If a hanger sustains a load (whipper), it can pop the nut, or perhaps the nut wasn't sufficiently tightened upon installation. A wobbly nut will eventually unwind from the bolt's threaded end, and the hanger will drop off. If you don't have a wrench, tighten the nut by hand as you climb past. If you have a wrench, tighten the nut until it feels snug, but don't go hog-wild (see the "Overtightening" sidebar). Also, orient the hanger in the direction of the fall so that the nut is less likely to pop loose again;

A wedge bolt.
FIXEhardware Inc.

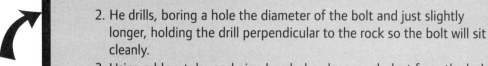

2. He drills, boring a hole the diameter of the bolt and just slightly longer, holding the drill perpendicular to the rock so the bolt will sit cleanly.
3. Using a blow tube and pipe brush, he cleans rock dust from the hole.
4. He hammers the bolt in, using strong, clean blows to avoid deforming the head or nut.
5. He tightens the bolt. Voilà, it's done!

6

you can also apply an adhesive/sealant (I use blue Loctite) to the nut and threads to prevent rotation.

Bad Bolts

A bad bolt is one that's placed in hollow, shattered, or loose rock (bang the facet with the heel of your hand to test it), that sits crookedly in its hole, whose head is deformed (however even bolts that tighten well can end up looking mushed for various reasons), or that juts out from the rock.

Here are a few other scenarios that indicate an expansion bolt might be untrustworthy. Also be aware that anchor hardware (chains, rings, quick links, fixed biners, etc.) is subject to the same types of corrosion as bolts and should likewise be inspected:

- **Mangled hangers.** Old SMC hangers, homemade hangers, and hangers subject to repeated sideways falls can deform and should be replaced with more-bomber alternatives. Your carabiner can break on or unclip from a bad hanger.
- **Spider-webbing.** If you see telltale spider-web fracturing leading from or around a bolt, it's in friable, fractured, untrustworthy rock. The bolt as well as rock panel could fail.
- **Mixed metals.** Stainless-steel and plated-steel components (bolts and hangers) should not be mixed; contact between the two different metal types plus an electrolyte (salts in the rock and/or carried by water) can foster galvanic corrosion, which degrades the components. Also, in cases of a stainless hanger and a plated bolt, say, in a water streak, a bolt might be rusted

OVERTiGHTENiNG

The main reason climbers seem reluctant to do field repairs is because they worry about overtightening a bolt and blowing it out. They figure an "expert" would be better suited to address such important matters. But there isn't some crack squad of bolt ninjas out maintaining the cliffs. Almost all such work is done by volunteers, sporadically and somewhat haphazardly, and said volunteers often rely on information from other climbers. So if you see a loose bolt, first do your best to make it "safe enough," and then post about it online (www.badbolts.com) or get in touch with your local climbing organization.

It's quite hard to overtighten to failure with a garden-variety crescent wrench, especially with sleeve bolts. Metals have a yield curve of stress (tightening) relative to strain (holding power). Each bolt has its manufacturer's tightness specifications, and true safety nuts will even use a torque wrench to tighten each bolt to manufacturers' specs. But the good news is, especially with sleeve bolts, even if you surpass that sweet spot, the metal's not going to automatically fail: It instead stretches along a slightly rising plateau of increased strain and thus reduced holding power, not a precipitous climb along the yield curve to sudden, catastrophic failure. In other words, even an overtightened sleeve bolt is not necessarily on the brink of rupture, especially given the incredibly high forces bolts can withstand.

Wedge bolts are a little different: Overtightening the nut can shear the bolt, a technique I'll often use to remove old wedge bolts when rebolting vintage climbs. With all bolts, but especially wedge bolts, reduce the risk of overtightening by not using a wrench with a super-long handle (a foot or more) and by learning, through experience, where the sweet spot lies. Basically, don't crank past the point where the head or nut naturally stops turning, and don't use a giant socket bar as a super-lever you practically jump up and down on. *Let common sense prevail—bolts are like any other hardware.* If in doubt, borrow a torque wrench and experiment with installing different bolts on a chunk of rock or concrete at home, exactly to the manufacturer's specifications. With practice, you'll soon recognize when to stop tightening, even without a torque wrench.

out behind the hanger, but you wouldn't realize it because the hanger still looks good. Stainless steel has a dull grey color like brushed nickel, while plated steel has a shinier blue or chrome-like sheen. With camouflaged hardware, though, you might not be able to tell the difference.

- **Rust or oxidation corrosion.** Minor surface oxidation on the bolt or hanger may be no big deal, but without removing the bolt, you have no idea how corroded it is inside. If a bolt has a telltale red-orange rust streak below it and sees lots of water, or if the components are so rusty they're uniformly brown or furry like an old ship's anchor, don't trust them. The same goes for bolts in marine and rainy or tropical environments, which may also experience stress-corrosion cracking (see below).

- **Stress-corrosion cracking (SCC).** Common in marine or tropical environments, especially in wet, porous rock like limestone, this severe weakening of steel happens when chloride ions from dissolved salts pervade the metal as they follow stress lines in the bolt, nut, or hanger. The metal then becomes riddled with internal cracks and subsequently fails in a fall or even under body weight. Most insidiously, SCC often isn't visible. For example, at sea cliffs on the island of Cayman Brac, recently placed (within 18 months), rust-free, visibly intact bolts snapped solely from the weight of a hanging climber. View any bolt at marine crags or on porous, consistently seepy rock that's not a titanium glue-in with suspicion. Even stainless-steel glue-ins can be subject to SCC!

CLIMBING SHOES

We demand more from our climbing shoes than from any other piece of gear. Rock shoes are indeed safety gear, because good footwork coupled with faith in reliable shoes is what keeps us attached to the rock. Sadly, many climbers neglect and disrespect their shoes. Protect yourself by caring for your rock shoes and understanding when it's appropriate to have them resoled.

Rock That Resole

Only a few climbers (most sponsored) retire shoes after they burn through the factory sole. The rest of us have our shoes resoled, which at $25 to $45 a pop is much cheaper than buying a new pair. There are, however, a few things to know both about resoling and extending your shoes' life span such that they remain good candidates for repeated resoles. Eric Pauwels opened the Boulder, Colorado, resoling outfit Rock & Resole in 1989 and has since slapped new soles on untold thousands of shoes. He and fellow cobbler Colby Rickard have gleaned tips from the "bootload" of footwear that's passed through their shop, presented here as an FAQ:

When do I need resoles?
Pauwels says that 90 percent of sole wear takes place in the big-toe area, so that should be where you evaluate rubber thickness when deciding to resole. "Keep in mind that you start with a four-millimeter sole there, and it will gradually decrease to the point where it's paper thin," says Pauwels. "At that point you want to resole." Climbers often make the mistake of looking at general sole condition or the outside of the shoe, but the big toe (our foot's power point) invariably wears thin first.

Do I need toe caps?
Toe caps are patches of sticky rubber used to repair holes in the rand, the thinner (two-millimeter) band of rubber that wraps laterally around a shoe's upper. Your resoler might replace the full rand or just cut away a small crescent-shaped swatch and glue on new rand rubber. If your rand has a visible hole in it, you need a toe cap, but you might also need a toe cap absent a hole, as a rand can develop weaknesses around the toe box, depending on wear patterns. (Maybe you are a "toe dragger" or do lots of gym climbing where you stab at sharp little jibs.)

To inspect a rand that's not visibly holey:
- Start by the pinkie toe, which generally has the least amount of rand wear, and pinch the rand with your thumb, working toward the big toe.
- With this perspective of a full-thickness rand, inspect for areas of reduced resistance; they can be focused like a pinhead or as large as a pencil eraser.
- Pay particular attention to rand wear on shoes that have stiff

(plastic) midsoles, as these tend to spread your feet outward and create pressure against the outside of the shoe.
- ○ Point out any trouble spots to your resoler, and ask about a toe cap. Note that getting a toe cap will also mean getting a new half-sole: You have to remove the old sole to put on the toe cap because rand rubber wraps a quarter inch around beneath the outsole. In a perfect world, you'll time needing a toe cap with needing a new sole.

6

What if I've punched through the suede or synthetic upper?
Are your shoes kaput? Not necessarily. Cobblers can layer a netting or mesh fabric to repair these sorts of holes and firm up the upper, including in high-impact areas like the toe box. Even if you've punched a hole through your rand *and* upper, your shoes might be salvageable. A cobbler can mend smaller holes with a leather patch and then overlay new rubber.

How many times can I resole my shoes?
Pauwels says that a looked-after pair of performance shoes, without any rotting or deterioration in the footbed and midsole, and with the uppers and closure system still intact, should stand up well to resoling three or four times. After that, the shoes generally won't hold their shape. "If you're climbing moderate slabs up the Flatirons, you might get a dozen," says Pauwels. "But if you're crack climbing, you might get two."

How can I make my shoes last?
The biggest deterioration problem Rock & Resole sees is interior rotting, most often from dampness or sweat. Maybe it's the pH in certain people's perspiration, the amount they perspire, a humid climate, or that climbers often leave their shoes inside crag packs, where they never fully dry out, but sweaty shoes aren't a good thing, and both Pauwels and Rickard emphasize the importance of airing them out. You could slip your shoes outside your pack for transport to the crags, and bring at least two pairs so that one pair can dry while you climb in the others. When you get home after a hot day climbing, set your shoes in a dry, open area, undo the laces or velcro closures, and pull up the tongue to increase airflow. Remember that a poorly cared-for shoe is less easily resurrected.

6

What do I do with old shoes I can't use anymore?
If your shoes are so beat up that you can't use them, chances are no one else wants them either. Pauwels says it's best to just throw them away—there is limited demand for recycled rubber, and the rubber from climbing shoes represents such a small fraction of this that the shoes usually end up in the landfill anyway.

LiFE SPAN OF PERFORMANCE SHOES

Professional climber Tommy Caldwell demands a lot from his rock shoes, putting them through their paces on thin, technical Yosemite Valley granite where matchstick-sized holds might be considered jugs. For his 2008 in-a-day redpoint of El Capitan's 2800-foot 5.13d/5.14a *Magic Mushroom,* Caldwell even stashed a fresh, just-broken-in pair of boots 18 pitches up, before the crux, flared chimneys on which he estimates he applied 250 pounds of force to his feet. These rigors demanded a fresh, stiff midsole; the pair he'd worn to that point were too broken down. For supertechnical slab and thin-face climbing, Caldwell thinks shoes are best after a one-pitch break-in, assuming you don't wear them too tight, and will hold their performance edge for around 20 pitches of highly technical climbing. After that, he reserves those shoes for easier climbs.

When evaluating whether to retire or resole a performance shoe, look for:

- **Rounding of the toe,** with the seam between the rand and outsole becoming blurred and indistinct. By comparison, this transition will be quite apparent on fresh, brand-new shoes.
- **Mushiness in the sole.** While wearing his shoes, Caldwell says, "If I can take one finger and press it through the sole and feel my finger pushing up into my foot, it means the midsole is broken down too much and it won't be great for super-hard pitches."
- **Integrity of the big-toe area.** With your shoe off, if you can press into the sole and make a serious dent in the big-toe focal point, the shoe has likely outlived its useful span.

Some Other Dos:

- **Keep your entire shoe clean.** You can safely machine-wash rock shoes a few times over their life span, to keep dirt from building up throughout the shoe and contributing to deterioration. Use cold water and a delicate cycle, and then air-dry the shoes.
- **Use a liquid urethane rubber**, such as Freesole Urethane Formula Shoe Repair, for field repairs like emergency bonding or patching. (Pauwels recommends against Shoe Goo, which is a contact adhesive.) You can also use Freesole or Five Ten's Stealth Paint to coat and reinforce high-impact points on the shoe, such as those that wear out crack climbing like the cinching buckles on velcro closures.
- **Keep your soles clean and grit free** to prolong the life of the rubber. Wipe them down with water, saliva, or rubbing alcohol; put them on, and then place a towel, crash pad, or flat rock in the dirt below the climb so that the rubber stays clean as you step onto the rock. You can also wipe your sole down on your opposite pant leg as a final gesture.
- **Keep your feet clean at the cliff, or clean them before you put on your rock shoes.** Dirt, grime, and bacteria lead to odor and decay issues. A few baby wipes go a long way, and you can even scrub your nasty old dogs in the shower with an antibacterial soap and burly brush after climbing.

And Don'ts:

- **Dry your shoes with talcum powder.** Rickard says that it can migrate throughout a shoe and infiltrate between the midsole and the sole, compromising the bond between sole and shoe. Neither does he recommend fabric-softener sheets, whose oils and scent chemicals likewise permeate the shoe—so deeply that he's been able to smell the perfume in the rubber when grinding off old soles. For odor issues caused by bacteria, it's best to simply air-dry your kicks before trying other measures (see the "Odor Eaters" sidebar).

6

○ **Leave your shoes out in excessive heat** (130 degrees Fahrenheit or hotter), such as in the direct sun in your car on a hot day—it leads to delamination. According to Pauwels, the glues that hold soles on are very heat sensitive. In fact, "If you want to loosen up a glue bond, you apply heat," he says.

○ **Wear your shoes while not climbing.** Approaching climbs in performance shoes or wearing them to belay will break down the midsole until your shoe loses it shape and supportive foundation. Taking the shoes half off and standing on the heels while you belay will further deform them. If you don't like fussing with approach or tennis shoes between climbs, bring flip-flops or slip-on shoes.

ODOR EATERS: KILL THE STANK

If air-drying isn't working and your shoes are still boggy and rancid, try the following (with the caveat that these tips might shorten your shoes' life span):

○ Put coffee beans, cat litter, or baking soda in a sock, and place it in your shoes when not wearing them.
○ Freeze your shoes to kill the bacteria.
○ Stuff crumpled-up newspaper in your footbed.
○ Use a scrub brush and a mild detergent to wash the funk out of the footbed.

GEAR INSPECTION

Your equipment is only as good as your last inspection; evaluate it regularly, even when it's brand new. Climbing gear is made and inspected by people, and people are fallible, so become the final word on the safety of your equipment since you have to live with the consequences. If a piece looks funky, send it back for inspection or replacement, and stay informed of any recall notices.

Most importantly, don't be cheap. Almost as a dirtbag point of pride, climbers love to stretch out gear as long as possible, but this is magical if not downright fatal thinking. *It's your life at stake.* I'd sacrifice every last piece of gear in my closet if it meant living to climb another day. You can, after all, always buy new climbing gear—but not a new you.

6

7 ARE YOU FIT FOR PUBLIC CONSUMPTION?

IT'S A LONG VOYAGE from apprentice to journeyman to master, not unlike standing below El Capitan for your first time and looking up in awe if not despair, thinking, "How am I ever going to climb that? It goes on *forever* . . ." The answer, of course, is pitch by pitch, move by move, hold by hold, crystal by crystal. Anything worth mastering, especially a rich, prismatic sport like climbing, takes time. True improvement remains a lifelong process, and you should remain an apprentice in your own mind right up until your very last pitch as a 92-year-old crag wizard. The stone will always have something new to teach if you stop to listen.

No one becomes a climber overnight. Sure, you can learn to *climb* in a few weeks or a few days or even a few hours, but that doesn't make you a *climber* any more than heating up a frozen pizza makes you a chef. All the things that go into climbing, that happen both on and off the rock, are what make you a climber. Our sport is a journey, personal evolution, and metaphor for thoughtful living, connected to something larger than ourselves.

To be a bit cheesy and maybe even poetic, when we climb, we're essentially in outer space where terrain meets sky, where the earth opens up to the cold black vastness of the universe, hanging on by our fingers and toes to a little scrap of rock that thrusts audaciously into the heavens. We're like astronauts, and when we fall, we hurtle through the ether just as rocket ships come back to Earth. Climbing isn't only about ticking 5.13-plus, launching sick dynos, or taking epic road trips with your bros and broettes. It's a vital communion with a timeless medium, a chance to improve and better understand ourselves while also engaging in athletic congress with the world's coolest playground apparatus.

It takes considerable responsibility to be a "climber" in the classic sense. With climbing's boom phase, it's more important now than ever for us to pass along our collective wisdom. If we don't, the tribe risks dying out; the lore of the elders will turn to ash and blow away, the crags becoming but crowded, battered, used-up outdoor gyms where we're disconnected from nature. All this expert advice has been meant to push you in the opposite direction.

Do you want to be a *climber* or just another person who *climbs?* Do you want to make the crags a better place for everyone or just tick your route and go home? Do you want to respect yourself, others, and the stone in the ways that this book challenges you to or do you simply not care? There are few outright rules in climbing, which is exactly why so many of us got into it. So please don't feel that the *Crag Survival Handbook* either prescribes or proscribes certain behaviors or that it's a "How-Not-To" book that like a magpie on your shoulder nag, nag, nags at you. This book is designed to present a spectrum, to present solutions, and to make you *think* about our collective impacts; it's completely up to you what changes you'll make.

NORBERT'S RELATIVELY TAME ADVENTURE

Well, we've come full circle, friendos, back to the topic we started with: how to be a safe, conscientious, and respectful crag citizen. And now it's also time to check back in with Norbert N00b—these days just "Norbert". After recovering from his injuries, our buddy Norbert took classes through his local mountain club, found older and wiser climbers to mentor him, and read this book. We were all once Norbert N00b to one degree or another, and we all eventually figured out (or are still figuring out) how to step up our game. So let's see how he's doing.

7

Norbert wakes up at 7:30 AM, grabs a quick breakfast of coffee, orange juice, and oatmeal, and heads out to a ride-share lot at the base of Gnar-Gnar Canyon, where he is meeting his longtime partner, Tommy, to carpool to the cliff. Tommy and Norbert trust each other implicitly and know each other's rhythms, without the distraction of a massive posse. They'd planned the night before to head to the Enormodome, a crag with an exposed ledge below the routes, so Norbert opts to leave Rommel at home where the dog will be safer and happier.

At the ride-share lot, Norbert is careful to keep his rope wrapped in its tarp and moves his gear right from his trunk to Tommy's so that his crag pack doesn't touch any spilled oil, antifreeze, or other gunk on the ground. As they wend their way up canyon, they talk about which routes they want to try, and Norbert reads the route descriptions to Tommy from the guidebook. Neither of them is feeling too heroic this morning, so they opt for the left side of the Enormodome Ledge where the climbs are shorter and better protected.

Tommy pulls into the trailhead, parking straight-in as per the signs. While Tommy pays their four-dollar day-use fee, Norbert visits a pit toilet: better to take care of business now rather than futz around at the cliff with a Wag Bag or cathole. The climbers hike uphill, following the designated path. They pass by the super-steep, ever-popular Total Sickness Cave, but it is signed as closed for another couple months because of nesting raptors.

"Too bad," says Tommy. "I was pretty close on *MegaMondoThon*."

"Yeah, well, no worries," says Norbert. "It'll open back up in August, and I'd be psyched to head up there with you." Norbert did *MegaMondoThon* six months earlier, but he doesn't say anything—it will give him just as much pleasure to see a buddy succeed as it did for him to send, and besides, another lap on *MegaMondoThon* will be good training.

They reach the crag, conversing quietly, catching up on life, but there is already another party below the two routes Norbert and Tommy most want to try. "No biggie," thinks Norbert. "We'll just warm up on something else and then check those routes later, or maybe those guys will let us surf their draws." Instead of walking over to crowd the other climbers on the narrow ledge, Norbert and Tommy give them a friendly wave and then consult their guidebook. There is a nice 5.9 around to the right in the shade, and since it is a fairly warm morning, the rock will still be cool.

Norbert and Tommy head up the gully, taking care to step on solid slabs and to avoid knocking rocks onto the approach trail below. The first ascentionists have built a good belay platform with a rock retaining wall below the climb, and the boys stage themselves here after looking up to make sure no one is climbing above and that there is no obviously loose choss. Tommy pulls his draws from his pack and lays them out on a flat rock, to keep them out of the dirt, while Norbert unrolls the rope bag below and just to the side of the first bolt.

"Kind of a high first clip," says Tommy, looking up and scratching his head. Norbert's first instinct is to say, "Yeah, but when did you last fall on a 5.9?" but he checks himself. Tommy decked and sprained his ankle on a 5.9 only months earlier, trying to reach the first bolt when a hold broke and spat him into the talus. He is only now getting his sea legs back.

"Here, I'll go find a stick," offers Norbert. "Let's preclip this-here 'rock staple!'" He returns, sets up a stick-clip, tags the draw onto the bolt with the rope properly clipped, then takes the tape off the stick and puts it in a trash sack in his pack. Norbert notices a few other odds and ends of old tape, food wrappers, and cigarette butts on the ground, so he picks those up as well.

"You can leave the draws on—I'll lead it too," says Norbert. "I'll just lower you from the anchors, OK?"

"Bueno," says Tommy, putting a stopper knot in the end of the rope, as the guidebook notes that the pitch is 28 meters long and a 60-meter rope *barely* reaches.

Tommy ties-in, cleans his shoes with his palms, stands on a rock, and wipes his soles against each pant leg.

"You good, man? Harness doubled back, buckles buckled, knot solid?" asks Norbert. Tommy looks down, double-checks his harness and knot, and then points to Norbert's setup: "I'm good. You?" Norbert checks his harness as well, then reconfirms that his Grigri is on and threaded correctly, that the locking biner is locked, and that the rope has a stopper knot. As a final safeguard, Tommy tugs on the rope to lock it up in Norbert's device, then Norbert pulls back to test Tommy's knot. The climbers are ready.

Norbert stands directly below the first bolt and just to the side, looking up, paying out slack to match Tommy's pace, and anticipating each clip. As Tommy, climbing fluidly and staying balanced over his feet, reaches the fourth bolt a good

25 feet up, Norbert starts to keep a lazy smile in the rope to give a dynamic catch. But Tommy doesn't fall: he is in there, on a route three letter grades below his limit. Tommy reaches the anchors, clips draws onto the hangers so he won't wear out the rings while lowering, hollers down "Take!" to Norbert, waits until the rope becomes taut, and then lets go as Norbert lowers him. Back on the ground, the two climbers confirm their plan that Norbert will thread the anchors and have Tommy lower him after his lead. Finally, Norbert leads and cleans the pitch.

With both climbers back safely on the ground, they rest, drink some water, consult their guidebook again, power up with some almonds, and plan the rest of their day.

WHAT IF, WHAT IF, WHAT IF?

Mountain Project (www.mountainproject.com) is the preeminent climbing-information site, an interactive, user-created and volunteer-administrated guidebook and database that has filled a unique need in the community since its inception, in January 2000, as www.climbingboulder.com. The brainchild of computer programmer Michael Komarnitsky, who had an aha moment one day out in Eldorado Canyon, the site later expanded, with the help of other administrators, to include sites for dozens of regions across the United States. In 2005, Andy Laakman and Nick Wilder amalgamated these sites into Mountain Project, which today also features a smartphone app that lets you download an area and take it to the cliffs offline. It has become the go-to online resource for route beta.

Top Mountain Project Forum FAQs

Mountain Project has a lively user forum, and newer or intermediate climbers often solicit answers to common technical questions. Laakman and the site's administrators have compiled the following Top Mountain Project Forum FAQs.

1. Do bolts ever break?

Yes, unfortunately they do, either by pulling out or shearing. So if a bolt, nut, or hanger looks ancient, suspect, corroded, or otherwise compromised, don't trust it. Some US cliffs have relic, time-bomb nail drives, star drives, buttonheads, and other quarter-inchers; sketchy, thin-metaled SMC hangers and defective Leeper hangers; and other ancient mank. Learn to identify and avoid these and/or supplement them with traditional protection. The American Safe Climbing Association (ASCA, www.safeclimbing.org) has a great series of articles in the education section of their website.

Meanwhile, try not to put all your eggs in one basket, even with an apparently bomber bolt. In situations where failure would be catastrophic, such as on the second or third clip, or a high first bolt over a bad landing, back yourself up. When placed well in compact, dry rock, modern $3/8$- and $1/2$-inch steel bolts can endure for decades and rarely, if ever, fail. Thus many climbs put up in the last 10 or 15 years are much safer than their older counterparts. For more information about bolts, see the "Metal" section in Chapter 6.

2. Which brand or model of gear should I buy?

The annual gear guides put out by publications such as *Climbing* and *Rock & Ice* spell out the different categories of gear, the various products, and their general features and specs. Also, the staff at your local shop can give you guidance. Climbing gear has become highly specialized, and each item has been designed for a specific, intended use. Instead of comparing brands across a certain category, look instead at what kind of climbing you intend to do and which specific tool is best for the job, whatever the brand. For example, that brand of microcams with a single stem and narrow head profile might work better in the incipient seams at your local area than other options. To get an overall feel for the gear landscape, read manufacturer literature as well as reviews in print magazines and online (I recommend the Gear Institute, Super-Topo, and OutdoorGearLab, all online).

3. What about that cheap Ukrainian gear?

Good question! First of all, you don't necessarily look to official certification for your answer. Even though that Ukrainian gear might have a CE (Conformité Européene), International Mountaineering and Climbing Federation (UIAA), or 3-Sigma stamp, these are simply agreed-upon standards the gear must meet to obtain that stamp and don't imply that a specific item has been inspected or is reliable. It's all a bit arbitrary: CE, for example, is required for all items sold within the European Union; for climbing, it's based on UIAA standards for climbing gear. Thus gear without these certifications, perhaps that cut-rate Ukrainian stuff, might be fine—it's just not sold in Europe. Certification is therefore a useful guideline, but it's not the end-all be-all. If you're concerned, research the gear's specs pertaining to loads, break strength, and holding power, and then compare them to similar items from a brand you trust. Really, it's *your* call.

Let me put it another way: Would you buy a sketchy Ukrainian minivan to chauffer your kids around, or would you stick with a brand you trusted? Put the same care into each climbing purchase. I'd rather spend extra money to go with a known, top-shelf brand, but that's just me. You could also buy one piece from that mystery manufacturer, put it through its rigors, and then consider buying more from them if it holds up.

4. Should I say anything to someone doing something unsafe?

Yes, you should before they fulfill their lifetime goal of maiming or killing themselves in some avoidable, boneheaded manner that also involves you in a rescue. Be polite, point out the consequences of what they're doing, and then offer safer alternatives or the best, most common practice. (See the "The Top Five Ways to Stay Alive" section in Chapter 1.)

5. Should I bring my dog to the crag?

That depends on you, area regulations concerning dogs, the crag environment, and your dog. See the "Dog Management 101" section in Chapter 2 for advice from climber and dog expert Melissa Lipani.

6. Should I bring my kids to the crag?

That depends on you, the venue, conditions, your child, and to some degree your child's age. See the "Kids and Cragging" section in Chapter 2 for advice from climber-parents Lucia Hyde Robinson and Jonathan and Jackie Koehne.

7. Where are good places for family climbing?

"Kids and Cragging" in Chapter 2 delves into this topic at greater length, but briefly, the best venues are: easily accessed bouldering areas; cliffs with safe, flat, unexposed staging areas and short, easy approaches; cliffs that aren't too exposed to harsh elements like wind, storms, and blazing sun; cliffs with solid rock or that aren't known for choss; cliffs with a lack of crowds (or popular crags at off times); cliffs with fun nonclimbing things for kids to do like explore caves or the forest, or play in a stream; and cliffs with short, easily top-roped moderate routes for your kids to try.

8. Is it OK to bring 87 people with me to the crag?

That depends. If the crag is on your own private property, then sure, go for it. Bring a keg and a BBQ grill and have a party. Otherwise, local land-management agencies likely have regulations about organizing such a large group, so check with them first. Also, in terms of etiquette, consider the venue and your impact on other climbers and the environment, as outlined in the "Ten Commandments of Cragging Etiquette," the "Minimum Impact" section, and the "Leave

No Trace" sidebar, all in Chapter 2. Personally, I'd warrant that climbing in giant groups is lame and that anyone who'd bring 87 people to the cliffs is a jackass, but that's just me.

9. *What do I do when I get to the crag and every easy line is being gang-top roped?* Scream, "What the hell is wrong with you chuffers? What are you doing at *my* crag!" and then run around pulling the top ropes down, howling, and tugging at your hair. Well, actually, don't. If crowds bother you and you value your solitude, head elsewhere. Or if you're gung-ho to climb a specific occupied route, approach the group leader and ask if you can work in when no one's climbing. If this doesn't meet with good results, utilize the authority of the resource technique (see Chapter 2). Explain that perhaps this cliff isn't the best venue for such a large group, and that in the interest of sharing the limited number of climbs, it would be more equitable and in line with what the crag has to offer all users for their group to let others work in.

ARE YOU FIT FOR PUBLIC CONSUMPTION?

Perhaps Norbert's original tale, from his Norbert N0Ob days, was a bit extreme, but then again perhaps not. (At least he went on to redeem himself!) On any given day at a busy cliff, you've probably noticed someone evincing at least one of Norbert's behaviors, or you've behaved that way yourself. My description of Norbert's bad behavior was inspired by things I've seen at crags, some of which have closed because of climber misfeasance, such as Roadside Crag and Torrent Falls at the Red River Gorge in Kentucky. In any case, I'm human and have made mistakes of my own—this book is not a manifesto. It's a handbook of ideas and suggestions for crag survival and etiquette—nothing more, nothing less.

The final big question is whether you are fit for public consumption. In other words, are you ready to be out at the crags in a way that's fun and positive for you, as well as everyone else? Only *you* have the answer. Only *you* can cultivate your awareness of what it means to be a solid cragging citizen.

In her work, climbing ranger Bernadette Regan of Joshua Tree National Park sees all manner of climber behavior—the good, the bad, and the ugly—given the park's proximity to the Los Angeles and San Diego megalopolis. Still she remains

7

optimistic."Be a good example," she urges. Do small, simple things: "If you see trash, pick it up. Don't put your pack on a plant, and maybe your partner won't." In other words it all starts with *you* so, as Regan concludes, "Be the climber you want everyone else to be."

FURTHER RESOURCES

The following web, print, and organizational resources form the cornerstone of a well-educated, responsible, and citizenship-minded climber, and they have been part of my climbing world either since their inception or since I first touched stone. I hope you find them as useful as I have.

ORGANIZATIONS

Access Fund (AF, www.accessfund.org): An advocacy organization dedicated since 1991 to helping keep crags open.

American Alpine Club (AAC, www.americanalpineclub.org): America's oldest and largest climbing club, and publishers of the *American Alpine Journal* and *Accidents in North American Mountaineering*.

American Safe Climbing Association (ASCA, www.safeclimbing.org): A climber-funded nonprofit dedicated to education about and action around replacing dangerous outdated hardware.

Leave No Trace (www.lnt.org): Curator and developers of the most widely accepted outdoor ethics program used on public lands.

Mountain Project (www.mountainproject.com): An online route-info database/interactive guidebook with untold thousands of climbs.

The Mountaineers (www.mountaineers.org): Founded in 1906, an outdoors education and conservation organization based in the Pacific Northwest; publishers of many instructional climbing titles including *Mountaineering: The Freedom of the Hills.*

Professional Climbers International (www.proclimbers.com): Association founded to create a better future for athletes through programs that develop and inspire the next generation of climbers; also offers educational seminars, clinics, slideshows, etc.

BOOKS

American Alpine Club. *Accidents in North American Mountaineering.* Golden, CO: American Alpine Club, annual. *Annual roundup of accidents in North America with analyses of what went wrong.*

Beal, Peter. *Bouldering: Movement, Tactics, and Problem Solving.* Seattle: Mountaineers Books, 2011. *The boulderer's bible of techniques and best practices.*

Bisharat, Andrew. *Sport Climbing: From Toprope to Redpoint, Techniques for Climbing Success.* Seattle: Mountaineers Books, 2009. *The sport climber's bible of techniques and best practices.*

Burbach, Matt. *Gym Climbing: Maximizing Your Indoor Experience.* Seattle: Mountaineers Books, 2005. *A primer on making gym climbing effective and fun.*

Eng, Ronald, Editor. *Mountaineering: The Freedom of the Hills: 8th edition.* Seattle: Mountaineers Books, 2010. *The all-encompassing resource for anyone who ventures into the vertical world, be it the crags or the mountains.*

Ilgner, Arno. *The Rock Warrior's Way.* La Vergne, TN: Desiderata Institute, 2003. *A philosophical as well as practical look at honing your mental edge and getting the better of the fear that holds us back. (See also www.warriorsway.com.)*

Lewis, S. Peter, and Dan Cauthorn. *Climbing from Gym to Crag: Building Skills for Real Rock.* Seattle: Mountaineers Books, 2000. *How to safely and methodically transfer your indoor skills outside.*

Long, John. *How to Rock Climb.* Guilford, CT: Globe Pequot Press, 2010. *John Long's classic and lively how-to manual, first published in 1989.*

Luebben, Craig. *Rock Climbing Anchors: A Comprehensive Guide.* Seattle: Mountaineers Books, 2006. *Exhaustive look at climbing anchors and the best, safest anchor-building practices.*

———. *Rock Climbing: Mastering Basic Skills.* Seattle: Mountaineers Books, 2004. *Comprehensive how-to rock-climbing manual.*

MacLeod, Dave. *9 out of 10 Climbers Make the Same Mistakes.* Ardlarach, Scotland: Rare Breed Productions, 2009. *Training manual from one of the world's best all-around climbers.*

INDEX

ABOUT THE AUTHOR

Chris Weidner

MATT SAMET is a freelance writer and editor based in Boulder, Colorado, and has been climbing since 1986. He is the author of *Climbing Dictionary* (Mountaineers Books, 2011) and the memoir *Death Grip* (St. Martin's Press, 2013). The former editor in chief of *Climbing* magazine, Samet can be often found climbing on the local rocks in the Flatirons, as well as Eldorado and Boulder Canyons. His goal is to keep at his beloved sport as long as his battered knees, shoulders, elbows, and fingers will permit.

MOUNTAINEERS BOOKS

SKIPSTONE   BRAIDED RIVER

recreation · lifestyle · conservation

MOUNTAINEERS BOOKS is a leading publisher of mountaineering literature and guides—including our flagship title, *Mountaineering: The Freedom of the Hills*—as well as adventure narratives, natural history, and general outdoor recreation. Through our two imprints, Skipstone and Braided River, we also publish titles on sustainability and conservation. As a 501(c)(3) nonprofit, we are committed to supporting the environmental and educational goals of our organization by providing expert information on human-powered adventure, sustainable practices at home and on the trail, and preservation of wilderness.

The Mountaineers, founded in 1906, is a nonprofit outdoor activity and conservation organization whose mission is "to explore, study, preserve, and enjoy the natural beauty of the outdoors." One of the largest such organizations in the United States, it sponsors classes and year-round outdoor activities throughout the Pacific Northwest, including climbing, hiking, backcountry skiing, snowshoeing, bicycling, camping, paddling, and more. The Mountaineers also supports its mission through its publishing division, Mountaineers Books, and promotes environmental causes through educational activities and sponsorship of legislation. For more information, visit The Mountaineers Program Center, 7700 Sand Point Way NE, Seattle, WA 98115-3996; phone 206-521-6001; www .mountaineers.org; or email info@mountaineers.org.

MOUNTAINEERS BOOKS

All of our publications are made possible through the generosity of donors and through sales of more than 500 titles on outdoor recreation, sustainable lifestyle, and conservation. To donate, purchase books, or learn more, visit us online:

1001 SW Klickitat Way, Suite 201 • Seattle, WA 98134
800-553-4453 • mbooks@mountaineersbooks.org
www.mountaineersbooks.org

Mountaineers Books is proud to be a corporate sponsor of the Leave No Trace Center for Outdoor Ethics, whose mission is to promote and inspire responsible outdoor recreation through education, research, and partnerships. The Leave No Trace program is focused specifically on human-powered (nonmotorized) recreation.

Leave No Trace strives to educate visitors about the nature of their recreational impacts and offers techniques to prevent and minimize such impacts. Leave No Trace is best understood as an educational and ethical program, not as a set of rules and regulations.

For more information, visit www.lnt.org, or call 800-332-4100.